Mastering Apache Solr 7.x

An expert guide to advancing, optimizing, and scaling your
enterprise search

Sandeep Nair
Chintan Mehta
Dharmesh Vasoya

BIRMINGHAM - MUMBAI

Mastering Apache Solr 7.x

Commissioning Editor: Pravin Dhandre
Acquisition Editor: Aman Singh
Content Development Editor: Aishwarya Pandere
Technical Editor: Dinesh Pawar
Copy Editor: Vikrant Phadkay
Project Coordinator: Nidhi Joshi
Proofreader: Safis Editing
Indexer: Aishwarya Gangawane
Graphics: Tania Dutta
Production Coordinator: Arvindkumar Gupta

First published: February 2018

Production reference: 1160218

Published by Packt Publishing Ltd.
Livery Place
35 Livery Street
Birmingham
B3 2PB, UK.

ISBN 978-1-78883-738-5

www.packtpub.com

mapt.io

Mapt is an online digital library that gives you full access to over 5,000 books and videos, as well as industry leading tools to help you plan your personal development and advance your career. For more information, please visit our website.

Why subscribe?

- Spend less time learning and more time coding with practical eBooks and Videos from over 4,000 industry professionals

- Improve your learning with Skill Plans built especially for you

- Get a free eBook or video every month

- Mapt is fully searchable

- Copy and paste, print, and bookmark content

PacktPub.com

Did you know that Packt offers eBook versions of every book published, with PDF and ePub files available? You can upgrade to the eBook version at www.PacktPub.com and as a print book customer, you are entitled to a discount on the eBook copy. Get in touch with us at service@packtpub.com for more details.

At www.PacktPub.com, you can also read a collection of free technical articles, sign up for a range of free newsletters, and receive exclusive discounts and offers on Packt books and eBooks.

Contributors

About the authors

Sandeep Nair has more than 11 years of experience of Java and Java EE technologies. His keen interest is in developing enterprise solutions using the Liferay platform, and he has been doing so for the past 9 years. He has executed projects using Liferay across various verticals, providing solutions for collaboration, enterprise content management, and web content management systems. He is also experienced with Java and Java EE.

He has authored *Liferay Beginner's Guide* and *Instant Liferay Portal 6 Starter*.

Travel, food, and books are his passions, besides coding.

> *I would like to thank my dad, Uday, for believing in me; my mom, Savithri, for loving me the most in the world; my brother, Sanju, who cheers me up at every moment of my life; my wife, Iesha, all I will say is I Love You; and finally, that little life that may come to this world hopefully before this book gets published. Thanks to KNOWARTH, my coauthors, and the entire Packt team, especially Aishwarya, for making this happen.*

Chintan Mehta is a cofounder of KNOWARTH Technologies and heads the cloud/RIMS/DevOps team. He has rich, progressive experience in server administration of Linux, AWS Cloud, DevOps, and RIMS, and server administration on open source technologies. He is also an AWS Certified Solutions Architect.

Chintan has authored *MySQL 8 for BigData*, *MySQL 8 Administrator's Guide*, and *Hadoop Backup and Recovery Solutions*, and has reviewed *Liferay Portal Performance Best Practices* and *Building Serverless Web Applications*.

> *I would like to thank my coauthors. I would like to especially thank my wonderful wife, Mittal, and my sweet son, Devam, for putting up with the long days, nights, and weekends when I was camped out in front of my laptop. Last but not least, I want to thank my Mom and Dad, friends, family, and colleagues for supporting me throughout.*

Dharmesh Vasoya is a Liferay 6.2 certified developer. He has 5.5 years of experience in application development with technologies such as Java, Liferay, Spring, Hibernate, Portlet, and JSF. He has successfully delivered projects in various domains, such as healthcare, collaboration, communication, and enterprise CMS, using Liferay.

Dharmesh has good command of the configuration setup of servers such as Solr, Tomcat, JBOSS, and Apache Web Server. He has good experience of clustering, load balancing and performance tuning. He completed his MCA at Ahmedabad University.

I had a wonderful experience as an author of this book. It was an awesome journey and I would like to thank each and every contributor. I would like to thank all my coauthors, Packt team members, and all the reviewers for their great support and effort. Big thanks to my family members for their great support during the entire course of writing.

About the reviewers

Marcelo Ochoa works at the system laboratory of Facultad de Ciencias Exactas of Universidad Nacional del Centro de la Provincia de Buenos Aires and is the CTO at Scotas. He has worked on several Oracle-related projects, such as translating Oracle manuals and multimedia CBTs. Since 2006, he has been part of an Oracle ACE program and was recently inducted into a Docker mentor program.

He has coauthored *Oracle Database Programming using Java and Web Services* by Digital Press and *Professional XML Databases* by Wrox Press. He has been a technical reviewer on several Packt Publishing books.

Krunal Patel has been working on the Liferay portal for 5+ years and has 9+ years of experience in enterprise application development using Java and Java EE. He has also executed enterprise CMS projects using Solr, Apache web server, and Apache Lucene. He has good experience in setup and configuration of servers (Solr, Tomcat, JBOSS, and Jenkins (CI)), performance tuning, LDAP integration, and so on. He has an ITIL Foundation certification in IT service management, Liferay 6.1 Developer certification, Brainbench Java 6 certification, and MongoDB for Java Developers certification.

Packt is searching for authors like you

If you're interested in becoming an author for Packt, please visit authors.packtpub.com and apply today. We have worked with thousands of developers and tech professionals, just like you, to help them share their insight with the global tech community. You can make a general application, apply for a specific hot topic that we are recruiting an author for, or submit your own idea.

Table of Contents

Preface

In today's digital enterprise world, every business has complex search requirements. With big data coming into the picture, the volume of data on which search filters have to be applied has massively increased. It becomes absolutely crucial to have an enterprise search platform that caters to your enterprise application.

Solr is a leading open source Java-based enterprise search platform that has been adopted by many organizations. It offers a plethora of features, such as handling rich documents, faceted search, and full-text searching, to name a few.

With the recent release of Solr 7, the arsenal of features that Solr provides has widened. We hope that this book will provide you with everything you need to not only learn but also master the various features and functionalities that Solr provides. We believe you will enjoy reading this as much as we did writing it. Happy learning!

Who this book is for

This book is for anyone who wants to not only learn Solr 7.0 but also understand various advanced concepts of Solr. You'll learn why you should search on an enterprise search platform like Solr by the time you finish this book.

What this book covers

Chapter 1, *Introduction to Solr 7*, gets you acquainted with what Solr is all about and explains why you should use Solr.

Chapter 2, *Getting Started*, shows you how to set up Solr and how everything is laid out under the Solr umbrella.

Chapter 3, *Designing Schemas*, takes us through schema design using the schema API and gives an understanding of schemaless mode.

Chapter 4, *Mastering Text Analysis Methodologies*, shows us features related to text analysis, tokenizers, filters, and analyzers.

Chapter 5, *Data Indexing and Operations*, teaches us how to use the client API to do indexing. We also learn about index handlers.

Chapter 6, *Advanced Queries – Part I*, looks at querying Solr, velocity search UI, relevance, query parsing, faceting, and highlighting.

Chapter 7, *Advanced Queries – Part II*, continues where the last chapter ended. We go through suggester, pagination, result grouping, clustering, and spatial search.

Chapter 8, *Managing and Fine-Tuning Solr*, shows how to make Solr ready for production.

Chapter 9, *Client APIs – An Overview*, gives an overview of the various APIs that are available for JavaScript, Ruby, Python, and Java to interact with Solr.

To get the most out of this book

1. It would be great if you know a bit of Java, but it is not mandatory as this book will teach you from the ground up

Download the example code files

You can download the example code files for this book from your account at www.packtpub.com. If you purchased this book elsewhere, you can visit www.packtpub.com/support and register to have the files emailed directly to you.

You can download the code files by following these steps:

1. Log in or register at www.packtpub.com.
2. Select the **SUPPORT** tab.
3. Click on **Code Downloads & Errata**.
4. Enter the name of the book in the **Search** box and follow the onscreen instructions.

Once the file is downloaded, please make sure that you unzip or extract the folder using the latest version of:

- WinRAR/7-Zip for Windows
- Zipeg/iZip/UnRarX for Mac
- 7-Zip/PeaZip for Linux

The code bundle for the book is also hosted on GitHub at `https://github.com/PacktPublishing/Mastering-Apache-Solr-7x`. We also have other code bundles from our rich catalog of books and videos available at `https://github.com/PacktPublishing/`. Check them out!

Download the color images

We also provide a PDF file that has color images of the screenshots/diagrams used in this book. You can download it here: `https://www.packtpub.com/sites/default/files/downloads/MasteringApacheSolr7x_ColorImages.pdf`.

Conventions used

There are a number of text conventions used throughout this book.

`CodeInText`: Indicates code words in text, database table names, folder names, filenames, file extensions, pathnames, dummy URLs, user input, and Twitter handles. Here is an example: "Also, the `PATH` variable should point to JRE 1.8."

A block of code is set as follows:

```
<requestHandler name="/dataimport" class="solr.DataImportHandler">
  <lst name="defaults">
    <str name="config">db-data-config.xml</str>
  </lst>
</requestHandler>
```

When we wish to draw your attention to a particular part of a code block, the relevant lines or items are set in bold:

```
<field column="category_id" name="category_id" />
<field column="category_name" name="category_name" />
<field column="remarks" name="remarks" />
```

Any command-line input or output is written as follows:

```
brew install solr

solr start
```

Bold: Indicates a new term, an important word, or words that you see onscreen. For example, words in menus or dialog boxes appear in the text like this. Here is an example: "Go to the **Query** screen; at the bottom, click on **facet**."

Warnings or important notes appear like this.

 Tips and tricks appear like this.

Get in touch

Feedback from our readers is always welcome.

General feedback: Email feedback@packtpub.com and mention the book title in the subject of your message. If you have questions about any aspect of this book, please email us at questions@packtpub.com.

Errata: Although we have taken every care to ensure the accuracy of our content, mistakes do happen. If you have found a mistake in this book, we would be grateful if you would report this to us. Please visit www.packtpub.com/submit-errata, selecting your book, clicking on the Errata Submission Form link, and entering the details.

Piracy: If you come across any illegal copies of our works in any form on the Internet, we would be grateful if you would provide us with the location address or website name. Please contact us at copyright@packtpub.com with a link to the material.

If you are interested in becoming an author: If there is a topic that you have expertise in and you are interested in either writing or contributing to a book, please visit authors.packtpub.com.

Reviews

Please leave a review. Once you have read and used this book, why not leave a review on the site that you purchased it from? Potential readers can then see and use your unbiased opinion to make purchase decisions, we at Packt can understand what you think about our products, and our authors can see your feedback on their book. Thank you!

For more information about Packt, please visit packtpub.com.

1
Introduction to Solr 7

Today we are in the age of digitization. People are generating data in different ways: they take pictures, upload images, write blogs, comment on someone's blog or picture, change their status on social networking sites, tweet on Twitter, update details on LinkedIn, do financial transactions, write emails, store data on the cloud, and so on. Data size has grown not only in the personal space but also in professional services, where people have to deal with a humongous amount of data. Think of the data managed by players such as Google, Facebook, the New York Stock Exchange, Amazon, and many others. For this data tsunami, we need the appropriate tools to fetch data, in an organized way, that can be used in various fields, such as scientific research, real-time traffic, fighting crime, fraud detection, digital personalization, and so on. All of this data needs to be captured, stored, searched, shared, transferred, analyzed, and visualized.

Analyzing structured, unstructured, or semi-structured ubiquitous data helps us discover hidden patterns, market trends, correlations, and personal preferences. With the help of the right tools to process and analyze data, organizations can expect much better marketing plans, additional revenue opportunities, improved customer services, healthier operational efficiency, competitive benefits, and much more. It is important to not only store data but also process it in order to generate information that is necessary. Every company collects data and uses it; however, to potentially flourish more effectively, a company needs to search relevant data. Every company must carve out direct search-produced data, which can improve their business either directly or indirectly.

Okay, now you have Solr, which is generally referred to as search server, and you are doing searches. Is that what you need? Hold on! This allows a lot more than a simple search. So get ready and hold your breath to take a deep dive into Solr—a scalable, flexible, and enterprise NoSQL search platform!

We will go through the following topics in this chapter:

- Introduction to Solr
- Why Solr?
- Solr use cases
- What's new in Solr 7

Introduction to Solr

Solr is one of the most popular enterprise search servers and is widely used across the world. It is written based on Java and uses the Lucene Java search library. Solr is an open source project from **Apache Software Foundation** (**ASF**) and is amazingly fast, scalable, and ideal for searching relevant data. Some of the major Solr users are Netfix, SourceForge, Instagram, CNET, and Flipkart. You can check out more such use cases at `https://wiki.apache.org/solr/PublicServers`.

Some of the features included are as follows:

- Full-text search
- Faceted search
- Dynamic clustering
- GEO search
- Hit highlighting
- Near-real-time indexing
- Rich document handling
- Geospatial search
- **Structured Query Language** (**SQL**) support
- Textual search
- Rest API
- JSON, XML, PHP, Ruby, Python, XSLT, velocity, and custom Java binary output formats over HTTP
- GUI admin interface
- Replication
- Distributed search
- Caching of queries, documents, and filters

- Auto-suggest
- Streaming
- Many more features

Solr has enabled many such Internet sites, government sites, and Intranet sites too, providing solutions for e-commerce, blogs, science, research, and so on. Solr can index billions of documents/rows via XML, JSON, CSV, or HTTP APIs. It can secure your data with the help of authentication and can be drilled down to role-based authentication. Solr is now an integral part of many big data solutions too.

History of Solr

Doug Cutting created `Lucene` in 2000, which is the core technology behind Solr.

Solr was made in 2004 by Yonik Seeley at CNET Networks for a homegrown project to provide search capability for the CNET Networks website.

Later in 2006, CNET Networks published the Solr source code to ASF. By early 2007, Solr had found its place in some of the top projects. It was then that Solr kept on adding new features to attract customers and contributors.

Solr 1.3 was released in September 2008. It included major performance enhancements and features such as distributed search.

In January 2009, Yonik Seeley, Grant Ingersoll, and Erik Hatcher joined Lucidworks; they are the prime faces of Solr and enterprise search. Lucidworks started providing commercial support and training for Solr.

Solr 1.4 was released in November 2009. Solr had never stopped providing enhancements; 1.4 was no exception, with indexing, searching, faceting, rich document processing, database integration, plugins, and more.

In 2011, Solr versioning was revised to match up with the versions of Lucene. Sometime in 2010, the Lucence and Solr projects were merged; Solr had then became an integral subproject of Lucene. Solr downloads were still available separately; however, it was developed together by the same set of contributors. Solr was then marked as 3.1.

Solr 4.0 was released in October 2012, which introduced the SolrCloud feature. There were a number of follow-ups released over a couple of years in the 4.x line. Solr kept on adding new features, becoming more scalable and further focusing on reliability.

Solr 5.0 was released in February 2015. It was with this release that official support for the WAR bundle package ended. It was packaged as a standalone application. And later, in version 5.3, it also included an authentication and authorization framework.

Solr 6.0 was released in April 2016. It included support for executing parallel SQL queries across SolrCloud. It also included stream expression support and JDBC driver for the SQL interface.

Finally, Solr 7.0 was released in September 2017, followed by 7.1.0 in October 2017, as shown in the following diagram. We will discuss the new features as we move ahead in this chapter, in the *What is new in Solr 7 section*.

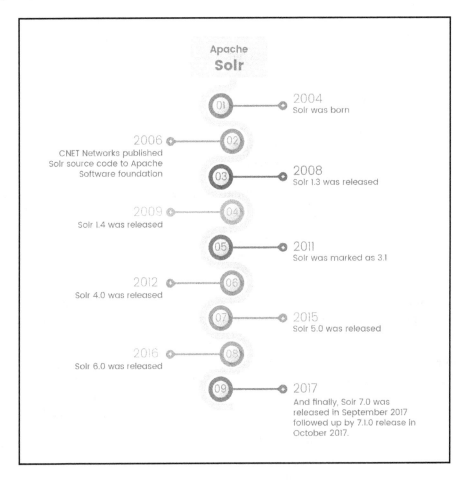

We have depicted the history of Solr in the preceding image for a much better view and understanding.

So by now, we have a brief understanding of Solr, along with its history. We must also have a good understanding of why we should be using Solr. Let's get the answer to this question too.

Lucene – the backbone of Solr

Lucene is an open source project that provides text search engine libraries. It is widely adopted for many search engine technologies. It has strong community contributions, which makes it much stronger as a technology backend. Lucene is a simple code library that you can use to write your own code by using the API available for searching, indexing, and much more.

For Lucene, a document consists of a collection of fields; they are name-value pairs consisting of either text or numbers. Lucene can be configured as a text analyzer that tokenizes a field's text to a series of words. It can also do further processing, such as substituting with synonyms or other similar processes. Lucene stores its index on the disk of the server, which consists of indexing for each of the documents. The index is an inverted index that stores the mapping of a field to its relevant document, along with the position of the word from the text of the document. Once you have the index in place, you can search for documents with the input of a query string that is parsed accordingly to Lucence. Lucene manages to score a value for each of the relevant documents and the ones that are high-scoring documents are displayed.

Why choose Solr?

If we already have a relational database, then why should we use Solr? It's simple; if there is a use case that needs you to search, you need a search engine platform like Solr. There are various use cases that we will be discussing further in the chapter.

Databases and Solr have their own pros and cons. In one place where we use a database, SQL supports limited wildcard-based text search with some basic normalization, such as matching uppercase to lowercase. It might be a costly query as it does full table scans. Whereas in Solr, a searchable word index is stored in an inverse index, which is much faster than traditional database searches.

Let's look at the following diagram to understand this better:

Solr v.s. 🛢 relationalDB

Lucene	Solr	Relational DB
Text Search	Fast and sophisticated	Minimal and slow
Features	Few, targeted to text search	Many
Deployment Complexity	Medium	Medium
Administration Tools	Minimal open source projects	Many open source & commercial
Monitoring Tools	Weak	Very Strong
Scaling Tools	Automated, medium scale	Large scale
Support Availability	Weak	Strong
Schema Flexibility	Must in general rebuild	Changes immediately visible
Indexing Speed	Slow	Faster and adjustable
Query Speed	Text search is fast & predictable	Very dependent on design & use case
Row Addition/Extraction Speed	Slow	Fast
Partial Record Modification	No	Yes
Time to visibility after addition	Slow	Immediate
Access to internal data structures	High	None
Technical knowledge required	Java (minimal),web server deployment, IT	SQL, DB-specific factors, IT
Regular maintenance tasks		

Having an enterprise search engine solution is must for an organization nowadays, it is having a prominent role in the aspect of getting information quickly with the help of searches. Not having such a search engine platform can result in insufficient information, inefficiency of productivity, and additional efforts due to duplication of work. Why? Just because of not having the right information available quickly, without a search; it is something that we can't even think of. Most such use cases comprise the following key requirements:

1. Data collected should be parsed and indexed. So, parsing and indexing is one of the important requirements of any enterprise search engine platform.
2. A search should provide the required results almost at runtime on the required datasets. Performance and relevance are two more key requirements.
3. The search engine platform should be able to crawl or collect all of the data that it would require to perform the search.
4. Integration of the search engine along with administration, monitoring, log management, and customization is something that we would be expecting.

Solr has been designed to have a powerful and flexible search that can be used by applications; whenever you want to serve data based on search patterns, Solr is the right fit.

Here is a high-level diagram that shows how Solr is integrated with an application:

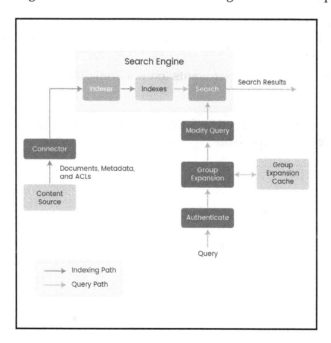

The majority of popular websites, including many Intranet websites, have integrated search solutions to help users find relevant information quickly. User experience is a key element for any solution that we develop; and searching is one of the major features that cannot be ignored when we talk about user experience.

Benefits of keyword search

One of the basic needs a search engine should support is a keyword search, as that's the primary goal behind the search engine platform. In fact it is the first thing a user will start with. Keyword search is the most common technique used for a search engine and also for end users on our websites. It is a pretty common expectation nowadays to punch in a few keywords and quickly retrieve the relevant results. But what happens in the backend is something we need to take care of to ensure that the user experience doesn't deteriorate. Let's look at a few areas that we must consider in order to provide better outcomes for search engine platforms using Solr:

- Relevant search with quick turnaround
- Auto-correct spelling
- Auto-suggestions
- Synonyms
- Multilingual support
- Phrase handling—an option to search for a specific keyword or all keywords in a phrase provided
- Expanded results if the user wants to view something beyond the top-ranked results

These features can be easily managed by Solr; so our next challenge is to provide relevant results with improved user experience.

Benefits of ranked results

Solr is not limited to finding relevant results for a user's search. Providing the end user with selection of the most relevant results, that are sorted, is important as well. We will be doing this using SQL to find relevant matching pattern results and sorting them into columns in either ascending or descending order. Similarly, Solr also does sorting of the result set retrieved based on the search pattern, with a score that would match the relevancy strength in the dataset.

Ranked results is very important, primarily because the volume of data that search engine platforms have to dig through is huge. If there is no control on ranked results, then the result set would be filled with no relevancy and would have so much data that it wouldn't be feasible to display it either. The other important aspect is user experience. All of us are now used to expecting a search engine to provide relevant results using limited keywords. We are getting restless, aren't we? But we expect a search engine platform to not get annoyed and provide us relevant ranked results with few keywords. Hold on, we are not talking of Google search here! So for users like us, Solr can help address such situations by providing higher rankings based on various criteria: fields, terms, document name, and a few more. The ranking of the dataset can vary based on many factors, but a higher ranking would generally be based on the relevancy of the search pattern. With this, we can also have criteria such as gender; with the rankings of certain documents being at the top.

Solr use cases

Solr is widely accepted and used by big companies such as Netflix, Disney, Instagram, The Guardian, and many more. Let us see with the help of a few use cases the real-life importance that Solr has made on renowned scenarios.

For an extended but incomplete list of use cases and sites that leverage Solr, you can refer to the official web page of Solr at `https://wiki.apache.org/solr/PublicServers`:

This diagram helps us understand Solr as a solution serving various industries. Though it's not an exhaustive list of industries where Solr has been playing a prominent role in business decisions, let's discuss a few of the industries.

Social media

LinkedIn, a well known professional social media site, uses Lucene/Solr search. Lucene has a powerful faceting system that allows us to pivot and navigate by user or company attributes abstracted from user profile data. LinkedIn has an excellent feature that is backed up by Solr: its ranking of results by people's relationship with you. This data is not fixed, and being derived by Lucene in real time, it's all based on the arithmetic calculations of the relationships in your connections list.

One more use case is Myspace. Myspace is considered one of the world's largest search sites, with almost 200 million active users and adding up to almost 2.5k new users daily. It is expected to have around 50 million videos and adding around 75,000 daily. Myspace consists of almost 900 billion rows of data and 15 billion friend relationship searches by Lucene, with about 1 terabyte of data added every week.

Science and research

NASA (https://www.nasa.gov/open/nebula.html) uses Solr for its Nebula Cloud Computing Platform. Similarly, **Public Library of Science** (**PLOS**) that is a non-profit publisher of research articles on various subjects. VUFind (https://vufind.org/vufind/) is another powerful open source discovery portal of libraries. It is known to have around 25 million records for a few of its implementations.

Search engine

Having Google using Solr is a milestone for Solr. **Google Search Appliance** (**GSA**), is backed up with Solr. GSA uses many features of Solr: metadata sorting, recommendations, spellcheck, auto-suggest, and more.

Similarly, Open Test Search (http://www.opentestsearch.com/) uses Solr to provide a comparison of a few common search engines.

E-commerce

Flipkart is a leading example of Solr. It has more than 900k users and sees more than 20k searches per second. Flipkart product search has a backbone of 175 million listings, ~250 million documents, and ~5,500 categories. The major challenge was real-time results, ranking, autocompletion, high-update rates, and inverted index. It has become a huge success by using Solr for product searches for its e-commerce business.

Media and entertainment

Netflix uses Solr for the site search feature. Netflix has more than 2 million queries per day for searches and more than 15 million subscribers. It is available in more than 190 countries and supports around 23 languages. The search works based on video title name, genre name, or person name. Features such as autocompletion and ranked results are used by Netflix.

The Guardian, one of the leading newspapers, also uses Solr for its API search platform. There are other users too: MTV, Digg, cnet.com, and many more.

Government

The White House uses Solr for `https://www.whitehouse.gov/`. It uses features such as search, highlighting, and faceting. Similarly, **Federal Communications Commission** (**FCC**) uses Solr for its website search.

Education

Hathitrust is another wonderful use case of Solr. It has almost a couple of terabytes of index, with more than 10 million books provided online. Solr plays a prominent role in searches through its huge library of books. There are many such examples having similar use cases:

- **Internet Archive**: `https://archive.org/`
- **National Library of Australia**: `http://trove.nla.gov.au/`
- **FictFact**: `https://www.fictfact.com/`
- **Biblio**: `https://www.biblio.com/`
- **A Norwegian online book store**: `https://www.akademika.no/`

What's new in Solr 7?

With a major release of Solr, lots of new features have been introduced. Overall, there are 51 new small-to-major features introduced in Solr 7. Along with these features, lots of bug fixes, optimization, and updates have been introduced. Let us go through some of the major changes introduced in Solr 7.

Replication for SolrCloud

Before we understand the new replication methods introduced in Solr 7, let's go through what was available for replication before Solr 7.

Until Solr 7, Solr had two options for replication purposes:

- Master-slave replication or index replication
- Solr Cloud

In master-slave replication, also known as **index replication**, the master shares a copy of indexed data with one or more slave servers. The master server's job is to index the data that is being added into Solr and share it with the slave servers while all read operations are performed in the slaves.

SolrCloud is a clustered environment of Solr that provides high availability and failover capability so that the content indexed using Solr can be distributed equally among multiple servers for scaling. In SolrCloud, one of the servers act as the leader and the rest of the servers in the cluster work as replica shards. Until Solr 7, in case of any issue on the leader server, any of the replica servers could act as a leader and form the leader-replica cluster. So in that case, data had to be shared with each of the nodes in the cluster, as leader shards and replica shards must remain in sync at any time. Each replica node performed the same operations as the leader. This replication, method available in SolrCloud before Solr 7, was known as NRT replicas.

In Solr 7, two new replication methods have been introduced:

- TLOG replicas
- PULL replicas

TLOG replicas

TLOG replica means transaction log replica. Instead of indexing the data again, a TLOG replica reads the transactions logs of the master or leader shard and replicates the segment or indexed data using a replication handler. In case of failure of the leader shard, one of the TLOG replicas acts as a leader and performs real-time indexing. It also makes a copy of the transaction log. Once the leader shard is available again, it again goes to the replica shard mode and performs only binary replication of segments. Replication done using the TLOG replication method is not as real-time as the one done using NRT replicas.

PULL replicas

A PULL replica pulls the data from the leader shard instead of indexing data locally as in NTR replicas or maintaining the transaction logs as in TLOG replicas. In case of failure of the leader shard, a PULL replica cannot become the new leader shard. For that, we may have to use either TLOG or NRT only. PULL replicas provide faster data replication from leader shards to replica shards.

Schemaless improvements

Solr has improved its schemaless mode functionality, the way it now detects data for indexing of an incoming field would be text based. By default, it will now be indexed as `text_general` for incoming fields, which can be modified if required. The name of the field will be the one defined in the document. A copy field rule will now be added in the schema when a collection is created if config set is not defined. It is now schemaless, which would insert the first 256 characters from the text field in a new strings field. It would be named as `<name>_str`.

The relevant schemaless behavior can be customized to remove a copy field rule or to update the number of characters added into the strings field or type of field used.

Copy field rules can impact the index size as well as slow down the indexing process. It is recommended to use the copy field rule when it is required. If there is no need to do a sort or facet on a field, you should ideally disable the copy field rule that is generated automatically.

The field creation rule can be disabled via the `update.autoCreateFields` property. You can also use the configuration API with the following command to disable it:

```
curl http://hostname:8983/solr/collection/config -d '{"set-user-property":
{"update.autoCreateFields":"false"}}'
```

Autoscaling

As termed in the documentation of `http://lucene.apache.org`, the goal of autoscaling is to make SolrCloud cluster management easier by providing a way for changes to the cluster to be more automatic and more intelligent.

So in Solr 7, there are some APIs that monitor some predefined preferences and policies. If any of the rules provided in the policies are violated, Solr changes its configuration automatically as defined in the preferences. With the updated autoscaling feature, we can now have Solr spin up new replicas depending on the monitoring metrics, such as disk space.

Default numeric types

`Trie*`-based numeric files are now replaced by `*PointField` from Solr 7 onwards. Going forward, from Solr 8, all `*PointField` types will be removed. You need to work towards moving from `*PointFields` to the new `Trie*` fields for your schema. After changing to the new `*Pointfields` type, data will need to be reindexed in Solr.

Spatial fields

Here is the list of spatial fields that have been deprecated:

- `SpatialVectorFieldType`
- `SpatialTermQueryPrefixTreeFieldType`
- `LatLonType`
- `GeoHashField`

The following is the list of spatial fields that can be used moving forward:

- `SpatialRecursivePrefixTreeField`
- `RptWithGeometrySpatialField`
- `LatLonPointSpatialField`

SolrJ

Here are the changes made in SolrJ:

- `HttpClientBuilderPlugin` is replaced with `HttpClientInterceptorPlugin` and would work with a `SolrHttpClientBuilder` rather than `HttpClientConfigurer` that was the case earlier.
- `HttpClient` instances configuration can be done now with help of `SolrHttpClientBuilder` rather than the earlier `HttpClientConfigurer` with the help of `HttpClientUtil`.
- `SOLR_AUTHENTICATION_CLIENT_BUILDER` is now being used in variable instead of `SOLR_AUTHENTICATION_CLIENT_CONFIGURER` in environment variable.
- `HttpSolrClient#setMaxTotalConnections` along with `HttpSolrClient#setDefaultMaxConnectionsPerHost` has now been removed. By default, these parameters are now set on the higher side and can be changed with the help of parameters when an `HttpClient` instance is created.

JMX and MBeans

Here are the changes made in **Java Management Extensions (JMX)** and MBeans:

- We notice there is now a hierarchical format for names used in metrics in MBeans attributes. For reference we can have look at `/admin/plugins` and `/admin/mbeans`. And the UI plugins tab is now using a similar approach as now all the APIs fetch data from a metrics API. The earlier approach of having a flat JMX view has been removed.

- `<metric><reporter>` has now replaced `<jmx>` elements in `solrconfig.xml`. And `<metric><reporter>` needs to be defined in the `solr.xml` configuration file. Default instances of `SolrJmxReporter` supports automatically limited backward compatibility when a local MBean server is discovered. If we want to enable a local MBean server we can use `ENABLE_REMOTE_JMX_OPTS` in `solr.sh` configuration file or via system properties that uses – `Dcom.sun.management.jmxremote`. With default instance all registries are exported using Solr metrics.

- If we want to disable the behavior of `SolrJmxReporter` we can do it by using `SolrJmxReporter` configuration with a `Boolean` argument set to `false`. Backward compatibility support might be removed from Solr 8 for `SolrJmxReporter`.

Other changes

Apart from these changes, there are many other features and improvements that have been made in Solr 7:

- In Solr 7 the default response type is set to `JSON` that was previously in XML format. If you want a response in XML then you will need to defined `wt=xml` in the request parameter.

- Default value for the `legacyCloud` parameter is set to `false`. That means if an entry is not found for the replica in `state.json`, it will not be registered in the cluster shard.

- By default, the new incoming field will be indexed as `text_general`. The name of the field will be the same as defined in the incoming document.

- The `_default` config set is introduced to replace `data_driven_configset` and `basic_configset`. So while creating a new collection if no configuration value is defined, it will use `_default` configuration. In case of SolrCloud, ZooKeeper will use `_default` configuration if no configuration parameter is defined. While in standalone mode, `instanceDir` will be created using the `_default` configuration parameter.

- New configuration set is defined for the SolrClient. So now configuration of socket timeout or connect timeouts are not dependent on `HttpClient` and can be defined specifically for SolrClient.

- In SolrJ, `HttpSolrClient#setAllowCompression` that was earlier used to define enabling compression has been removed. Now this parameter must be enabled from the `Constructor` parameter only.
- New V2 **Application Program Interface (API)** is available at `/api/` as a preferred method and to leverage old API `/solr/` continues to be available.
- The standard query parser now has the default `sow=false` which means that text fields will not split on whitespace before handing text to the analyzer. It will help analyzer to match synonyms of multi-words.

Summary

This was an interesting chapter with important content to learn, right? In this chapter, we started with an introduction to Solr. We went through the impressive history of Solr and its backbone, Lucene. We learned and understood the characteristics and why we use Solr. Besides, we saw a wonderful list of use cases around the globe that have adopted Solr to serve many of the key features of the solution. In the later section of the chapter, we learned about the exciting new features of Solr 7 that briefly covered replication, SolrJ, schemaless improvements, spatial fields, and more.

Moving on to the next chapter, we will learn how to get started with Solr. The chapter will focus on Solr installation, understanding various files and the folder structure, along with loading sample data into Solr. The chapter will explain how we can browse the Solr interface and how to use the Solr admin interface.

2
Getting Started

"Information is the oil of the 21st Century, and analytics is the combustion engine."

– Peter Sondergaard

Apache Solr is one tool that has some common features such as full-text search, facets-based search, clustering on demand, the ability to select highlighters, indexing on demand, database integration, geospatial searches, NoSQL features, fault tolerance, scaling on demand, and the ability to handle all sorts of documents (such as PDF, docx, ppt, and more). Solr finds its intense use in enterprise searches and huge analytics. Due to such powerful features, major players in the world such as Instagram, Netflix, NASA, and eBay are using Solr.

Solr runs as a standalone server with the option of having clusters as per demand. Internally, it makes use of the Lucene Java search library and has full support of REST like HTTP/XML and JSON APIs. This makes it possible to use most of the available programming languages even without Java coding. You feed Solr data over HTTP and Solr responds with an output in formats of JSON, CSV, and binary. Apache Lucene and Apache Solr were merged in 2010 and they are collectively termed Lucene/Solr or Solr/Lucene. This chapter focuses mainly on the following points:

- Solr installation
- Understanding various files and the folder structure
- Running and configuring Solr
- Loading sample data
- Understanding the browser interface
- Using the Solr admin interface

Solr installation

Let's get up and running with Solr. At the time of writing of this book, the latest stable version of Solr was 7.1.0. This book focuses all its aspects on Apache Solr 7.1.0.

Getting up and running with Apache Solr requires the following prerequisites:

- Java 8 (mandatory)
- Cygwin (optional, recommended for Windows)
- curl (optional, recommended)

So, you will necessarily require JRE version 1.8 or higher for Solr to run. Go ahead! Open Command Prompt, type the following command, and check your Java version:

```
java -version
```

It should show the following output:

```
C:\WINDOWS\system32\cmd.exe

Microsoft Windows [Version 10.0.16299.19]
(c) 2017 Microsoft Corporation. All rights reserved.

C:\Users\chint>java -version
java version "1.8.0_151"
Java(TM) SE Runtime Environment (build 1.8.0_151-b12)
Java HotSpot(TM) 64-Bit Server VM (build 25.151-b12, mixed mode)

C:\Users\chint>
```

If your output is something different, it means Java is not properly installed and it needs to be installed properly. Also, the PATH variable should point to JRE 1.8. You can download Java from http://www.oracle.com/technetwork/java/javase/downloads/index.html if needed.

Cygwin and curl utilities are not mandatory but will be helpful when we go deeper.

The next step is to download Apache Solr. An important point to keep in mind is that Apache Solr can also run as a standalone unit and is operating system independent. It would be the same across the operating systems; the difference would be in the way we reach there. To install Solr, follow along steps:

1. Go to http://lucene.apache.org/solr/.
2. Click on **DOWNLOAD**.

3. You will be redirected to `http://www.apache.org/dyn/closer.lua/lucene/solr/7.1.0`.

4. Select the mirror site, which will open up the following page:

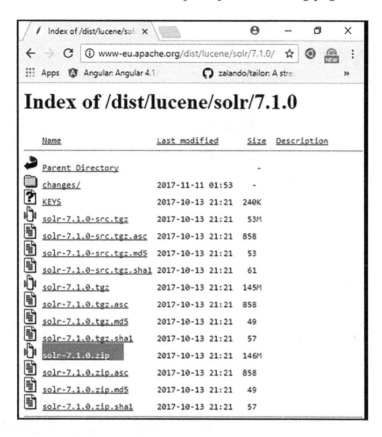

5. If you are on Windows, download the `solr-7.1.0.zip` file and extract it to a location of your choice.

6. If you are on Linux/Unix or macOS, download the `.tgz` file and extract it to the local home directory:

```
wget http://www-eu.apache.org/dist/lucene/solr/7.1.0/solr-7.1.0.tgz

cd ~/

tar zxf solr-7.1.0.tgz
```

The same command should work for macOS also, provided the `wget` utility is installed. If not, you can use another alternative.

7. For macOS, if you don't have `wget` installed, you can use the native `brew` command:

   brew install solr

   solr start

Irrespective of the way you install Solr for your OS, the extracted location should be something like this, with the folder structure as follows:

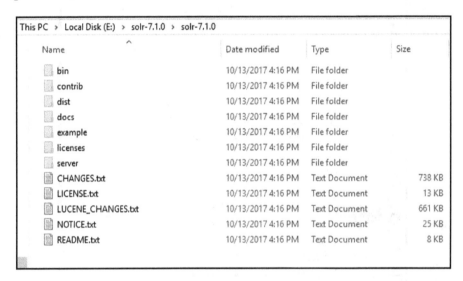

Now that we have Solr installed, the next step is to get it up and running. Navigate to the `bin` folder, which contains the Solr startup script. Open the terminal and hit the following command, which will open up an interactive prompt screen, as shown in the following screenshot:

solr -e cloud

Let's look at the following steps:

1. The very first question it asks us is the number of nodes we want to run in parallel for Solr. Let's keep it at 2 since 2 is the default. Just press *Enter* without typing anything.

2. Next, we need to specify the port on which Solr will run. The default ports are 8983 and 7574. Change the port if they are already occupied, or simply press *Enter* to go ahead with the default ports.

3. Next, it will ask us to provide the name of a collection in which we want to add data. Let's go with the default one.

4. The bin/solr and bin/solr.cmd contains Solr preconfigurations. When we start Solr, it asks us whether we want to change those configurations. We can simply press *Enter* to keep the preconfigurations as default, or we can type in to define our own configurations.

If everything goes well, you should see the following screen:

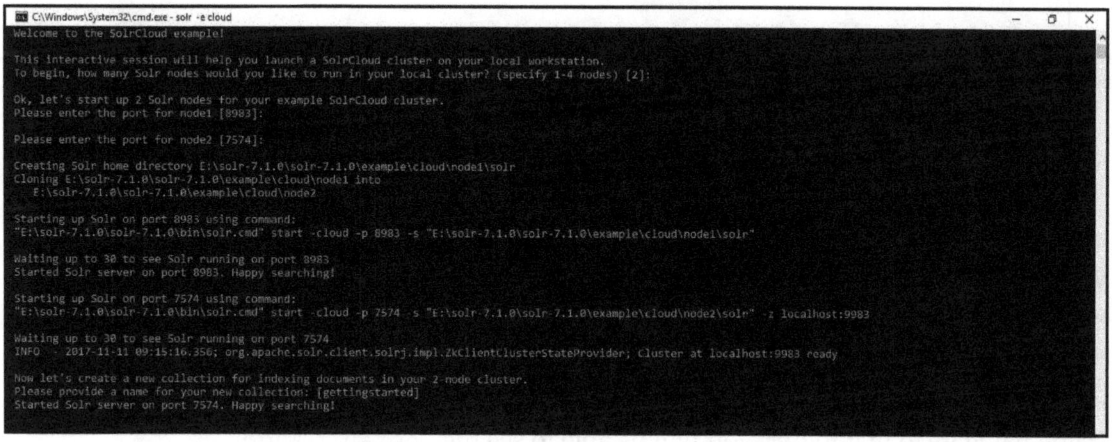

You can now navigate either to `http://localhost:8983/solr/#/` or
`http://localhost:7574/solr/#/` as you have started Solr in cluster mode. You should
be able to see the following admin interface:

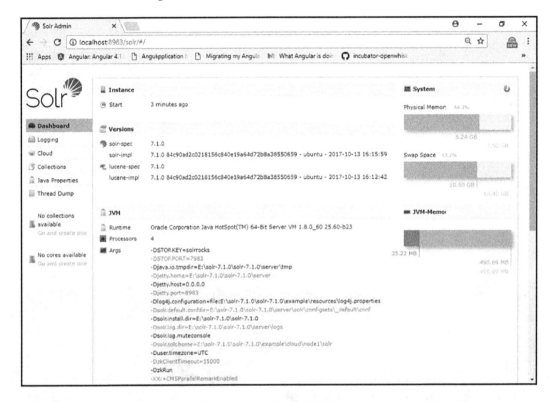

What did we just do? While running this command, we started Solr in cloud mode. When
we specified the number of hosts, port number, and collection name, it created an initial
configuration set. Solr comes with an example configuration set, which we can use with
cloud mode. It can be found at: `$SOLR_HOME/server/solr/configsets`.

If you navigate to that folder, you will be able to see the `_default` and
`sample_techproducts_configs` config sets.

However, cloud mode is not the only mode Solr comes with. Solr comes with tailor made
configuration sets, which we can use if they fit our purpose. The following config sets are
available in Solr 7.1.0 and they can be viewed at `$SOLR_HOME/example`. If you navigate to
that folder, you will be able to find config sets for an instance of `cloud`, `example-DIH`,
`films`, and `techproducts`.

To start Solr with any of the example config sets, you have to navigate to the `bin` directory and type the following command in the terminal:

```
solr start -e <name_of_example_config_set>
```

Now that we are up and running with Solr, let's look at the folder structure to get a deeper idea of Solr.

Understanding various files and the folder structure

Let's now understand the constituents of Solr, its directory structure, and the significance of each folder and the configurations involved. This diagram shows the parent-level directory of Solr, along with an explanation of each folder:

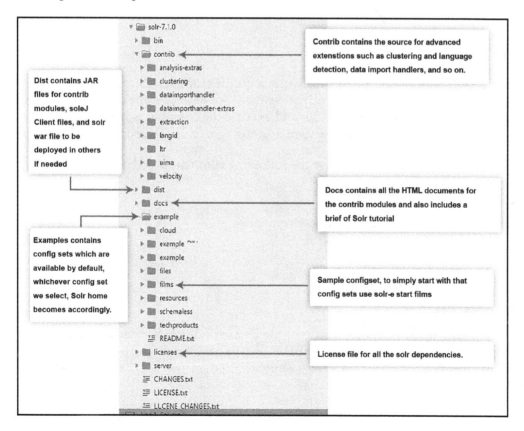

Let's look at the major folders and files we will be dealing with.

bin

The bin folder has all the scripts primarily needed to get up and running with Solr. Mainly, we will be using Solr and post scripts for our day-to-day purposes. It is also the location to place the replication scripts for more advanced setup, if needed. The `bin` folder is home to the following utilities: it contains the `solr.in.sh` and `solr.in.cmd` files, from where you can provide input parameters to Solr. It has the `install_solr_service.sh` script and the `oom_solr.sh` and `init.d` folders, if you want to run it as a service on any Linux/Unix service.

Since we will be using Solr scripts very often, it is advisable to add `$SOLR_HOME/bin` (for example, `E:\solr-7.1.0\solr-7.1.0\bin`) in the path environment variable so that we can use it anywhere.

Solr script

The Solr script in this folder is used for various utilities for managing Solr. You can pass various parameters to Solr from here. Now we will see a list of some of the things you can do with Solr script. Go to the `bin` folder and execute the commands in the terminal to check the output. Based on the operating system, use the `.cmd` or `.sh` version accordingly:

- If you are on Windows, use the following command:

    bin\solr.cmd start

- If you are on Linux, use this command:

    bin/solr.sh start

Post script

Solr, by default, includes a post script for indexing various kinds of documents directly to the Solr server. This utility is very helpful when you have huge files present and you want to end up writing a program that reads each line and then sends it to the Solr server via HTTP end points.

To run this utility on Windows, please install Cygwin. Otherwise, you will have to navigate to `$solr_home\example\exampledocs\post.jar`.

The following screenshot helps us to understand how we can execute a post script from the command line:

```
Select C:\Windows\System32\cmd.exe                                                    —    ⏷    ✕

Microsoft Windows [Version 10.0.15063]
(c) 2017 Microsoft Corporation. All rights reserved.

E:\solr-7.1.0\solr-7.1.0\example\exampledocs>java -jar post.jar -h
SimplePostTool version 5.0.0
Usage: java [SystemProperties] -jar post.jar [-h|-] [<file|folder|url|arg> [<file|folder|url|arg>...]]

Supported System Properties and their defaults:
  -Dc=<core/collection>
  -Durl=<base Solr update URL> (overrides -Dc option if specified)
  -Ddata=files|web|args|stdin (default=files)
  -Dtype=<content-type> (default=application/xml)
  -Dhost=<host> (default: localhost)
  -Dport=<port> (default: 8983)
  -Dbasicauth=<user:pass> (sets Basic Authentication credentials)
  -Dauto=yes|no (default=no)
  -Drecursive=yes|no|<depth> (default=0)
  -Ddelay=<seconds> (default=0 for files, 10 for web)
  -Dfiletypes=<type>[,<type>,...] (default=xml,json,jsonl,csv,pdf,doc,docx,ppt,pptx,xls,xlsx,odt,odp,ods,ott,otp,ots,rtf,htm,html,txt,log)
  -Dparams="<key>=<value>[&<key>=<value>...]" (values must be URL-encoded)
  -Dcommit=yes|no (default=yes)
  -Doptimize=yes|no (default=no)
  -Dout=yes|no (default=no)

This is a simple command line tool for POSTing raw data to a Solr port.
NOTE: Specifying the url/core/collection name is mandatory.
Data can be read from files specified as commandline args,
URLs specified as args, as raw commandline arg strings or via STDIN.
Examples:
  java -Dc=gettingstarted -jar post.jar *.xml
  java -Ddata=args -Dc=gettingstarted -jar post.jar '<delete><id>42</id></delete>'
  java -Ddata=stdin -Dc=gettingstarted -jar post.jar < hd.xml
  java -Ddata=web -Dc=gettingstarted -jar post.jar http://example.com/
  java -Dtype=text/csv -Dc=gettingstarted -jar post.jar *.csv
  java -Dtype=application/json -Dc=gettingstarted -jar post.jar *.json
  java -Durl=http://localhost:8983/solr/techproducts/update/extract -Dparams=literal.id=pdf1 -jar post.jar solr-word.pdf
  java -Dauto -Dc=gettingstarted -jar post.jar *
  java -Dauto -Dc=gettingstarted -Drecursive -jar post.jar afolder
  java -Dauto -Dc=gettingstarted -Dfiletypes=ppt,html -jar post.jar afolder
The options controlled by System Properties include the Solr
URL to POST to, the Content-Type of the data, whether a commit
or optimize should be executed, and whether the response should
be written to STDOUT. If auto=yes the tool will try to set type
automatically from file name. When posting rich documents the
```

This table consists of some example commands used for the same purpose:

Command	Description
`post -c chintan *.xml`	This adds all files with extension `.xml` to the core or collection named chintan
`post -c chintan -d '<delete><id>42</id></delete>'`	Deletes a document from the chintan collection or core that has ID 42
`post -c chintan *.csv`	Indexes all CSV files with auto field mappings on
`post -c chintan *.json`	Indexed all JSON files
`post -c chintan *.pdf`	Indexes all PDF files
`post -c chintan abc/`	Indexes all files inside the `abc` folder
`post -c chintan -filetypes ppt,html abc/`	Indexes only PPT and HTML files inside the `abc` folder

contrib

The `contrib` folder is one where you will be able to see all of Solr's contribution modules. All the extensions to Solr, which do advanced things beyond core Solr, can be found here.

Note that the runnable Java files of all of these extensions can be found in the `dist` folder; here it's just the source and the `README.md` files.

Some of the useful extensions are as follows.

DataImportHandler

`DataImportHandler` is an import tool for Solr that helps in importing data from databases, XML files, and HTTP data sources very smoothly and easily. The data sources for importing go beyond relational databases and cover filesystems, websites, emails, FTP servers, NoSQL databases, LDAP, and so on. You can set default locales, time zones, or charsets via this extension. You can find two JAR files of this extension in the `dist` folder: `solr-dataimporthandler-7.1.0.jar` and `solr-dataimporthandler-extras-7.1.0.jar`.

ContentExtractionLibrary

This contrib module provides a way to extract and index content contained in rich documents, such as Word, Excel, PDF, and so on. This module uses Apache Tika (a toolkit that extracts metadata and text from over a thousand different files). This contrib module provides automatic MIME type detection so that it can use that based on the file provided.

LanguageIdentifier

This module is meant to be used while indexing documents with a multitude of languages. The implementation of this document is such that it creates an `UpdateProcessor`, which can be placed in `UpdateChain`. It identifies the language and tags that document with that `languageId`. For example, if the input is `surname` and it detects English as the language, then it will be `surname_en`. Language detection can be per field or for the whole document.

Clustering

This module is used when we want to add third-party implementations. At the time of writing this book, it provides clustering support for search results using the Carrot2 project (`https://project.carrot2.org/`).

VelocityIntegration

This contrib helps us to integrate Solr with Apache Velocity. It gives us a writer that, behind the scenes, uses the Apache Velocity template engine on the GUI to render Solr responses.

dist and docs

The `dist` folder contains all the distributions that can be used as deployment artifacts in other servers. It contains the main Solr file, which is `solr-core.7.1.0.jar`. This folder also contains JAR files of all the contribs we discussed earlier. You can deploy these artifacts to any application server as per your needs.

The `docs` folder contains online documentation for all the help needed in Solr. It has Wiki Docs, new changes in the current version, minimum system requirements, tutorials, Lucene documentation, and Java API docs for all the contrib modules.

example

This directory contains all Solr examples and config sets that are provided by default. Each example is self-contained in a separate directory. It contains a fully self-contained Solr installation. It has a sample configuration, some documents, and ZooKeeper data.

Solr provides the following sample data out of the box:

- `films`
- `files`
- `exampledocs`

Solr provides the following config sets:

- `schemaless`
- `DIH`
- `techproducts`

Let's look at one such directory structure of an out-of-the-box example of Solr `cloud`:

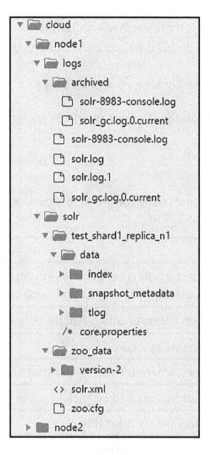

Here is the detailed directory structure of our out-of-the-box example of Solr `cloud`:

- The parent-level directory contains `node1` and `node2`, stating that Solr has been started in cluster mode for this config set.
- Each node contains two folders, `solr` and `logs`.
- The `solr` folder contains two folders, `test_shard1_replica_n1` and `zoo_data`. Since we have started Solr in clusters, it creates one replication folder, `test_shard1_replica_n1`. It contains the `data` folder and one file, `core.properties`, which has information about the other node.

- Apache Solr comes with embedded ZooKeeper. `zoo_data` is the ZooKeeper data directory.
- In the `solr` directory, there are two configuration files: `solr.xml` and `zoo.cfg`.
- `solr.xml` has some global configuration options that apply to all or defined cores.
- `zoo.cfg` contains the ZooKeeper-related files.

Let's look at all the configuration files that we would be using on a day-to-day basis.

core.properties

The core.properties contains some of the following properties, which we can configure as per our needs for our Solr core:

Property	Description
name	The name of the Solr core. Whenever you need to reference `SolrCore` with `CoreAdminHandler`, you will need this name.
config	Configuration filename and path. By default, this is `solrconfig.xml`.
schema	Schema filename of a core.
dataDir	Data directory where indexes are stored.
configSet	The config set that should be picked up to configure the core.
properties	The properties file path for this core.
transient	This decides whether the core can be unloaded or not if Solr reaches `transientCacheSize`.
loadOnStartUp	This decides whether or not to load the core on startup.
coreCodeName	A unique identifier for the node hosting the core. It can be helpful when you are replacing a machine that has had a hardware failure.
ulogDir	Directory for the update log.
Shard	The name of the shard to which the core would be assigned.
Roles	The name of the collection of the core in which you will index data.

zoo.cfg

This contains some of the following properties, by which we can configure for ZooKeeper:

Property	Description
tickTime	The tickTime decides actually how long eachTick has to be. This part of ZooKeeper determines which servers are up and running at any point in time by sending ticks.
initLimit	The amount of time in ticks for a forwarder to connect to the leader. It's the number of ticks that can be allowed for the initial synchronization phase to take place.
syncLimit	The amount of time that can be allowed for followers to keep in sync with ZooKeeper. If the followers cross this limit and yet don't sync up, they will be dropped.
dataDir	This is the directory in which cluster data information would be stored in ZooKeeper. It should initially be empty.
clientPort	This is the port at which Solr will access ZooKeeper; when this file is in place, you can start a ZooKeeper instance.
maxClientCnxns	The maximum number of client connections you want to handle.
autopurge.snapRetainCount	The number of snapshots to retain in the data directory.
Autopurge.purgeInterval	The purge task interval in hours. After this much time, it will start the retain task.

 It is not recommended to use embedded ZooKeeper in production.

solr.xml

The solr.xml contains Solr configuration that can apply to single or multiple cores as needed. The following table briefly summarizes the configurations available in this file:

Parent element	Property	Description
solrCloud	distribUpdateConnTimeout	Used to define the connection timeout limit for intra-cluster updates
solrCloud	distribUpdateSoTimeout	Used to define the socket time for intra-cluster updates
solrCloud	host	The hostname that Solr will use to access cores
solrCloud	hostContext	The context path
solrCloud	hostPort	The port that Solr will use to access cores
solrCloud	genericCoreNodeNames	Decides whether the node names should be based on the address of the node or not
solrCloud	zkClientTimeout	The timeout limit for connection to the ZooKeeper server
solrCloud	zkCredentialsProvider and zkACLProvider	The parameters used for ZooKeeper access control
solrCloud	leaderVoteWait	The Solr node will wait for this much time for all known replicas of that shard to be found
solrCloud	leaderConflictResolveWait	The maximum time the replica will wait to see conflicting state information to be resolved
shardHandlerFactory	socketTimeOut	The read time out for querying among intra-clusters

shardHandlerFactory	connTimeOut	The connection timeout for intra-cluster queries and administrative requests
shardHandlerFactory	urlScheme	The urlScheme to be used in distributed search
shardHandlerFactory	maxConnectionsPerHost	Maximum connections allowed per hosts
shardHandlerFactory	maxConnections	Maximum total connections allowed
shardHandlerFactory	corePoolSize	Initial core size of threadpool servicing requests
shardHandlerFactory	maximumPoolSize	Maximum size of threadpool servicing requests
shardHandlerFactory	maxThreadIdleTime	The amount of time in seconds that a thread persists in queue before getting killed

server

This directory contains an instance of the Jetty servlet and a container setup to run Solr. Given here is the server directory layout:

- server/contexts: This contains the Jetty web application deployment descriptors required by the Solr web app.
- server/etc: This contains Jetty configurations and has an example SSL keystore.
- server/lib: This has Jetty and other third-party libraries that are needed. It has folder ext; any external JAR you want you can keep there.
- server/logs: This has the Solr log files.
- server/solr-webapp: This contains files used by the Solr server. As Solr is not a Java web application, don't edit the files in this directory.
- server/solr: This is the default solr.home directory where Solr will create the core directories. It must contain solr.xml.
- server/resources: This must contain configuration files such as various Log4j configurations (log4j.properties) required for configuring Solr loggers.

- `server/scripts/cloud-scripts`: This is the command-line utility for working with ZooKeeper when we are running Solr with SolrCloud mode. You can check out `zkcli.sh` or `zkcli.bat` for usage information.
- `server/solr/configsets`: Contains various directories; they contain configuration options essential for running Solr.
- `_default`: This has some bare minimum configurations, with the options of field guessing and managed schema turned on by default so as to start indexing data in Solr without having to design any schema upfront. Schema management can be done via the REST API as you refine your index.
- `sample_techproducts_configs`: This has example configurations that show many powerful features based on the use case of building a search solution for tech products.

Now that we have a detailed idea about Solr's directory and file structure, let us get acquainted with running and configuring Solr for our needs.

Running Solr

Let's start with running and configuring our Solr. We will see several ways of running Solr, some configurations needed for Solr to be in production mode, and more. The following topics will be covered:

- Solr startup
- Production-level Solr setup and configurations

Running basic Solr commands

Earlier, we started Solr in interactive mode, where we picked up the cloud as the default config set. Let's revisit the Solr startup commands.

If you want to start Solr with a custom port, then you can use the following command:

```
bin\solr.cmd start -p 8984
```

 Based on your operating system, you have to use `bin/solr` or `bin\solr.cmd`.

Similar to `start`, there's a command `stop`. To stop Solr, simply use the following command:

```
bin\solr.cmd stop -all
```

The `-all` parameter stops all Solr instances; if you want to stop a specific port, then pass that port number with an argument with parameter `-p`. Let's say you start Solr with any key; then you can stop that particular instance by passing the key as a parameter:

```
bin\solr.cmd stop -k <key_name>
```

As seen earlier, you can launch examples by passing the `-e` flag:

```
bin\solr.cmd -e <example_name>
```

Let's start Solr in cloud mode; hitting `bin\solr.cmd -e cloud` will start the interactive process as follows:

- Specifying the number of nodes on which we would like to run Solr in the local cluster
- Port number for each Solr instance
- Creating a Solr instance home directory with node 1, node 2, and node 3
- Specifying the name for a new collection
- Specifying the shards, the new collection should split
- The replicas per shard we want to create
- The configuration for collection which we want

After this, the config API will be called and updated with the selected configurations. Then you can see the Solr running status on hitting `http://localhost:8983/solr/#/~cloud`. It should show something like this:

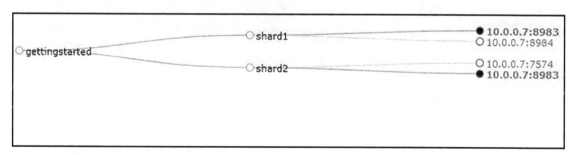

Now, to check the status of the running instances of Solr, it provides the command status. Let's check out the number of Solr instances we have up and running:

```
bin\solr.cmd status
```

The following screenshot is the output that shows the status of the Solr service, with a few more details such as uptime, solr_home, memory, and so on:

```
C:\Windows\System32\cmd.exe                                              —   □   ×

E:\solr-7.1.0\solr-7.1.0>bin\solr.cmd status

Found Solr process 7260 running on port 7574
{
  "solr_home":"E:\\solr-7.1.0\\solr-7.1.0\\example\\cloud\\node2\\solr",
  "version":"7.1.0 84c90ad2c0218156c840e19a64d72b8a38550659 - ubuntu - 2017-10-13 16:15:59",
  "startTime":"2017-11-12T16:16:48.718Z",
  "uptime":"0 days, 0 hours, 2 minutes, 48 seconds",
  "memory":"90.7 MB (%18.5) of 490.7 MB",
  "cloud":{
    "ZooKeeper":"localhost:9983",
    "liveNodes":"3",
    "collections":"1"}}


Found Solr process 8040 running on port 8983
{
  "solr_home":"E:\\solr-7.1.0\\solr-7.1.0\\example\\cloud\\node1\\solr",
  "version":"7.1.0 84c90ad2c0218156c840e19a64d72b8a38550659 - ubuntu - 2017-10-13 16:15:59",
  "startTime":"2017-11-12T16:16:37.100Z",
  "uptime":"0 days, 0 hours, 3 minutes, 1 seconds",
  "memory":"102.6 MB (%20.9) of 490.7 MB",
  "cloud":{
    "ZooKeeper":"localhost:9983",
    "liveNodes":"3",
    "collections":"1"}}


Found Solr process 9240 running on port 8984
{
  "solr_home":"E:\\solr-7.1.0\\solr-7.1.0\\example\\cloud\\node3\\solr",
  "version":"7.1.0 84c90ad2c0218156c840e19a64d72b8a38550659 - ubuntu - 2017-10-13 16:15:59",
  "startTime":"2017-11-12T16:16:59.966Z",
  "uptime":"0 days, 0 hours, 2 minutes, 39 seconds",
  "memory":"88.5 MB (%18) of 490.7 MB",
  "cloud":{
    "ZooKeeper":"localhost:9983",
    "liveNodes":"3",
    "collections":"1"}}
```

Now, if you haven't started Solr with example config sets, you will find no core created. Simply put, a core is just like a database in an SQL table. To create a new core at any time, just use the following command:

```
bin\solr.cmd create -c <name>
```

This command essentially creates a core or collection based on whether Solr is running in standalone (core) mode or SolrCloud (collection) mode. Based on the running instance of Solr, this command does its action.

By default, any new core created follows the _default config set, which is not a recommended practice in production.

If you want to delete a collection, just invoke the following rest point:

```
http://localhost:8983/solr/admin/collections?action=DELETE&name=<name_of_co
llection>
```

Now let's add some sample documents to our collection. I have some PDF documents on microservices and Node.js, and I am indexing in Solr. Open up your terminal.

If you are on Linux, hit the following command:

```
bin/post -c chintan <path_to_documents>/*.pdf
```

If you are on Windows, do this:

```
java -Dauto -Dc=chintan -jar post.jar E:\\books\\solr\\chintan\\*.pdf
```

In both cases, it looks for all the PDF documents in the folder, indexes them, and adds them into the collection or core: chintan.

If you want to use the post utility in Windows, download Cygwin and try the same command as in Linux.

Now that the documents are successfully indexed, let's verify by asking Solr questions. Open up the terminal and query collection getting started by asking questions about the query parameter nodejs by hitting the following end point, which would be http://localhost:8983/solr/gettingstarted/select?q=nodejs.

You should get a response like this:

```
{"responseHeader":{ "zkConnected":true, "status":0, "QTime":22, "params":{
"q":"nodejs"}},
"response":{"numFound":2,"start":0,"maxScore":2.283722,"docs":[ {},{}]
```

Production Solr setup

Now that we are done playing around in Solr, let's take a step further and look into installing Solr as a service. This is specifically useful in servers and Linux systems. Follow these steps:

1. The Solr bundle you downloaded earlier contains the `solr` directory, which includes a shell script `bin/install_solr_service.sh`. This will help to install Solr as a service on Linux. As some prerequisites, it will need the path where you want to install Solr and the user who should be owning Solr, that is, privileges.

2. While installing Solr, make sure that the `indexed` directory and `logs` directory stay out of the `solr` installation folder; this will be very helpful when we upgrade Solr.

3. The Solr service script, by default, extracts the archive in `/opt`. If you want to change that path, just add the `-i` option while running the Solr script. You can install the Solr service by simply hitting:

   ```
   sudo bash ./install_solr_service.sh solr-7.1.0.tgz
   ```

   It will install in the `opt` folder and also create a symbolic link:

   ```
   /opt/solr --> /opt/solr-7.1.0
   ```

   This helps in easy and smooth upgrades.

4. The data directory should be different; the script takes care of it. By default, it adds a directory at `/var/solr`, but if you want to change that, you can pass a location using `-d`.

5. Running Solr as a root user is not recommended. This script creates a Solr user by default, so `/var/solr` and `/opt/solr` can be fully owned by the Solr admin. No need to give them root privileges!

Now that the script is installed, you can start/stop Solr at any time with the following commands:

```
sudo service solr start
sudo service solr stop
```

So after getting up and running with basic utilities in Solr, covering the various available options in Solr, and getting to install and run a Solr service in Linux, let us now play with data. We will load some sample data and understand the various ways to load and query data.

Loading sample data

Now that we've got acquainted with Solr and the various commands involved in Solr's day-to-day usage, let's populate it with data so that we can query it as needed. Solr comes with sample data in examples. We will use the same $solr_home/example/films for our queries.

Fire up the terminal and create a collection films with 10 shards:

```
solr\bin create -c films -shards 10
```

Now, in $solr_home/example/films there is file called file.json. Let's import it into our collection, films. Based on your OS, hit the appropriate command for the post script or post.jar.

Uh Oh!! It throws an error, as follows:

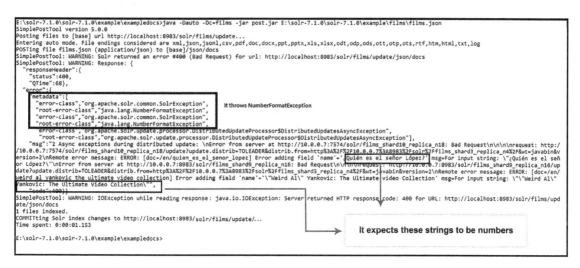

What must have gone wrong? By checking the logs while creating the collection, you must have seen a warning.

Warning

Using `_default` config set data driven schema functionality is enabled by default, which is not recommended for production use.

To turn it off, use the following command:

```
curl http://localhost:8983/solr/test11/config -d '{"set-user-property":
{"update.autoCreateFields":"false"}}'
```

While creating the collection, we went on with the `_default` config set. The `_default` config set does two things: we make use of the managed schema meaning, the schema can be modified only through Solr's schema API. We don't specify the field mapping and let the config set to do the guessing. It may seem advantageous at one point because we don't have to restrict Solr to know any pre-fields and we can adopt the concept of schemaless. Solr will create fields on demand as it encounters documents. Now, this very advantage had become a problem. If you open up `films.json` and check the name of the first field, you will see it as `.45`. Solr, guessing it as Float type, keeps the datatype of the filmname as Float; the moment it encounters text, it spits out the error. We end up with huge trouble as we can't change the mapping fields once the index contains data.

For the same reason, it is not recommended to go with the `_default` schema config set. So, let's solve this issue by leveraging the schema API to modify our schema definition.

Delete the films collection by hitting the rest point:

```
http://localhost:8983/solr/admin/collections?action=DELETE&name=films
```

Create the collection again using the following command:

```
bin\solr.cmd -c films -shards 10 -n schemaless
```

We will be passing -n so that it will pick up the schemaless configuration instead of the previous default configuration.

Now make a post call with the following details, which will basically tell Solr to expect a field's name as a text rather than letting it auto-guess as Float:

End point	http://localhost:8983/solr/films/schema
Header	{"Content-Type":application/json}
Body	{"add-field": {"name":"name", "type":"text_general", "multiValued":false, "stored":true}}

You should get a successful response.

Now try hitting the import command again:
```
java -Dauto -Dc=films -jar post.jar
E:\solr-7.1.0\solr-7.1.0\example\films\films.json
```

You should be able to do so successfully. Go to the browser and open `http://localhost:8983/solr/films/select?q=*:*`. You should be able to see 1,100 records. You can similarly import CSV and XML files.

While importing a CSV file, you need to specify that if a field has multiple values, it should split; and you need to specify what the separator would be. If you check out `films.csv`, then you will notice that genres and `directed_by` are such fields. In this case, our import command would be:

```
java -jar -Dc=films -Dparams=f.genre.split=true & f.directed_by.split=true
& f.genre.separator=| & f.directed_by.separator=| -Dauto
example\exampledocs\post.jar example\films\*.csv
```

This is how we can load unstructured data in Solr. Let's now look at how to load structured data in Solr.

Loading data from MySQL

Solr's contrib provides the `datahandlerimport` module, and one of the examples in Solr is also focused on `DataImportHandler`, also known as DIH. Let's run the DIH example given by default. Hit `solr -e dih` to start Solr with the example of DIH. It will pick the configuration set in `$solr_home/example/example-DIH`. Create sample data in MySQL as follows:

```
Oracle is a registered trademark of Oracle Corporation and/or its
affiliates. Other names may be trademarks of their respective
owners.

Type 'help;' or '\h' for help. Type '\c' to clear the current input stat

mysql> use parth;
Database changed
mysql> desc archives;
+---------------+--------------+------+-----+---------+----------------
| Field         | Type         | Null | Key | Default | Extra
+---------------+--------------+------+-----+---------+----------------
| category_id   | int(11)      | NO   | PRI | NULL    | auto_increment
| category_name | varchar(150) | YES  |     | NULL    |
| remarks       | varchar(500) | YES  |     | NULL    |
+---------------+--------------+------+-----+---------+----------------
3 rows in set (0.00 sec)

mysql> select * from archives;
+-------------+---------------+-------------+
| category_id | category_name | remarks     |
+-------------+---------------+-------------+
|           1 | parth         | test test   |
|           2 | ghiya         | test1 test1 |
|           3 | random        | test1 test1 |
|           4 | perplex       | test1 test1 |
|           5 | mystified     | test1 test1 |
+-------------+---------------+-------------+
5 rows in set (0.00 sec)
```

Now it's time to integrate it into Solr. Follow these steps to find out the necessary configurations:

1. As stated earlier, any Solr installation would require the `solrconfig.xml` file, which has the necessary config information. This file usually resides in `$solr_home/<config_set_selected>/conf`. As we have selected `-e dih` and we are specifically looking for the database utility, we will find our `solrconfig.xml` at `$solr_home/example/example-DIH/solr/db/conf/solrconfig.xml`. Add the following lines of code in this file.

   Since we are going to use MySql, we need to download the MySQL connector JAR (`http://central.maven.org/maven2/mysql/mysql-connector-java/8.0.8-dmr/mysql-connector-java-8.0.8-dmr.jar`), place it in the `dist` folder `$solr_home/dist`, and let Solr know where to find the connector JAR by adding the following lines of code. Make sure that the `dataimporthandler` module is available in `dist`:

   ```
   <lib dir="${solr.install.dir:../../../..}/dist/" regex="solr-
   dataimporthandler-.*\.jar" />
     <lib dir="${solr.install.dir:../../../..}/contrib/extraction/lib"
   regex=".*\.jar" />
     <lib dir="${solr.install.dir:../../../..}/dist" regex="mysql-
   connector-java-\d.*\.jar" />
   ```

2. Next, we need to tell Solr where our database configuration file is. Add the following lines of code and create a file `db-data-config.xml` parallel to `solrconfig.xml`:

```
<requestHandler name="/dataimport" class="solr.DataImportHandler">
   <lst name="defaults">
    <str name="config">db-data-config.xml</str>
   </lst>
  </requestHandler>
```

3. `db-data-config.xml` is the file where we will define our database and Solr mapping. Create one file and define that file with the following schema:

```
<dataConfig>
    <dataSource driver="com.mysql.jdbc.Driver"
            url="jdbc:mysql://localhost:3306/chintan" user="root"
password="root" />
        <document>
        <entity name="archives" query="select * from archives"
 deltaImportQuery="SELECT * from archives WHERE
category_id='${dih.delta.id}'">
        <field column="category_id" name="category_id" />
        <field column="category_name" name="category_name" />
        <field column="remarks" name="remarks" />
        </entity>
        </document>
        </dataConfig>
```

4. The last part is to let Solr know about the new entity we have added. Go to `${solr_home}/example/example-DIH/solr/db/conf/managed-schema` and make the following changes. Change the primary key from `id` to `category_id`:

```
<field name="category_id" type="string" indexed="true" stored="true"
required="true" multiValued="false" />
...
<uniqueKey>category_id</uniqueKey>
```

 This is just a method to show how to import data from MySQL, and hence we are changing the primary key. In the real world, doing this is strongly not recommended.

5. Now let's add the new fields you introduced in `db-data-config.xml`:

```
<field name="category_name" type="string" indexed="true"
stored="true"/>
<field name="remarks" type="string" indexed="true" stored="true"/>
```

That's done. Now restart the server by hitting `solr/bin stop -all && solr/bin start -e dih`.

Go to the Solr admin panel. On the core selector, select the database and follow the steps shown in this screenshot:

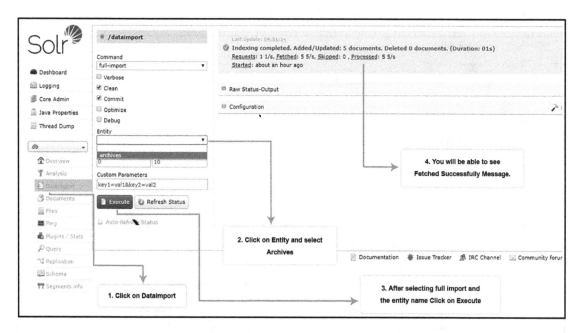

You can hit on the browser to see MySQL data in Solr.

Let's look at ways to browse data in Solr through the browse interface.

Understanding the browse interface

Now that our Solr is loaded up with data, we will look at multiple queries and the browse interface, through which we can query without actually knowing the end points. The data provided in `techproducts` includes a wide variety of fields along with geospatial indexes. So let's use that for a change. Open up the terminal and hit `bin\solr.cmd -e techproducts -p 4202`. As we have loaded a sample `techproducts` config set, it will import a bunch of files into the collection while starting up the server.

Once the server is up and running, hit
`http://localhost:4202/solr/techproducts/browse` to check out the browse
interface provided by Solr, as shown in the following screenshot:

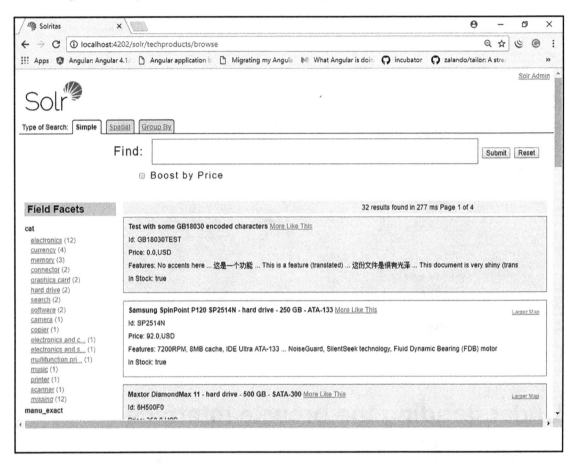

It is just another Google search for electronics now. Go ahead and type the query string
parameter. It will autocomplete and display the results as needed.

The following screenshot explains the browse interface in a lot of detail:

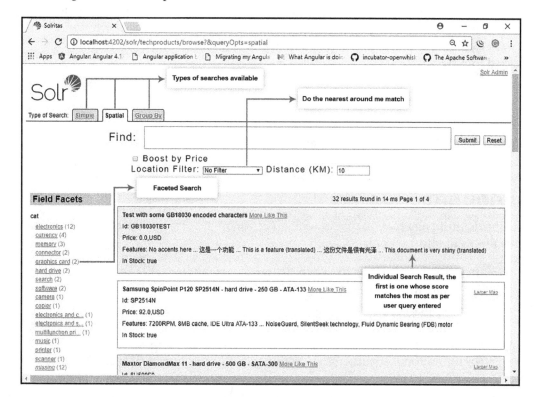

This feature makes use of the solariatis velocity contrib, which we saw earlier. This is useful for generating textual (it may or may not be HTML) from the Solr request.

Using the Solr admin interface

Solr provides a web interface for feasibility of Solr administrators and programmers to perform the following operations easily:

- View Solr configuration details
- Run different queries against indexes
- Analyze document fields to fine-tune the Solr config set
- Provide a schema browser for easy querying
- Show the java properties of each core

And much more... Under the hood, Solr reuses the same HTTP APIs that are available to all clients. Let us look at the Solr admin panel in detail. Go and start up Solr with the config set we created earlier. Accessing `http://localhost:7574/solr` or `http://localhost:8983/solr` will open up the Solr admin dashboard. The whole screen is divided into two parts:

- The left part showing the navigational menu
- The right part showing the interface selected menu

Let's take a deep dive into each of the sections.

Dashboard

This is the default page that opens up whenever we open Solr. The dashboard contains various pieces of information:

- **Instance details**: Tells us when the instance was started.
- **Versions information**: This gives us detailed information about the Solr and Lucene specs and implementation versions.
- **JVM information**: This details out information about JVM. It covers the JVM runtime environment found, processors, and arguments supplied to Solr. All the configurational arguments passed in various Solr config files can be seen combined here.
- **System**: This shows a pictorial view of the system status occupied right now and how much is available. The first and last gray bars show the physical and JVM memory available. The first is a measure of the amount of memory available in the hosting machine. The second shows the amount assigned to the startup of Solr in units of -Xms and -Xmx options.
- **JVM memory**: This shows info about the JVM memory and the memory and percentage that Solr occupies at any point in time.

Logging

Logs are a way to know what's going in the system at any point in time. When you click on logging, a screen similar to the following screenshot comes up. This is the interface where real-time logs of Solr are shown. It even supports multi-core logs. You can see various log levels, time, message, the core from which it comes, and so on:

Log4j (org.slf4j.impl.Log4jLoggerFactory)						
Time (Local)	Level	Level	Core	Logger	Message	1
11/11/2017, 1:37:00 PM	WARN false			ClientCnxn	Client session timed out, have not heard from server in 1184144ms for sessionid 0x15fa9dc7cb50000	
11/11/2017, 1:37:00 PM	WARN true			NIOServerCnxn	caught end of stream exception	ⓘ
EndOfStreamException: Unable to read additional data from client sessionid 0x15fa9dc7cb50000, likely cl at org.apache.zookeeper.server.NIOServerCnxn.doIO(NIOServerCnxn.java:239) at org.apache.zookeeper.server.NIOServerCnxnFactory.run(NIOServerCnxnFactory.java:203) at java.lang.Thread.run(Thread.java:745)						
11/11/2017, 1:37:00 PM	WARN false			ConnectionManager	Watcher org.apache.solr.common.cloud.ConnectionManager@4e85ac7 name: ZooKeeperConnection Watcher:localhost:9983 got event WatchedEvent state:Disconnected type:None path:null path: null type: None	
11/11/2017, 1:37:00 PM	WARN false			ConnectionManager	zkClient has disconnected	
11/11/2017, 1:37:00 PM	WARN false			ClientCnxn	Unable to reconnect to ZooKeeper service, session 0x15fa9dc7cb50000 has expired	
11/11/2017, 1:37:00 PM	WARN false			ConnectionManager	Watcher org.apache.solr.common.cloud.ConnectionManager@4e85ac7 name: ZooKeeperConnection Watcher:localhost:9983 got event WatchedEvent state:Expired type:None path:null path: null type: None	
11/11/2017, 1:37:00 PM	WARN false			ConnectionManager	Our previous ZooKeeper session was expired. Attempting to reconnect to recover relationship with ZooKeeper...	
11/11/2017, 1:37:01 PM	WARN false			Overseer	Solr cannot talk to ZK, exiting Overseer main queue loop	ⓘ
11/11/2017, 1:37:01 PM	WARN false			OverseerTriggerThread	OverseerTriggerThread woken up but we are closed, exiting.	
11/11/2017, 1:37:01 PM	ERROR false			Overseer	could not read the data	ⓘ
11/11/2017, 1:37:01 PM	WARN false			DefaultConnectionStrategy	Connection expired - starting a new one...	

Here are a few highlights of the logging details of our out-of-the-box Solr example:

- It shows logs based on time, level, core, logger class, and message.
- Some of the messages have an informative icon at the end. Clicking on it prints the stack trace.
- There are different log levels. The red ones are error level logs, and the yellow ones are warning level logs.

Solr provides a way to change the log level at any running system instance. You can adjust the level of logs for any class. The various options for the log level you can select are all, trace, debug, info, warn, error, fatal, off, and unset.

You can change the log levels of any class at any point of the running instance.

When you open up the level in Solr, you will see all of the hierarchy of class paths and class names. Any class that has logging capabilities would be marked in yellow. Click on the highlighted row and you will be able to change the log level of that class.

One interesting parameter you will see is unset. Any category that is unset will have log levels of its parents. This simple feature allows us to change many categories at once by just changing the log level of the parent:

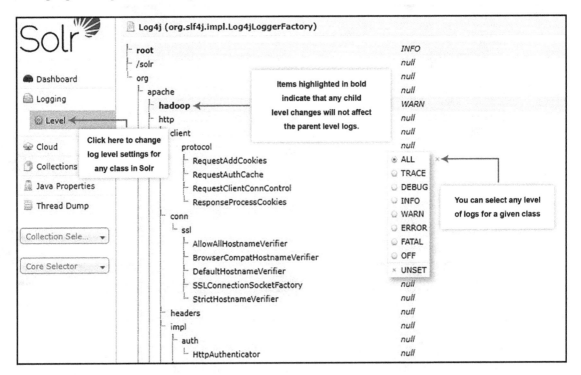

 This is a runtime setting and is not persisted, so if you open Solr again, it will be lost.

This isn't the only way we can change the log levels. Log levels can also be changed in the following ways:

- Using the log level API as mentioned here:

```
# Set the root logger to level WARN curl -s
http://localhost:8983/solr/admin/info/logging --data-binary
"set=root:WARN"
```

- Log levels can also be selected at startup. Again, this can be done in two ways:
  - Search for the string SOLR_LOGS_LEVEL in bin/solr.in.cmd or bin\solr.in.sh. Change it as needed.
  - The second alternative is to pass at startup with the -v or -q options. For example:

```
bin\solr start -f -v
bin\solr start -f -q
```

- A more permanent solution can be to change log4j.properties directly, which can be found at $solr_home/server/resources.

Cloud screens

When we run Solr in cloud mode, a cloud option will appear between logging and collections. This screen gives us the details of each collection and node in the cluster. It gives information about the level data stored in ZooKeeper. An important point to note is that this option is not visible when a single node is running or master-slave replication instances of Solr are running. It provides three different views: tree, graph, and graph (radial).

Tree view

This shows the directory structure of data residing in ZooKeeper and according to ZooKeeper configurations. It has cluster-wide information such as the number of live nodes, overseer, and overseer election status. It also has collection-specific information, such as `state.json` (which has a definition of the collection), the shard leaders, and the configuration files in use.

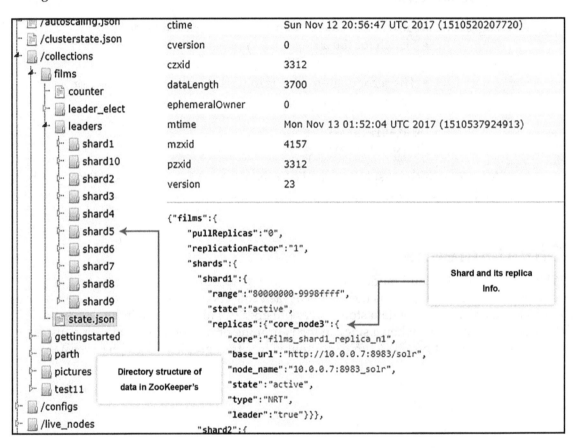

Graph view

This shows a graph of each collection, the number of shards that constitute that collection, and the address of each of the replicas of that shard. At the bottom of the screen, it shows labels for the leader shard, active shards, recovering shards, failed shards, inactive shards, and gone shards:

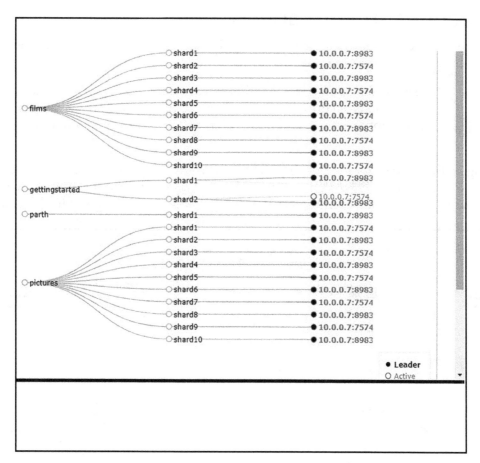

As you can see, there are multiple collections: films, gettingstarted, chintan, pictures, and so on. Most of the shards are active but notice a difference in the gettingstarted collection. Its shard 2 node has one blacked-out circle and another empty circle. This means that it is just an active node and not the leader. Also, if you check out shard 1 of gettingstarted, you will see a faint color; this means that this shard is no longer active.

Now let's look at some of the core admin stuff that we will be using in day-to-day life. The next section of collections is just a visual interface for the available collections API. Behind the scenes, this interface calls the very same APIs exposed over the rest. As a matter of fact, the Solr admin UI is made in AngularJS.

Collections or core admin

This screen provides some of the basic functionalities for managing collections in Solr, which runs the collections API under the hood.

Based on the number of instances you are running, you will see the option as collections or core admin. If you are running a single instance, you will see the option as core admin, which runs `CoreAdminApi` under the hood.

Clicking on **Collections** for the first time opens the list of collections you have. Clicking on any of the collections will give you metadata about it, which has various options such as shard count, config set name, and so on. It enables various options, as seen in this diagram:

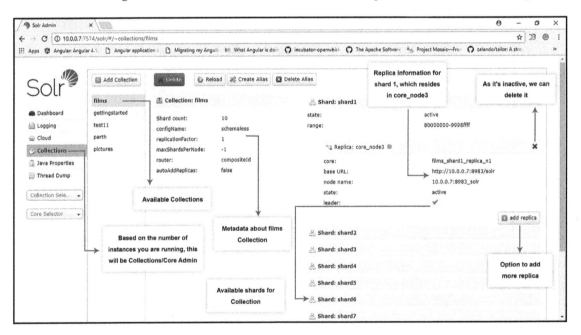

Java properties

With this screen, you can see all configured properties of JVM, which is running Solr. It includes the class path, encoding type, external libraries, and so on.

	Angular application bundles www.syntaxsuccess.com/viewarticle/angular-application-bundles
STOP.KEY	solrrocks
STOP.PORT	6574
awt.toolkit	sun.awt.windows.WToolkit
file.encoding	Cp1252
file.encoding.pkg	sun.io
file.separator	\
java.awt.graphicsenv	sun.awt.Win32GraphicsEnvironment
java.awt.printerjob	sun.awt.windows.WPrinterJob
java.class.path	E:\solr-7.1.0\solr-7.1.0\server\lib\gmetric4j-1.0.7.jar
	E:\solr-7.1.0\solr-7.1.0\server\lib\javax.servlet-api-3.1.0.jar
	E:\solr-7.1.0\solr-7.1.0\server\lib\jetty-continuation-9.3.20.v20170531.jar
	E:\solr-7.1.0\solr-7.1.0\server\lib\jetty-deploy-9.3.20.v20170531.jar
	E:\solr-7.1.0\solr-7.1.0\server\lib\jetty-http-9.3.20.v20170531.jar
	E:\solr-7.1.0\solr-7.1.0\server\lib\jetty-io-9.3.20.v20170531.jar
	E:\solr-7.1.0\solr-7.1.0\server\lib\jetty-jmx-9.3.20.v20170531.jar
	E:\solr-7.1.0\solr-7.1.0\server\lib\jetty-rewrite-9.3.20.v20170531.jar
	E:\solr-7.1.0\solr-7.1.0\server\lib\jetty-security-9.3.20.v20170531.jar
	E:\solr-7.1.0\solr-7.1.0\server\lib\jetty-server-9.3.20.v20170531.jar
	E:\solr-7.1.0\solr-7.1.0\server\lib\jetty-servlet-9.3.20.v20170531.jar
	E:\solr-7.1.0\solr-7.1.0\server\lib\jetty-servlets-9.3.20.v20170531.jar
	E:\solr-7.1.0\solr-7.1.0\server\lib\jetty-util-9.3.20.v20170531.jar
	E:\solr-7.1.0\solr-7.1.0\server\lib\jetty-webapp-9.3.20.v20170531.jar
	E:\solr-7.1.0\solr-7.1.0\server\lib\jetty-xml-9.3.20.v20170531.jar
	E:\solr-7.1.0\solr-7.1.0\server\lib\metrics-core-3.2.2.jar
	E:\solr-7.1.0\solr-7.1.0\server\lib\metrics-ganglia-3.2.2.jar
	E:\solr-7.1.0\solr-7.1.0\server\lib\metrics-graphite-3.2.2.jar
	E:\solr-7.1.0\solr-7.1.0\server\lib\metrics-jetty9-3.2.2.jar
	E:\solr-7.1.0\solr-7.1.0\server\lib\metrics-jvm-3.2.2.jar
	E:\solr-7.1.0\solr-7.1.0\server\lib\ext\jcl-over-slf4j-1.7.7.jar

Thread dump

This is the screen that lets you view and analyze the active threads on the server in Solr. Each thread is mentioned with a number and the stacktrace access if applicable. Each icon preceding the thread name indicates the state of the thread. A thread can be in any one of `new`, `runnable`, `blocked`, `waiting`, `timed_waiting` or `terminated` states.

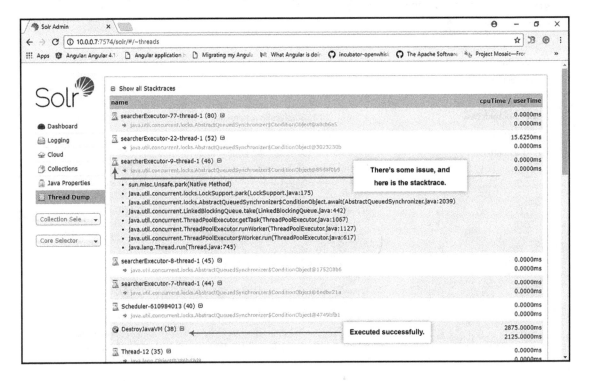

Collection-specific tools

Clicking on any one of the collections in the collection dropdown opens up the various things that we can do on any collection. It has the following suboptions.

Overview

This just contains basic metadata about the collection: the number of shards, the replica per shard, the range of each shard, the config set of the instance, and whether auto-add replicas is enabled or not.

Analysis

This is the screen that helps us analyze data in the collections. We can inspect the field, field type, and configurations in our schema; furthermore, we will be able to know how the content would be applied during indexing or query processing. Let's analyze one such query that gives us a detailed output, as follows:

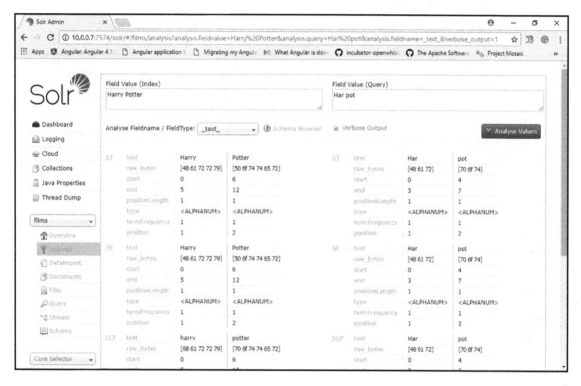

This screen is useful to study the analyzers applied on a collection. Analysis can be done in various phases where transformations such as uppercase, lowercase, singular/plural, synonyms, tenses, and so on will be taken into consideration.

DataImport

We saw this screen when we imported from MySQL. This screen allows us to monitor the status of all the import commands and the entities that we have defined in
`managed_schema`.

Documents

This screen allows us to directly run various Solr indexing commands right from the browser. You can do the following set of tasks:

1. Copy documents in any format, select the document type, and then index
2. Upload documents
3. Construct documents by the process of selecting field type and field values

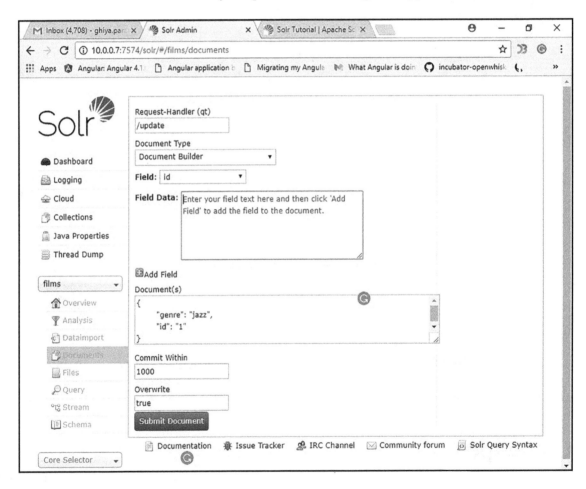

Files

The **Files** screen lets us browse and view various configuration and language-related files. These files cannot be edited with this screen. If you want to edit them, you have to visit the **Schema Browser** screen.

Query

You use this screen to query your existing collections. Various kinds of queries are available in Solr, right from normal queries to geospatial queries and faceted search.

Let's do a simple faceted query on genres in our `films` collection. Go to the **Query** screen; at the bottom, click on **facet**, and in `facet.field`, enter `genre`. Click on **execute query**:

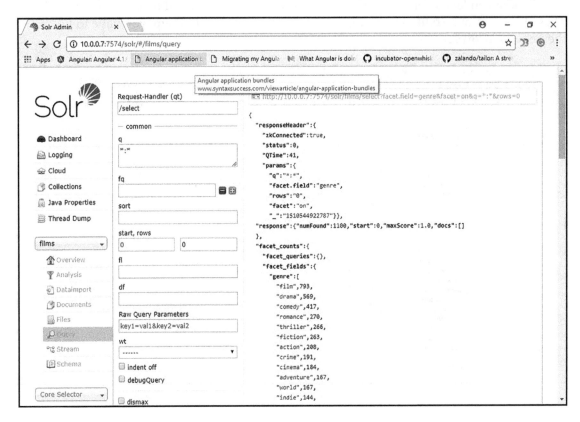

Stream

The streaming screen helps you understand the explanation of a query. It is very similar to the **Query** screen; it just adds an explanation part.

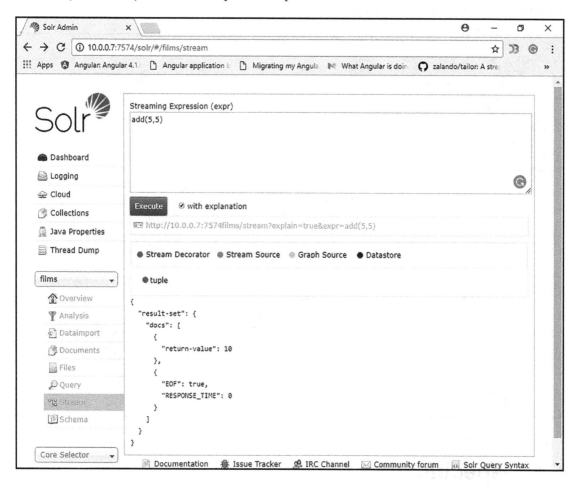

Schema

This screen lets us view the schema in a browser window. It provides in-depth information about each of the fields and its field type. It has options to add dynamic fields and copy field mapping from one field to another.

Core-specific tools

These are a group of UI utilities that give information about the core level. On selecting a **Core** in the dropdown, you will see the following screens:

- **Overview**: This will display some of the basic metadata about the running Solr core. You can add a file `admin-extra.html`, which consists of additional information if you would like to display in the **Admin Extra** block.
- **Ping**: This lets you send a ping to the selected core to determine whether the core is active or not.

- **Plugins / Stats**: Shows all the plugins installed and statistics. The performance factor of the Solr cache can be checked here.

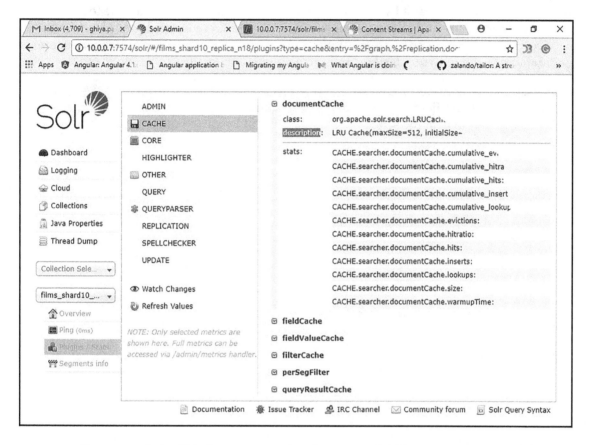

- **Segments info**: This lets you see visualizations of different segments by Lucene for the core selected. It shows information about the size of each segment, with units in both bytes and number of documents. You can also check out the number of deleted documents.

Summary

In this chapter, we got started with Solr. We saw the various options available to start Solr and saw the directory and folder structure of Solr in detail. We learned how to run Solr as service, Solr and ZooKeeper configurations, how to load some sample data from documents and databases, the browse interface, and the Admin UI in detail.

Let's move on to designing a schema in the next chapter. We will learn how to design it using documents and fields. We will go through various field types and see the schema API. We will also look at the schemaless mode.

3
Designing Schemas

Now that we have seen how to install Solr on our machine, let's dive deeper and understand the nitty-gritty of Solr.

Assume that you are building a home that you have always desired. How would you start? Will you just get all the bricks, cement, windows, doors, beams, and so on and ask the builders to start building? Nope! You would want to make sure you go through various designs based on the area that you have and decide on a design that you think will not only look good but also last long. Creating any application follows the same principle and demands proper schema design.

In this chapter, we will traverse through schema design. We will understand how to design a schema using documents and fields. We will also see various field types and get an understanding of the Schema API. We will finally look at schemaless mode.

How Solr works

The easiest way to understand how Solr works is to see how a telephone directory helps you to look something up. A telephone directory, or yellow pages as it is called in some places, is a book containing lots of phone numbers. It has lots of pages. Now, to find information in it would be a humongous task unless it had some sort of indexing and categorizing. For example, we can easily find all the restaurants by just navigating to the category of restaurants and finding the locality that we are living nearby.

Similarly, Solr can be imagined as a huge directory that has been fed data as per our requirement, and it can be queried to get the relevant data by using an appropriate search criteria that was indexed while feeding in the data. Let's have a look at the following diagram and understand how Solr search platform works:

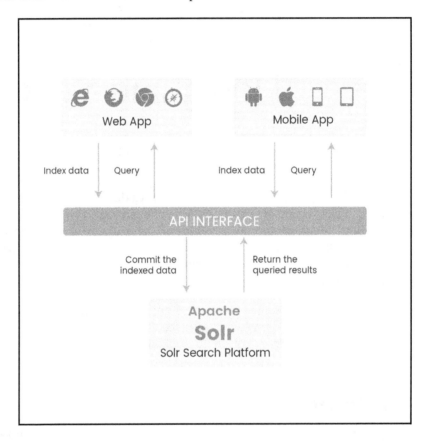

As you can see, the way to look at Solr is like this—it is basically fed with lots of information, which is correctly indexed. Then, in order to retrieve information, we query based on the index and get our results.

Suppose I am designing a data store for the world's largest online library using Solr. What I do is feed Solr with each book's information, such as the title, published date, author, price, genre, and so on. So, when I query all the books written by J.K. Rowling in the child fiction genre, it returns me my favorite *Harry Potter* book series.

Getting started with Solr's basics

Everything for Solr is a document, which forms the basic unit of information. Each document contains a set of fields, which can be of various types. If we take an example of a book store, each book forms a document. Now the author, publication date, and so on become fields of the document book, which can be a text or date format if we take up the example of the two fields quoted. Let's take a look at the following diagram and understand how the documents, fields are laid out in index of Solr instance:

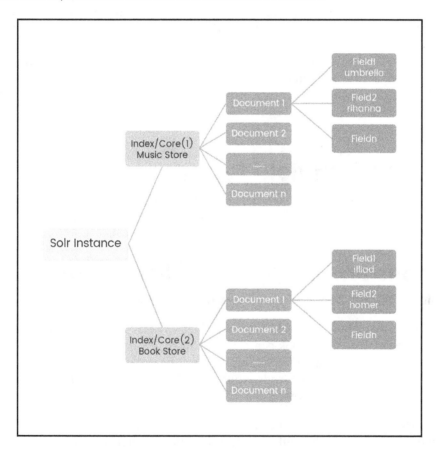

As you can see from the previous diagram, we can have as many indexes/cores in a Solr instance as we like. The first index/core in the previous case is for a music store, which can have various documents related to songs indexed in them. Each document has fields or metadata, such as singer, song title, and so on.

The schema file of Solr

All the information about fields and field types is mentioned in the schema file of Solr. Now, the schema file can be in one of the following places depending on how you have configured Solr:

- If you use `ClassicIndexSchemaFactory`, you would be manually editing the schema file which is named `schema.xml` by default
- If you decide to make schema changes at runtime using either the Schema API or schemaless mode, then the schema file is managed in the `managed-schema` file.

 In the case of SolrCloud, you will make changes to the schema using Solr's admin UI or Schema API if it is enabled. In such a case, you will not be able to find either `schema.xml` or `managed-schema.xml`.

Understanding field types

As discussed earlier, we are able to tell Solr how it should interpret the incoming data in a field and how we can query a field using the information specified in field types.

Definitions and properties of field types

Before going to the definitions and properties, we will see what field analysis means.

What Solr should do or how it should interpret data whenever data is indexed is important. For example, a description of a book can contain lots of useless words: helping verbs such as *is*, *was*, and *are*; pronouns such as *they*, *we*, and so on; and other general words such as *the*, *a*, *this*, and so on. Querying these words will bring all the data. Similarly what should we do with words that have capital letters?

All of these problems can be catered using field analysis to ignore common words or casing while indexing or querying. We will dive deep into field analysis in the next chapter.

Now, coming back to field types, all analyses on a field are done by the field type, whether documents are indexed or a query is made on the index.

All field types are specified in schema.xml. A field type can have the following attributes:

- The name field, which is mandatory.
- The class field, which is also mandatory. This tells us which class to implement.
- In the case of TextField, you can mention description to convey what the TextField does.
- Based on the Implementation class certain field type properties which may or may not be mandatory.

The field type is defined within the fieldType tags. Let's take a look at a field type definition for text_en:

```
<fieldType name="text_en" class="solr.TextField"
  positionIncrementGap="100">
    <analyzer type="index">
        <tokenizer class="solr.StandardTokenizerFactory"/>
        <!-- in this example, we will only use synonyms at query
          time
        <filter class="solr.SynonymGraphFilterFactory"
          synonyms="index_synonyms.txt" ignoreCase="true"
          expand="false"/>
        <filter class="solr.FlattenGraphFilterFactory"/>
        -->
        <!-- Case insensitive stop word removal-->
        <filter class="solr.StopFilterFactory"
            ignoreCase="true"
            words="lang/stopwords_en.txt"
        />
        <filter class="solr.LowerCaseFilterFactory"/>
        <filter class="solr.EnglishPossessiveFilterFactory"/>
        <filter class="solr.KeywordMarkerFilterFactory"
          protected="protwords.txt"/>
        <filter class="solr.PorterStemFilterFactory"/>
    </analyzer>
    <analyzer type="query">
        <tokenizer class="solr.StandardTokenizerFactory"/>
        <filter class="solr.SynonymGraphFilterFactory"
          synonyms="synonyms.txt" ignoreCase="true"
          expand="true"/>
        <filter class="solr.StopFilterFactory"
            ignoreCase="true"
            words="lang/stopwords_en.txt"
        />
        <filter class="solr.LowerCaseFilterFactory"/>
        <filter class="solr.EnglishPossessiveFilterFactory"/>
```

```
          <filter class="solr.KeywordMarkerFilterFactory"
            protected="protwords.txt"/>
          <filter class="solr.PorterStemFilterFactory"/>
      </analyzer>
   </fieldType>
```

As you can see, the first line defines fieldType with name text_en, which implements the solr.TextField class. It also has an attribute, positionIncrementGap, which adds spaces between multi-value fields.

For example, let's say your text contains the following tokens:

```
writer: Sandeep Nair
writer: Dharmesh Vasoya
```

Now, without any positionIncrementGap attribute, it is possible to bring up the results when someone searches for Nair Dharmesh. But with the positionIncrementGap attribute, we can avoid this.

We will cover the rest of the details available in fieldType class in detail in the next chapter.

 You must have noticed that a class begins with solr in solr.TextField. This is a short form for the fully qualified package name org.apache.solr.schema.

Field type properties

All of field type is behavior generally controlled by the fieldType class and the optional properties:

```
<fieldType name="currency" class="solr.CurrencyFieldType"
amountLongSuffix="_l_ns" codeStrSuffix="_s_ns"
      defaultCurrency="USD" currencyConfig="currency.xml" />
```

We see that the defaultCurrency is USD and extra config-related information is specified in a file called currency.xml.

There are three types of properties that can be associated with a `fieldType` class:

- General properties, which can be applicable for any `fieldType` class
- Field default properties, as shown in the previous example where we default the currency value to USD if none is specified
- Finally, properties that are specific for a specific `fieldType` class

General properties are specified as follows:

Properties	Description
name	The name of the `fieldType`.
class	The name of the class that is used to index and store the data for this type.
positionIncrementGap	Specifically for multi-value fields. It is used to specify the distance between multiple values. This helps in preventing phrase matches that are spurious in nature.
autoGeneratePhraseQueries	This is used for `TextField`. If this value is true, Solr generates phrase queries intended for adjacent terms automatically. If it is false, then terms are supposed to be enclosed in double quotes in order for them to be treated as phrases.
enableGraphQueries	Used for only text fields. It is applicable only while querying `sow=false`.
docValuesFormat	This is used to define a custom `DocValuesFormat`.
postingsFormat	Helps in defining a custom `PostingsFormat` to be used for fields of this type.

Now let's take a look at the field default properties. The values can be defaulted in actual fields or can be inherited from the field types.

Property	Detail	Available values	Default value
indexed	Tells whether to index the field or not.	• true • false	true

stored	The actual value of the field can be retrieved using queries if the value is `true`.	• `true` • `false`	`true`
`sortMissingFirst` and `sortMissingLast`	If a sort field is not present, this decides the placement of the document.	• `true` • `false`	`false`
`docValues`	The value of this field is placed in a column-oriented `docValues` structure if set to `true`.	• `true` • `false`	`false`
`multiValued`	Indicates whether a single document can have multiple values for this field type.	• `true` • `false`	`false`
`omitNorms`	Used to disable field length normalization and to save some memory. For all primitive field types, the value is `true` by default. Norms are needed only for full-text fields.	• `true` • `false`	*
`omitTermFreqAndPositions`	Omits term frequency, position, and payloads from postings of this field when `true`. Defaults to `true` for non-text fields.	• `true` • `false`	*
`omitPositions`	This is similar to `omitTermFreqAndPositions`; however, in this case, it preserves information about the term frequency.	• `true` • `false`	*
`termVectors`, `termPositions`, `termOffsets`, and `termPayloads`	Solr maintains full term vectors for every single document if these properties are `true`. These vectors, may include position, offset, and payload information optionally for each term occurrence.	• `true` • `false`	`false`
`required`	Tells Solr not to accept any attempts to add a document that does not have a value for the field.	• `true` • `false`	`false`

useDocValuesAsStored	This is dependent on the docValues enabled. This is enabled if we set it to true and will allow the field to be returned as if it were a stored field while matching * in an fl parameter.	• true • false	true
large	This will work only when stored="true" and multiValued="false". In order not to get cached in memory, this is meant for fields that might have very large values.	• true • false	false

In order to score a document in searching, Solr uses similarity. For every collection, there is one global similarity and Solr implicitly uses BM25Similarity. You can declare a top-level <similarity/> element and override it.

Best Matching (BM)

BM25 is a ranking algorithm used by search engines such as Lucene to rank matching documents according to their relevance by a given search query.

Field types available in Solr

Let's see the various field types available with Solr:

- BinaryField: This is intended for binary data.
- BoolField: This is for Boolean data. It can either be true or false. If values 1, t, or T are encountered in the first character, then it is interpreted as true. All other values are interpreted as false.
- CollationField: This is used for collated sort keys, which can be used for locale-sensitive sort and range queries.
- CurrencyFieldType: This is used for currencies and exchange rates.

There is also a CurrencyField that does the same thing, but it is deprecated.

- `DateRangeField`: This is used for working with date ranges, as the name suggests. We will cover this in detail in the next section.
- `ExternalFileField`: This is used when values have to be pulled from an external file.
- `EnumFieldType`: This is used for enumerated sets of values.

> There is also an `EnumField` that does the same thing, but it is now deprecated.

- `ICUCollationField`: This is similar to `CollationField` and is recommended instead of `CollationField`.
- `LatLonPointSpatialField`: This is used for multi-value for multiple points of latitude and longitude coordinate pairs. It is usually specified as latitude, longitude in that order, with a comma to separate the two.
- `PointType`: This is used when we have a single-valued n-dimensional point, and if we have to sort spatial data that is non-latitude, non-longitude or handle rare use cases.
- `PreAnalyzedField`: This is used when we have to send serialized token streams to Solr to store and index without any additional text processing.
- `RandomSortField`: This does not contain values and is used to return results in a random order.
- `SpatialRecursivePrefixTreeFieldType`: This accepts latitude, longitude strings in **well-known text** (**WKT**) format.
- `StrField`: This is intended for small fields and is not tokenized or analyzed.
- `TextField`: This is used for multiple words or tokens.
- `DatePointField/DoublePointField/FloatPointField/IntPointField/LongPointField`: These are all similar to the analogous Trie-based fields. The only difference is that they use dimensional-points-based data structures and do not require any configuration of precision steps.

> As of Solr 7, all the `Trie[Datatype]Fields` are deprecated: `TrieField`, `TrieDateField`, `TrieDoubleField`, `TrieFloatField`, `TrieIntField`, and `TrieLongField`.

`UUIDField` will generate a new UUID when we pass a value of `NEW`. It is recommended to use `UUIDUpdateProcessorFactory` instead of `UUIDField` to generate UUID values when using `SolrCloud`, since doing so will make each document of each replica have a unique UUID value.

Understanding date fields

As seen before, Solr's date fields such as `DatePointField`, `DateRangeField`, and `TrieDateField` (deprecated) represent dates as points in time with millisecond precision. Solr uses `DateTimeFormatter.ISO_INSTANT` for formatting and parsing:

```
YYYY-MM-DDThh:mm:ssZ
```

Let's break up the preceding date pattern. Please take a look at the break up listed as follow:

- `YYYY` is the year. An example is 1985
- `MM` is the month. For example, `02` represents February
- `DD` is the day of the month
- `T` is a literal used to separate date and time
- `hh` is the hour of the day
- `mm` is minutes
- `ss` is seconds
- `Z` is a literal used to indicate the string representation of the date in **Coordiated Universal Time (UTC)**

 No time zone can be specified and all the string representations of dates are specified in UTC.

An example would be:

```
1985-02-21T06:33:19Z
```

We can optionally add fractional seconds, but as mentioned earlier, any precision beyond milliseconds will not be considered.

If we need a date prior to the year 0000, then the date should have a leading –; similarly for years after 9999, there should be a leading +.

In order to express date ranges, Solr's DateRangeField is used. Some of the examples are shown as follows:

- 1985-02: This represents the entire month of February 1985
- 1985-02T06: This also adds an hour element from 6 AM to 7 AM during February 1985
- -0002: Since there is a leading –, this represents 3 BC
- [1985-02-21 TO 1989-08-27]: The date range between these two dates
- [1985 TO 1985-02-21]: From the start of 1985 until February 21, 1985
- [* TO 1985-02-21]: From the earliest representable time to the end of the 21st day of February 1985

Date math expressions are one more interesting format. They help by adding some quantity of time in a specified unit or rounding off the current time by a specified unit. These expressions can also be chained and they are always evaluated from left to right, like every Math expression.

Some valid expressions are as follows:

- NOW+4DAYS: Specifies 4 days from today.
- NOW-6MONTHS: Specifies 6 months before now.
- NOW/HOUR: Here, the slash indicates rounding. This tells us to round off to the beginning of the current hour.
- NOW+4MONTHS+6DAYS/DAY: This expression specifies a point in the future four months and six days from now and rounds off to the beginning of that day.

Date math can be applied between any two times and not everything has to necessarily be relative to NOW.

The NOW parameter can also be used to specify an arbitrary moment in time and not necessarily the current time. It can be overridden using long-valued milliseconds since the epoch.

`DateRangeFields` also supports three relational predicates between the indexed data and the query range:

- `Intersects` (which is default)
- `Contains`
- `Within`

We can specify the predicate by querying using the `op` local parameter:

```
fq={!field f=dateRange op=Contains}[1985 TO 1989]
```

This would find documents with indexed ranges that contain the range `1985` to `1989`.

Understanding currencies and exchange rates

As the name implies, a currency field type is used for any monetary value. It supports currency conversion and exchange rates during a query.

Solr provides the following features for it:

- Range queries
- Point queries
- Sorting
- Function range queries
- Symmetric and asymmetric exchange rates
- Currency parsing

As with other field types, the `currency` field type is configured in `schema.xml`. Shown here is the default configuration:

```
<fieldType name="currency" class="solr.CurrencyFieldType"
amountLongSuffix="_l_ns" codeStrSuffix="_s_ns"
        defaultCurrency="USD" currencyConfig="currency.xml" />
```

As you can see, `name` is set as `currency` and `class` is specified as `solr.CurrencyFieldType`. We have defined the `defaultCurrency` as `INR` or Indian rupee. Also note `currencyConfig`, which says that the file location is set to `currency.xml`. This file specifies exchange rates between `INR` and other currencies.

In your open `managed-schema` file under the `SOLR_HOME/example/example-DIH/solr/solr/conf` folder, using a text editor, you will find the following dynamic field:

```
<dynamicField name="*_c" type="currency" indexed="true" stored="true"/>
```

This `dynamicField` matches any fields suffixed by `_c` and treats them as `currency` type fields.

Solr gives us the flexibility to index money fields in our native currency. We can specify `100,SGD` to index the money field in Singapore dollars:

```
<fieldType name="currency" class="solr.CurrencyFieldType"
amountLongSuffix="_l_ns" codeStrSuffix="_s_ns"
        defaultCurrency="USD" currencyConfig="currency.xml" />
```

Let's revisit the field type.

Here, you will notice one thing; there are a couple of subfield suffixes named `amountLongSuffix` and `codeStrSuffix`, which correspond to raw amount and currency code respectively. In this case, the raw amount field will make use of the `*_l_ns` dynamic field, which uses a long field type. The currency code field will make use of the `*_s_ns` dynamic field, which uses a string field type.

In the previous tag, you can also see `currencyConfig`, which refers to a file called `currency.xml`. This is used to specify exchange rates.

Solr supports two types of providers:

- `FileExchangeRateProvider`
- `OpenExchangeRatesOrgProvider`

`FileExchangeRateProvider` is the default provider. In order to use this, we specify the config file using `currencyConfig` as shown previously. The contents of `currency.xml` are as follows:

```
<?xml version="1.0" ?>
<!-- Example exchange rates file for CurrencyFieldType named "currency" in
example schema -->
<currencyConfig version="1.0">
 <rates>
 <!-- Updated from http://www.exchangerate.com/ at 2011-09-27 -->
 <rate from="USD" to="ARS" rate="4.333871" comment="ARGENTINA Peso" />
 <rate from="USD" to="AUD" rate="1.025768" comment="AUSTRALIA Dollar" />
 <rate from="USD" to="EUR" rate="0.743676" comment="European Euro" />
 <rate from="USD" to="BRL" rate="1.881093" comment="BRAZIL Real" />
```

```xml
<rate from="USD" to="CAD" rate="1.030815" comment="CANADA Dollar" />
<rate from="USD" to="CLP" rate="519.0996" comment="CHILE Peso" />
<rate from="USD" to="CNY" rate="6.387310" comment="CHINA Yuan" />
<rate from="USD" to="CZK" rate="18.47134" comment="CZECH REP. Koruna" />
<rate from="USD" to="DKK" rate="5.515436" comment="DENMARK Krone" />
<rate from="USD" to="HKD" rate="7.801922" comment="HONG KONG Dollar" />
<rate from="USD" to="HUF" rate="215.6169" comment="HUNGARY Forint" />
<rate from="USD" to="ISK" rate="118.1280" comment="ICELAND Krona" />
<rate from="USD" to="INR" rate="49.49088" comment="INDIA Rupee" />
<rate from="USD" to="XDR" rate="0.641358" comment="INTNL MON. FUND SDR" />
<rate from="USD" to="ILS" rate="3.709739" comment="ISRAEL Sheqel" />
<rate from="USD" to="JPY" rate="76.32419" comment="JAPAN Yen" />
<rate from="USD" to="KRW" rate="1169.173" comment="KOREA (SOUTH) Won" />
<rate from="USD" to="KWD" rate="0.275142" comment="KUWAIT Dinar" />
<rate from="USD" to="MXN" rate="13.85895" comment="MEXICO Peso" />
<rate from="USD" to="NZD" rate="1.285159" comment="NEW ZEALAND Dollar" />
<rate from="USD" to="NOK" rate="5.859035" comment="NORWAY Krone" />
<rate from="USD" to="PKR" rate="87.57007" comment="PAKISTAN Rupee" />
<rate from="USD" to="PEN" rate="2.730683" comment="PERU Sol" />
<rate from="USD" to="PHP" rate="43.62039" comment="PHILIPPINES Peso" />
<rate from="USD" to="PLN" rate="3.310139" comment="POLAND Zloty" />
<rate from="USD" to="RON" rate="3.100932" comment="ROMANIA Leu" />
<rate from="USD" to="RUB" rate="32.14663" comment="RUSSIA Ruble" />
<rate from="USD" to="SAR" rate="3.750465" comment="SAUDI ARABIA Riyal" />
<rate from="USD" to="SGD" rate="1.299352" comment="SINGAPORE Dollar" />
<rate from="USD" to="ZAR" rate="8.329761" comment="SOUTH AFRICA Rand" />
<rate from="USD" to="SEK" rate="6.883442" comment="SWEDEN Krona" />
<rate from="USD" to="CHF" rate="0.906035" comment="SWITZERLAND Franc" />
<rate from="USD" to="TWD" rate="30.40283" comment="TAIWAN Dollar" />
<rate from="USD" to="THB" rate="30.89487" comment="THAILAND Baht" />
<rate from="USD" to="AED" rate="3.672955" comment="U.A.E. Dirham" />
<rate from="USD" to="UAH" rate="7.988582" comment="UKRAINE Hryvnia" />
<rate from="USD" to="GBP" rate="0.647910" comment="UNITED KINGDOM Pound"
/>
<!-- Cross-rates for some common currencies -->
<rate from="EUR" to="GBP" rate="0.869914" />
<rate from="EUR" to="NOK" rate="7.800095" />
<rate from="GBP" to="NOK" rate="8.966508" />
</rates>
</currencyConfig>
```

Updating `currency.xml` becomes tedious manual work. In order to dynamically pull the latest exchange rates from the Web, we use `OpenExchangeRatesOrgProvider`. This will download the latest exchange rates from `https://openexchangerates.org`:

```
<fieldType name="currency" class="solr.CurrencyFieldType"
    amountLongSuffix="_l_ns" codeStrSuffix="_s_ns"
providerClass="solr.OpenExchangeRatesOrgProvider"
    refreshInterval="60"    ratesFileLocation=
"http://www.openexchangerates.org/api/latest.json?app_id=yourPersonalAppIdK
ey"/>
```

As shown in the previous tag, we have specified `providerClass` as `solr.OpenExchangeRatesOrgProvider` and specified the refresh interval as 1 hour. We have also specified the URL from which to pull the latest exchange rates.

> You need to register first at Open Exchange Rates to get your own personal app ID key, which you will then replace in the preceding URL.

Understanding enum fields

Just as Java has the enum data type to have something for a closed set of values, Solr has `EnumFieldType`, which lets us define closed set values. Here, the sort order is predetermined.

Defining an `EnumFieldType` is done as follows:

```
<fieldType name="genreList" class="solr.EnumFieldType" docValues="true"
enumsConfig= "enumsConfig.xml" enumName="genre"/>
```

Here, as you can see, we have defined the name as `genreList` and the class is specified as `solr.EnumFieldType`. We also have specified `enumConfig` to specify the path of the configuration file.

Last but not least, we have specified `enumName` to uniquely identify the name of the enumeration:

```
<?xml version="1.0" ?>
<enumsConfig>
    <enum name="genre">
        <value>Science Fiction</value>
        <value>Satire</value>
        <value>Drama</value>
```

```
        <value>Action</value>
        <value>Adventure</value>
        <value>Mystery</value>
        <value>Horror</value>
    </enum>
</enumsConfig>
```

The `enumsConfig` file can contain many enumeration value lists with different names as per your requirement. Take a look at the content of the enumeration file for the genres shown in the preceding code.

Field management

Once your primary work of field types setup is done, field definition is a small task. Just as with field types, the fields element of `schema.xml` holds the field definition.

Field properties

Let's first see a sample field definition:

```
<field name="weight" type="float" default="0.0" indexed="true"
stored="true"/>
```

In the preceding example, we have defined a field named `weight`, whose field type is `float` with a `default` value of `0.0`. Moreover, the `indexed` as well as `stored` properties are explicitly set to `true`.

Field definitions will have these properties:

- `name`: The field name. This has to be alphanumeric and can include underscore characters. It cannot begin with a digit. Reserved names should start and end with underscores (for example, `_root_`). Every field must have a name.
- `type`: The name of the `fieldType`. All the fields should have a type.
- `default`: The default value to be used for the field.

Fields and field types share many of the optional properties here. If there are two different values of a property specified in both field and field type, then the property value specified in the field takes precedence.

Copying fields

Copying fields is used when you want to interpret a field in more than one way. Solr provides a solution to copy fields so that one can apply distinct field types for the same field.

Let's see the following element that I have copied from one of the managed-schemas available in demo Solr projects:

```
<copyField source="name" dest="text"/>
```

In the previous example, we are copying the name field specified in the source attribute to a field name text, which is specified in dest.

The actual copying of fields occurs before analysis, which makes it possible to have two fields with the same content but different analyses.

The general use case of this functionality is when we have one global search for all fields. Let's say I want to search the word Harry in the title and description. Then I can create a copyField for the title and description fields and redirect them to a common destination. Look at the following snippet:

```
<copyField source="*_e" dest="text" maxChars="10000" />
```

Here, we are specifying a wildcard pattern that matches everything that ends with _e and indexes them to the destination text field.

 You cannot chain copyField; that is, the destination of one copyField cannot be a part of the source of another copyField. The workaround is to create multiple destination fields and use the same source field.

Dynamic fields

We use dynamic fields to index fields that we do not want to explicitly define in our schema.

This feature is handy when you want to use a wild card for indexing fields, where you want to index all the fields having a certain pattern. Let's see an example of dynamicField:

```
<dynamicField name="*_e" type="int" indexed="true" stored="true"/>
```

As you can see, dynamic fields also have name, type, and options. However, here you can see that the name has a wildcard pattern *_e, which means any field with _e will have the same indexing.

Mastering Schema API

Schema API is the one-stop shop for most operations on your schema. It provides a REST-like HTTP API for doing all these operations.

You can read, write, or delete dynamic fields, fields, copy field rules, and field types.

 Do not manually write any changes into the managed-schema file yourself. This will work only as long as you don't use Schema API. If you use Schema API by mistake, all your changes might be overwritten. So, it is highly recommend that you leave your managed-schema file alone.

The response of the API call is of either JSON or XML format.

Assuming that you are using the gettingstarted collection, the base address of API will be http://localhost:8983/solr/gettingstarted.

 Always reindex once you use Schema API for modifications. Only then will the changes that you have applied to the schema be reflected for existing documents that are already indexed.

Schema API in detail

Let's see some of the important schema endpoints. We will do all the examples on the gettingstarted collection.

Schema operations

In order to see the schema, we need to use the /schema endpoint, http://localhost:8983/solr/gettingstarted/schema/.

This will retrieve the entire schema information:

```
{
  "responseHeader":{
    "status":0,
    "QTime":2},
  "schema":{
    "name":"default-config",
    "version":1.6,
    "uniqueKey":"id",
    "fieldTypes":[{
        "name":"ancestor_path",
        "class":"solr.TextField",
        "indexAnalyzer":{
          "tokenizer":{
            "class":"solr.KeywordTokenizerFactory"}},
        "queryAnalyzer":{
          "tokenizer":{
            "class":"solr.PathHierarchyTokenizerFactory",
            "delimiter":"/"}}},
      {
        "name":"binary",
        "class":"solr.BinaryField"},
      {
        "name":"boolean",
        "class":"solr.BoolField",
        "sortMissingLast":true},
      {
        "name":"booleans",
        "class":"solr.BoolField",
        "sortMissingLast":true,
        "multiValued":true},
      {
        "name":"delimited_payloads_float",
        "class":"solr.TextField",
        "indexed":true,
        "stored":false,
        "analyzer":{
          "tokenizer":{
            "class":"solr.WhitespaceTokenizerFactory"},
          "filters":[{
            "class":"solr.DelimitedPayloadTokenFilterFactory",
            "encoder":"float"}]}},
      ...
      ...
```

In order to add a field, we will use the following command:

```
curl -X POST -H 'Content-type:application/json' --data-binary '{
    "add-field":{
    "name":"song-name",
    "type":"text_general",
    "stored":true }
}' http://localhost:8983/solr/gettingstarted/schema
```

The previous code will add a song-name field name whose type is text_general to the gettingstarted schema.

We can also replace a field's definition. To do so we can issue the following command:

```
curl -X POST -H 'Content-type:application/json' --data-binary '{
    "replace-field":{
    "name":"song-name",
    "type":"string",
    "stored":false }
}' http://localhost:8983/solr/gettingstarted/schema
```

This will replace the definition of song with string.

Now let's take a look at the snippet to delete the field:

```
curl -X POST -H 'Content-type:application/json' --data-binary '{
    "delete-field" : { "name":"song-name" }
}' http://localhost:8983/solr/gettingstarted/schema
```

This will delete the song-name field that we created just now.

Similarly, to add, delete, and replace dynamic field rules, we need to use the following endpoints:

- add-dynamic-field
- delete-dynamic-field
- replace-dynamic-field

We can also add, update, and delete field types using these endpoints:

- add-field-type
- delete-field-type
- replace-field-type

We will take a look at the syntax of making an API call to `add-field-type` as it has some additional parameters:

```
curl -X POST -H 'Content-type:application/json' --data-binary '{
    "add-field-type" : {
        "name":"song-description-field",
        "class":"solr.TextField",
        "positionIncrementGap":"100",
        "analyzer" : {
            "charFilters":[{
                "class":"solr.PatternReplaceCharFilterFactory",
                "replacement":"$1$1",
                "pattern":"([a-zA-Z])\\\\1+" }],
            "tokenizer":{
                "class":"solr.WhitespaceTokenizerFactory" },
            "filters":[{
                "class":"solr.WordDelimiterFilterFactory",
                "preserveOriginal":"0" }]}}
}' http://localhost:8983/solr/gettingstarted/schema
```

Here, we have added a new field type for song description, which is of type `TextField` and uses `WhitespaceTokenizerFactory` as a tokenizer using a filter `WordDelimiterFilterFactory`.

Finally, in order to add or delete a copy field rule, use the following:

- `add-copy-field`
- `delete-copy-field`

Listing fields, field types, DynamicFields, and CopyField rules

In order to list all the fields, type the following URL in the browser: `http://localhost:8983/solr/gettingstarted/schema/fields`:

```
{
  "responseHeader":{
    "status":0,
    "QTime":0},
  "fields":[{
      "name":"_root_",
      "type":"string",
      "docValues":false,
      "indexed":true,
```

```
    "stored":false},
  {
    "name":"_text_",
    "type":"text_general",
    "multiValued":true,
    "indexed":true,
    "stored":false},
  {
    "name":"_version_",
    "type":"plong",
    "indexed":false,
    "stored":false},
  {
    "name":"id",
    "type":"string",
    "multiValued":false,
    "indexed":true,
    "required":true,
    "stored":true}]}
```

This will list all the fields defined. Now, to see all the field types, enter this `http://localhost:8983/solr/gettingstarted/schema/fieldtypes`:

```
{
  "responseHeader":{
    "status":0,
    "QTime":2},
  "fieldTypes":[{
      "name":"ancestor_path",
      "class":"solr.TextField",
      "indexAnalyzer":{
        "tokenizer":{
          "class":"solr.KeywordTokenizerFactory"}},
      "queryAnalyzer":{
        "tokenizer":{
          "class":"solr.PathHierarchyTokenizerFactory",
          "delimiter":"/"}}},
  {
    "name":"binary",
    "class":"solr.BinaryField"},
  {
    "name":"boolean",
    "class":"solr.BoolField",
    "sortMissingLast":true},
  {
    "name":"booleans",
    "class":"solr.BoolField",
```

```
      "sortMissingLast":true,
      "multiValued":true},
    {
      "name":"delimited_payloads_float",
      "class":"solr.TextField",
      "indexed":true,
      "stored":false,
      "analyzer":{
        "tokenizer":{
          "class":"solr.WhitespaceTokenizerFactory"},
        "filters":[{
            "class":"solr.DelimitedPayloadTokenFilterFactory",
```

This will display all the field types. You can also see an individual field type by passing the field type name. Similarly, to display dynamic fields and copy field rules, we can use the following endpoints respectively, `http://localhost:8983/solr/gettingstarted/schema/dynamicfields`:

```
  {
    "responseHeader":{
      "status":0,
      "QTime":1},
    "dynamicFields":[{
        "name":"*_txt_en_split_tight",
        "type":"text_en_splitting_tight",
        "indexed":true,
        "stored":true},
      {
        "name":"*_descendent_path",
        "type":"descendent_path",
        "indexed":true,
        "stored":true},
      {
        "name":"*_ancestor_path",
        "type":"ancestor_path",
        "indexed":true,
        "stored":true},
      {
        "name":"*_txt_en_split",
        "type":"text_en_splitting",
        "indexed":true,
        "stored":true},
      {
        "name":"*_txt_rev",
        "type":"text_general_rev",
        "indexed":true,
```

```
      "stored":true},
    {
      "name":"*_phon_en",
      "type":"phonetic_en",
      "indexed":true,
      "stored":true},
    {
      "name":"*_s_lower",
      "type":"lowercase",
      "indexed":true,
      "stored":true},
  ...
  ...
```

We can see a list of all copy fields using the following URL:
`http://localhost:8983/solr/gettingstarted/schema/copyfields`.

We will see this response:

```
{
  "responseHeader":{
    "status":0,
    "QTime":0},
  "copyFields":[]}
```

In order to see the schema name, use this URL:
`http://localhost:8983/solr/gettingstarted/schema/name`.

This will display the schema name's details:

```
{
  "responseHeader":{
    "status":0,
    "QTime":0},
  "name":"default-config"}
```

Similarly, you can see the schema version using the following
URL, `http://localhost:8983/solr/gettingstarted/schema/version`:

```
{
  "responseHeader":{
    "status":0,
    "QTime":0},
  "version":1.6}
```

This shows that the current schema version is `1.6`.

Likewise, in order to see the unique key, we can use this URL, `http://localhost:8983/solr/gettingstarted/schema/uniquekey`:

```
{
  "responseHeader":{
    "status":0,
    "QTime":0},
  "uniqueKey":"id"}
```

Here we see that the `uniqueKey` of the schema is `id`.

Finally, in order to see the class name of the global similarity, we have to use the following URL, `http://localhost:8983/solr/gettingstarted/schema/similarity`:

```
{
  "responseHeader":{
    "status":0,
    "QTime":0},
  "similarity":{
    "class":"org.apache.solr.search.similarities.SchemaSimilarityFactory"}}
```

This shows that our schema uses `SchemaSimilarityFactory` as the global similarity.

Deciphering schemaless mode

Schemaless mode is used when we want to quickly create a useful schema by indexing sample data. It does not involve any manual editing of the data.

All of its features are managed by `solrconfig.xml`.

The features that we are particularly interested in are:

- **Managed schema**: All modifications in the schema are made via Solr API at runtime using `schemaFactory`, which supports these changes.
- **Field value class guessing**: This is a technique of using a cascading set of parsers on fields that have not been seen before. It then guesses whether the field is an Integer, Long, Float, Double, Boolean, or Date.

And finally used for automatic schema field addition that is based on field value classes.

Creating a schemaless example

All of the preceding three features are already configured in the Solr bundle. To start using schemaless mode, run the following command:

```
bin/solr start -e schemaless
```

This will start a single Solr server with the collection `gettingstarted`.

In order to see the schema fields, use the following URL, `http://localhost:8983/solr/gettingstarted/schema/fields`:

```
{
  "responseHeader":{
    "status":0,
    "QTime":66},
  "fields":[{
      "name":"_root_",
      "type":"string",
      "docValues":false,
      "indexed":true,
      "stored":false},
    {
      "name":"_text_",
      "type":"text_general",
      "multiValued":true,
      "indexed":true,
      "stored":false},
    {
      "name":"_version_",
      "type":"plong",
      "indexed":false,
      "stored":false},
    {
      "name":"id",
      "type":"string",
      "multiValued":false,
      "indexed":true,
      "required":true,
      "stored":true}]}
```

As you can see in the previous response, there are three predefined fields available, named `_text_`, `_version_`, and `_id_`.

Schemaless mode configuration

We have already discussed that the schemaless mode provides three configuration elements. In the _default config set, we already have these three preconfigured. Let's see how to make changes and get our own schemaless configuration.

Managed schema

The support for Managed schema is enabled by default if you don't specify anything in solr-config.xml.

However, if you wish to make changes, then you can explicitly add your own schemaFactory, as follows:

```
<schemaFactory class="ManagedIndexSchemaFactory">
    <bool name="mutable">true</bool>
    <str name="managedSchemaResourceName">managed-schema</str>
</schemaFactory>
```

In the previous code snippet, we have changed managedSchemaResourceName to managed-schema.

Field guessing

If you open solrconfig.xml for the new schemaless project that you have created, you will see there is a section for UpdateRequestProcessorChain. This is primarily used to automatically apply some operations to the documents before they get indexed and helps in field guessing. We will see some of the snippets from solrconfig.xml now:

```
<updateProcessor class="solr.RemoveBlankFieldUpdateProcessorFactory"
name="remove-blank"/>
```

The previous plugin will remove any blanks from indexing:

```
<updateProcessor class="solr.ParseBooleanFieldUpdateProcessorFactory"
name="parse-boolean"/>
 <updateProcessor class="solr.ParseLongFieldUpdateProcessorFactory"
name="parse-long"/>
 <updateProcessor class="solr.ParseDoubleFieldUpdateProcessorFactory"
name="parse-double"/>
 <updateProcessor class="solr.ParseDateFieldUpdateProcessorFactory"
name="parse-date">
```

```
    <arr name="format">
        <str>yyyy-MM-dd'T'HH:mm:ss.SSSZ</str>
        <str>yyyy-MM-dd'T'HH:mm:ss,SSSZ</str>
        <str>yyyy-MM-dd'T'HH:mm:ss.SSS</str>
        <str>yyyy-MM-dd'T'HH:mm:ss,SSS</str>
        <str>yyyy-MM-dd'T'HH:mm:ssZ</str>
        <str>yyyy-MM-dd'T'HH:mm:ss</str>
        <str>yyyy-MM-dd'T'HH:mmZ</str>
        <str>yyyy-MM-dd'T'HH:mm</str>
        <str>yyyy-MM-dd HH:mm:ss.SSSZ</str>
        <str>yyyy-MM-dd HH:mm:ss,SSSZ</str>
        <str>yyyy-MM-dd HH:mm:ss.SSS</str>
        <str>yyyy-MM-dd HH:mm:ss,SSS</str>
        <str>yyyy-MM-dd HH:mm:ssZ</str>
        <str>yyyy-MM-dd HH:mm:ss</str>
        <str>yyyy-MM-dd HH:mmZ</str>
        <str>yyyy-MM-dd HH:mm</str>
        <str>yyyy-MM-dd</str>
    </arr>
</updateProcessor>
```

Here, you can see that we have added many update request processors to parse various field types. In the case of dates, we can also specify various patterns of a date that we can interpret:

```
<updateProcessor class="solr.AddSchemaFieldsUpdateProcessorFactory"
name="add-schema-fields">
    <lst name="typeMapping">
        <str name="valueClass">java.lang.String</str>
        <str name="fieldType">text_general</str>
        <lst name="copyField">
            <str name="dest">*_str</str>
            <int name="maxChars">256</int>
        </lst>
        <!-- Use as default mapping instead of defaultFieldType -->
        <bool name="default">true</bool>
    </lst>
    <lst name="typeMapping">
        <str name="valueClass">java.lang.Boolean</str>
        <str name="fieldType">booleans</str>
    </lst>
    <lst name="typeMapping">
        <str name="valueClass">java.util.Date</str>
        <str name="fieldType">pdates</str>
    </lst>
    <lst name="typeMapping">
        <str name="valueClass">java.lang.Long</str>
```

```
            <str name="valueClass">java.lang.Integer</str>
            <str name="fieldType">plongs</str>
        </lst>
        <lst name="typeMapping">
            <str name="valueClass">java.lang.Number</str>
            <str name="fieldType">pdoubles</str>
        </lst>
    </updateProcessor>
```

In the preceding snippet, you can see that we have assigned a field type to the fields that we parsed. The default field type is String, as you can see highlighted in bold. We also made the copy field rule to copy the data to text_general_str with a max of 256 characters:

```
<updateRequestProcessorChain name="add-unknown-fields-to-the-schema"
default="${update.autoCreateFields:true}"
 processor="uuid,remove-blank,field-name-mutating,parse-boolean,parse-
long,parse-double,parse-date,add-schema-fields">
        <processor class="solr.LogUpdateProcessorFactory"/>
        <processor class="solr.DistributedUpdateProcessorFactory"/>
        <processor class="solr.RunUpdateProcessorFactory"/>
    </updateRequestProcessorChain>
```

Finally, we add an updateRequestProcessChain to add all the predefined processors and make it default.

Summary

In this chapter, we got an overview of how Solr works and saw schema design. We then jumped into Solr field types and saw how to define fields, copy fields, and create dynamic fields. We moved on to the Schema API, and finally we saw what schemaless mode is all about.

In the next chapter, we will get our hands dirty and learn all about analyzers, tokenizers, and filters.

4
Mastering Text Analysis Methodologies

So far we have seen the installation of Solr server, schema design, documents, fields, field types, the Schema API and schemaless mode.

In this chapter we will explore:

- Text analysis
- Analyzers
- Tokenizers
- Filters
- Multilingual analysis
- Phonetic matching

Understanding text analysis

Nowadays, the search engine plays an important role in any search application. End users always expect accurate, efficient, and fast results from searches. The job of a search engine is to fulfill the search requirement in an easy and faster way. To achieve the expected level of search accuracy, Solr executes multiple processes sequentially behind the scenes: it examines the input string, normalizes the text, generates the token stream, builds indexes, and so on. The set of all of these processes is called text analysis. Let's explore text analysis in detail.

What is text analysis?

Text analysis is a Solr mechanism that takes place in two phases:

- During index time, optimize the input terms, feeding the information, generates the token stream and builds the indexes
- During query time, optimize the query terms, generates the token stream, matches with the term generated at index time, and provides results

Let's dive deeper and understand:

- How exactly Solr works to build indexes
- How to optimize the query terms to match with indexes
- How we get accurate, efficient, and fast results

If someone is searching for the string `The Host Country of Soccer World Cup 2018` and someone else is searching for the string `The Host Nation of Football world cup 2018`, the result should be `Russia` in both the cases. We will learn later in this chapter how Solr matches a query containing `Nation` and `Football` to documents containing `Country` and `Soccer`.

We can't assume which type of search input comes from the end users during the search, for example:

- Searching for `Soccer` and `Football`
- Searching for `Unites States Of America` and `USA`
- Searching for `South Africa` and `RSA`
- Searching for `air-crew`, `aircrew`, and `air crew`

All of these are different input patters that contain ideally the same meaning in natural languages. But the user may provide input in a non-natural language also, like this:

- Searching for `Hundred GB` and `100 gigabyte`
- Searching for `Caffé` and `cafe`

There are also other complex search patterns that may be used by end users at query time. So, looking at the overall scope of possible search patterns used by end users during search time, Solr has to be ready to determine all possible search patterns, analyze them, and output them accurately with efficient results.

Here, however, we don't have to worry because *The Solr* is an intelligent search engine that handles all search input patterns being used across the world. So now, without thinking too much about Solr's searching capability, let's see how Solr actually works to meet all our search requirements.

How text analysis works

We have seen an overview of Solr's text analysis; now let's learn how Solr actually implements the analysis process. Here are the common steps normally used by Solr in an analysis process:

- **Removing stop words**:
    - Stop words (common letters/words) such as a, an, the, at, to, for, and so on are removed from the text string; so Solr will not give results for these common words. These words are configured in a text file (for example, stopwords_en.txt) and this file needs to be imported in the analysis configuration.
- **Adding synonyms**:
    - Solr reads synonyms from the text file (synonyms) and adds them to the token stream. All synonyms need to be preconfigured in the text file, such as Football and Soccer, Country and Nation, and so on.
- **Stemming the words**:
    - Solr transforms words into a base form using language-specific rules
    - It transforms **removing** → **remove** (removes **ing**)
    - It transforms **searches** → **search** (converts to singular)
- **Set all to lowercase**:
    - Solr converts all tokens to lowercase

These are the common steps that Solr performs in all normal scenarios. But in real life, things may not be that easy and straightforward. We can't assume which type of search input pattern in which language end users may use. To meet all possible requirements, Solr's intelligence is hidden in its three powerful tools:

- **Analyzer**: The task of the analyzer is to determine the text and generate the token stream accordingly

- **Tokenizer**: The tokenizer splits the input string at some delimiter and generates a token stream, say `Mastering Apache Solr` to `Mastering`, `Apache`, and `Solr` (splitting at white spaces)
- **Filter**: The filter performs one of these tasks:
    - **Adding**: Adds new tokens to the stream, such as adding synonyms
    - **Removing**: Removes tokens from the stream, such as stop words
    - **Conversation**: Converts tokens from one form to another, such as uppercase to lowercase

We will explore each one of these in detail later in this chapter. By using these three tools, Solr becomes a powerful search engine to meet any complex search requirement.

Solr provides a UI Admin Console for us to understand the analysis process. Here, we can easily understand what is actually happening and which steps are getting executed during index and query time analysis. To access the admin console, navigate to `http://localhost:8983/solr`.

In the Solr admin console, the user can easily understand text analysis, querying, and so on:

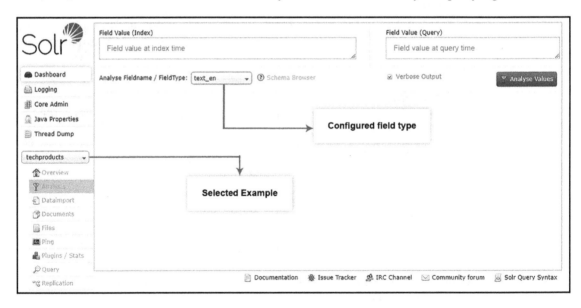

Go to **Dashboard** | **Core Selector**, select your configured example, and click on **Analysis**. Here we are using Solr's built-in example `techproducts`.

We have configured the `text_en` field as follows in the `managed-schema.xml` file:

```
<fieldType name="text_en" class="solr.TextField"
positionIncrementGap="100">
 <analyzer type="index">
 <tokenizer class="solr.StandardTokenizerFactory"/>
 <filter class="solr.StopFilterFactory" ignoreCase="true"
words="lang/stopwords_en.txt" />
 <filter class="solr.LowerCaseFilterFactory"/>
 </analyzer>
 <analyzer type="query">
 <tokenizer class="solr.StandardTokenizerFactory"/>
 <filter class="solr.StopFilterFactory" ignoreCase="true"
words="lang/stopwords_en.txt" />
 <filter class="solr.SynonymGraphFilterFactory" synonyms="synonyms.txt"
ignoreCase="true" expand="true"/>
 <filter class="solr.LowerCaseFilterFactory"/>
 </analyzer>
 </fieldType>
```

Applying **lower case filter** (**LCF**) during index time and query time:

Text analysis applied during index time on the input string.

Input: `The Nation of soccer`

Output: `nation, soccer`

Analysis applied:

- It is split at white spaces
- Stop words (`The`, `of`) removed
- All set to lowercase

Text analysis applied during query time on the input string.

Input: `Famous country for football`

Output: `famous`, `nation`, `country`, `soccer`, and `football`

Analysis applied:

- Split at white spaces
- Stop words (`for`) removed
- Synonyms added (`nation` for `country` and `soccer` for `football`)
- All set to lowercase

As we know that analysis takes place in both phases (index time and query time), we have configured two `<analyzer>` elements distinguished by type attribute value (`index` for index time and `query` for query time). And we've configured a set of tokenizers and filters in each phase. The configurations for each phase may vary based on requirements. It is also possible to define a single `<analyzer>` element without the `type` attribute and configure tokenizers and filters inside that `<analyzer>` element. This type of config set will apply the same configurations to both phases. This is useful for cases where we want perfect string matching. We will discuss this later when we explore the analyzer in detail. Now consider the preceding analysis example.

During the index and query phases, the configured set of configurations is executed by the respective tokenizers and filters and the final token stream is generated. This stream (`nation` and `soccer`) is stored as an index. Now, during query time, the final token stream of the query phase (`famous`, `nation`, `country`, `soccer`, and `football`) will match the final token stream of the index phase (`nation`, and `soccer`), and we can see that there are multiple similar tokens (`nation`, and `soccer`) available in both streams. So here, both `The Nation of soccer` and `Famous country for football` search for the same results. This is the way how text analysis process executing. Here we have just provided an overview of an analyzer, tokenizer, and filters. We will understand all of these analysis tools in detail later in this chapter.

Understanding analyzer

We have seen an overview of text analysis. Now let's dive deeper and understand the core processes running behind the scenes of analysis. As we have seen previously, the analyzer, tokenizer and filter are the three main components Solr uses for text analysis. Let's explore an analyzer.

What is an analyzer?

An analyzer examines the text of fields and generates a token stream. Normally, only fields of type `solr.TextField` will specify an analyzer. An analyzer is defined as a child element of the `<fieldType>` element in the `managed-schema.xml` file. Here is a simple analyzer configuration:

```
<fieldType name="text_en" class="solr.TextField"
positionIncrementGap="100">
 <analyzer class="org.apache.lucene.analysis.core.WhitespaceAnalyzer"/>
</fieldType>
```

Here, we have defined a single `<analyzer>` element. This is the simplest way to define an analyzer. We've already understood the `positionIncrementGap` attribute, which adds a space between multi-value fields, in the previous chapter.

The class attribute value is a fully qualified Java class name. The input text will be analyzed by the analyzer class (`WhitespaceAnalyzer`). Let's configure the following analyzer configuration in `managed-schema.xml` and verify through the admin console:

```
<fieldType name="text_en" class="solr.TextField">
    <analyzer class="org.apache.lucene.analysis.core.WhitespaceAnalyzer"/>
   </fieldType>
```

Applying WhitespaceAnalyzer on the input string:

Input: Running simple Solr analyzer through admin console

Output: Running, simple, Solr, analyzer, through, admin, and console

This is a very simple example. The analyzer class `WhitespaceAnalyzer` splits the string at white spaces and generates the token stream. The named class must derive from `org.apache.lucene.analysis.Analyzer`.

The analyzer may be a single class or may be composed of a series of tokenizers and filter classes. Configuring an analyzer along with tokenizers and filters is very easy and straightforward. Define the `<analyzer>` element with child elements that name factory classes for the tokenizer and filters. Always configure tokenizers and filters in the order you want to run them in. Here is an example:

```
<fieldType name="text_en" class="solr.TextField"
positionIncrementGap="100">
 <analyzer>
 <tokenizer class="solr.StandardTokenizerFactory"/>
 <filter class="solr.StopFilterFactory" ignoreCase="true"
words="lang/stopwords_en.txt" />
 <filter class="solr.LowerCaseFilterFactory"/>
 </analyzer>
</fieldType>
```

Solr will execute tokenizers and filters in the order in which they are configured. The execution order should be defined logically. For example, applying an LCF before a stop filter will impact the performance, as stop words are always going to be removed from the stream and still we would be unnecessarily applying an LCF.

The input text will be passed to the first element in the list (here it is `StandardTokenizerFactory`) and generate tokens accordingly. The output from this will be the input to the next (immediate successor; here it is `StopFilterFactory`). In this way, all the steps will be executed. The tokens generated from the last filter (`LowerCaseFilterFactory` here) will be the final token stream. Solr builds indexes using this stream.

How an analyzer works

Text analysis takes place in two phases, during index time and during query time. So we need to configure `<analyzer>` for both phases, distinguished by the type attribute. In the preceding example, we have configured a single `<analyzer>` element along with tokenizers and filters and not specified the `type` attribute. So Solr will apply the same configurations for the both phases (index and query). This type of configuration is required for some scenarios, say if we want to match strings exactly.

It is always advisable to define two separate `<analyzer>` for each phase distinguished by a `type` attribute. Doing so is required in some scenarios where we want to apply some steps at query time but not index time. For example:

```
<fieldType name="text_en" class="solr.TextField"
positionIncrementGap="100">
 <analyzer type="index">
 <tokenizer class="solr.StandardTokenizerFactory"/>
 <filter class="solr.StopFilterFactory" ignoreCase="true"
words="lang/stopwords_en.txt" />
 <filter class="solr.LowerCaseFilterFactory"/>
 </analyzer>
 <analyzer type="query">
 <tokenizer class="solr.StandardTokenizerFactory"/>
 <filter class="solr.StopFilterFactory" ignoreCase="true"
words="lang/stopwords_en.txt" />
 <filter class="solr.SynonymGraphFilterFactory" synonyms="synonyms.txt"
ignoreCase="true" expand="true"/>
 <filter class="solr.LowerCaseFilterFactory"/>
 </analyzer>
</fieldType>
```

Here, the synonyms filter (`SynonymGraphFilterFactory`) is injected at query time but not index time. If we inject this filter at index time, after adding a new synonym to the `synonyms.txt` file, we need to build document indexes again. Also the indexes for synonyms will be created and the index size will be increased.

At the time of configuring two separate `<analyzer>` for the index and query, we also need to bear in mind that configurations for both `<analyzer>` must be compatible with each other. For example, we have used the `LowerCaseFilterFactory` filter in both `<analyzer>` definitions in the preceding configurations. If we define an LCF only in the indexing phase and not in the querying phase, a query for `Soccer` will never match with the indexed term `soccer`.

So far we have learned the following:

- Solr performs text analysis in both phases: index and query time.
- Solr uses analyzers, tokenizers, and filters for text analysis.
- Using the analyzers, tokenizers, and filters, Solr examines the input string during index time. It normalizes accordingly and generates the token stream. Solr builds indexes based on this token stream.
- Using the same analyzer, tokenizers, and filters during query time, Solr examines the query string, normalizes accordingly, and generates a token stream. This token stream will be compared with the token stream generated at index time and return the matching output.
- The configuration of analyzer depends on the search requirements.
- Defining a single analyzer will be considered as the same analysis configuration for both phases.
- The advisable approach is always to define two separate analyzer for each phase so that we can apply friendlier configurations for each phase.
- When defining the tokenizers and filter, the ordering should be logical.
- Both the phase configurations should be compatible with each other.

So now we can apply text analysis on slightly more complex search strings. Let's apply more tokenizers and filters and understand their behavior. Previously, we mentioned an example of searching The Host Country of Soccer World Cup 2018 and searching for The Host Nation of Football world cup 2018; in both cases, the result should be Russia. Let's see how Solr analyzes this example. Up next are the analyzer configurations configured in the `managed-schema.xml` file. There are two separate `<analyzer>` elements for index time and query time, distinguished by the `type` attribute:

```
<fieldType name="text_en" class="solr.TextField"
```

```
positionIncrementGap="100">
    <analyzer type="index">
      <tokenizer class="solr.StandardTokenizerFactory"/>
      <filter class="solr.StopFilterFactory" ignoreCase="true"
words="lang/stopwords_en.txt" />
      <filter class="solr.LowerCaseFilterFactory"/>
    </analyzer>
    <analyzer type="query">
      <tokenizer class="solr.StandardTokenizerFactory"/>
      <filter class="solr.StopFilterFactory" ignoreCase="true"
words="lang/stopwords_en.txt" />
      <filter class="solr.SynonymGraphFilterFactory"
synonyms="synonyms.txt" ignoreCase="true" expand="true"/>
      <filter class="solr.LowerCaseFilterFactory"/>
    </analyzer>
  </fieldType>
```

Text analysis by configuring various tokenizers and filters during index time and query time:

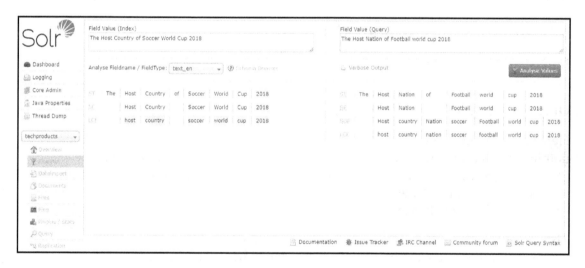

In the preceding screen, we have provided the string `The Host Country of Soccer World Cup 2018` at index time and `The Host Nation of Football world cup 2018` at query time.

An analyzer during index time.

String: `The Host Country of Soccer World Cup 2018`

Solr executes all tokenizers and filters sequentially configured inside the `<analyzer type="index">` definition and generates a token stream accordingly. It builds indexes using this token stream.

StandardTokenizerFactory (ST): Splits the string at white spaces:

```
<tokenizer class="solr.StandardTokenizerFactory"/>
```

Input: The Host Country of Soccer World Cup 2018

Output: The, Host, Country, of, Soccer, World, Cup, and 2018

The analyzer passes the input text to the first element from the list. Here, it is `StandardTokenizerFactory`. The entire string was split at white spaces using standard tokenizer. Now the output of this tokenizer will be the input to the next (immediate successor) in the sequence chain; here, it is `StopFilterFactory`.

StopFilterFactory: Removes all stop words (common) listed in the `stopwords_en.txt` file:

```
<filter class="solr.StopFilterFactory" ignoreCase="true"
words="lang/stopwords_en.txt" />
```

Input: The, Host, Country, of, Soccer, World, Cup, 2018 (output of immediate predecessor)

Output: Host,Country,Soccer,World,Cup,2018

Here all stop words (The, of, and so on) are removed from the steam. Stop words are nothing but all common words (a, an, the, of, at, for, in, and so on) listed in the `stopwords_en.txt` file. After the removal of these stop words, Solr will not give matching results for these words. Now the output of this filter will be the input to its immediate successor in the chain; here, it is `LowerCaseFilterFactory`.

The `attribute ignoreCase="true"` (default `false`) will ignore case when testing for stop words. If it is `true`, the stop list should contain lowercase words.

LowerCaseFilterFactory: Converts all tokens to lowercase:

```
<filter class="solr.LowerCaseFilterFactory"/>
```

Input: Host, Country, Soccer, World, Cup, 2018

Output: host, country, soccer, world, cup, X

All the incoming inputs will be converted to lowercase:

Now all three components (`StandardTokenizerFactory`, `StopFilterFactory`, and `LowerCaseFilterFactory`) have executed their job sequentially and generated the final token stream:

- **Final token stream**: `host, country, soccer, world, cup, 2018`

Next, Solr builds indexes based on this final token stream:

- **Analyzer**: Query time
- **String:** `The Host Nation of Football world cup 2018`

At query time, Solr executes all tokenizers and filters sequentially configured inside the `<analyzer type="query">` definition and generates a token stream accordingly. This token stream will be compared with the token stream generated during index time. The matching result will be given as output.

StandardTokenizerFactory: Splits the string at white spaces:

```
<tokenizer class="solr.StandardTokenizerFactory"/>
```

Input: `The Host Nation of Football world cup 2018`

Output: `The, Host, Nation, of, Football, world, cup,2018`

The analyzer passes the input text to the first element from the list. Here, it is `StandardTokenizerFactory`. The entire string was split at white spaces using Standard Tokenizer. The output of this tokenizer will be the input to the immediate successor in the chain; here, it is `StopFilterFactory`.

StopFilterFactory: Removes all stop words (common) listed in the `stopwords_en.txt` file.

```
<filter class="solr.StopFilterFactory" ignoreCase="true"
words="lang/stopwords_en.txt" />
```

Input: `The, Host, Nation, of, Football, world, cup, 2018` (output of immediate predecessor)

Output: `Host, Nation, Football, world, cup,2018`

Here all stop words are removed from the stream. The output of this filter will be the input to its immediate successor in the chain, `SynonymGraphFilterFactory`.

The `attribute ignoreCase="true"` (default: `false`) will ignore casing when testing for stop words. If it is `true`, the stop list should contain lowercase words.

SynonymGraphFilterFactory: Adds synonyms to the token stream:

```
<filter class="solr.SynonymGraphFilterFactory" synonyms="synonyms.txt"
ignoreCase="true" expand="true"/>
```

Input: Host, Nation, Football, world, cup, 2018
Output: Host, country, Nation, soccer, Football, world, cup, 2018

The synonyms (`country` for `nation` and `soccer` for `Football`) are added to the stream. All synonyms are configured in the `synonyms.txt` file, as follows. We will see this filter in detail later in this chapter.

`Synonyms.txt file`: Synonym mapping examples. Blank lines and lines that start with # will be ignored:

```
football,soccer
dumb,stupid,dull
country => nation
smart,clever,bright => intelligent,genius
```

Here, `SynonymGraphFilterFactory` is configured at query time but not at index time. Previously, we have seen the reason for this type of configuration variation for index time and query time.

The output will be passed to the next filter, `LowerCaseFilterFactory`.

LowerCaseFilterFactory: Converts all tokens to lowercase:

```
<filter class="solr.LowerCaseFilterFactory"/>
```

Input: Host, country, Nation, soccer, Football, world, cup, 2018

Output: host, country, nation, soccer, football, world, cup, 2018

All the incoming inputs will be converted to lowercase.

Solr has examined the query string and produced the final token stream using four components (`StandardTokenizerFactory`, `StopFilterFactory`, `SynonymGraphFilterFactory`, and `LowerCaseFilterFactory`).

Now, these are the final streams of both phases:

- **Indexed stream**: `host, country, soccer, world, cup, 2018`
- **Query stream**: `host, country, nation, soccer, football, world, cup, 2018`

We can see that many tokens from the query stream are matching tokens from the indexed stream, such as `country` and `soccer`. So in this way, Solr will bring the same output for the search string `The Host Country of Soccer World Cup 2018` and `The Host Nation of Football world cup 2018`.

Thus, we have covered:

- The Solr text analysis mechanism
- The tasks of analyzer, tokenizer, and filters
- Defining a single `<analyzer>` or multiple `<analyzer>` distinguished by the type attribute based on search requirements
- Defining configurations steps logically such as using a LCF after a stop filter and adding a synonym filter at query time only (we explained both the examples previously)

Now we are familiar with the Solr text analysis mechanism. Here we have tried to explain it by taking a little complex string example, but we can't assume which type of input may be entered during searches by end users. Providing accurate results for any pattern of input string is the main aim of any search engine. Solr comes with a number of tokenizers and filters to challenge any input pattern. Solr is also efficient at multiple language search. Here we have covered very few and common tokenizers and filters, but Solr's list for tokenizers and filters does not end there. There are many tokenizers and filters available. Let's understand the behavior of tokenizers in the next section.

Understanding tokenizers

We have previously seen that an analyzer may be a single class or a set of defined tokenizer and filter classes.

The analyzer executes the analysis process in two steps:

- **Tokenization (parsing)**: Using configured tokenizer classes
- **Filtering (transformation)**: Using configured filter classes

We can also do preprocessing on a character stream before tokenization; we can do this with the help of `CharFilters` (we will see this later in the chapter). An analyzer knows its configured field, but a tokenizer doesn't have any idea about the field. The job of the tokenizer is only to read from a character stream, apply a tokenization mechanism based on its behavior, and produce a new sequence of a token stream.

What is a tokenizer?

A tokenizer is a tool provided by Solr that runs a tokenization process, breaks a stream of text into tokens at some delimiter, and generates a token stream. Tokenizers are configured by their Java implementation factory class in the `managed-schema.xml` file. For example, we can define a standard tokenizer as:

```
<tokenizer class="solr.StandardTokenizerFactory"/>
```

Most tokenizer implementation classes do not provide a default no-arg constructor. So, always use a tokenizer factory class instead of a tokenizer class. Solr provides a standard way to define tokenizers in XML format using factory implementation classes. These factory classes translate XML configurations to create an instance of the respective tokenizer implementation class. An analyzer may contain only tokenizers or both tokenizers and filters. If only tokenizers are configured, the output produced from tokenization is ready to use; otherwise, the output will be passed to the first filter in the list.

After tokenization, a new token stream is generated. The newly generated token, along with its normalized text values, also holds some metadata, such as the location at which they are generated. Token metadata is important for things like highlighting search results in the field text. A newly generated token contains a value that may be different from its input text value. We can't assume that the text of a token is the same as the input text, or that the length is the same. It's also possible for more than one token to have the same position or refer to the same set in the original text.

Available tokenizers in Solr

Solr provides a large number of tokenizers. Let's explore the behavior of some of them.

Standard tokenizer

This splits the text field into tokens, treating white space and punctuation as delimiters. It considers white spaces and punctuation (comma, dots, hyphens, semicolons, colons, hashtags, and @) as delimiters and discards all of them, with these exceptions:

- Dots that are not followed by white spaces are kept as part of the token. An example is internet domains such as `www.google.com`.
- Factory class—`solr.StandardTokenizerFactory`.
- Arguments—`maxTokenLength` (integer, default 255) The max length of token characters. Tokens that exceed the number of characters specified by `maxTokenLength` will be ignored.

Example:

```
<fieldType name="text_en" class="solr.TextField"
positionIncrementGap="100">
 <analyzer>
 <tokenizer class="solr.StandardTokenizerFactory"/>
 </analyzer>
</fieldType>
```

Input: `Please send a mail at dharmesh.vasoya@example.com by 12-11.`

Output: `Please, send, a, mail, at, dharmesh.vasoya, example.com, by, 12, 11`

A total of 10 tokens have been generated by the standard tokenizer. These will be passed to its immediate successor in the chain. Standard tokenizer supports Unicode standard annex UAX#29, `http://unicode.org/reports/tr29/#Word_Boundaries` word boundaries with the following token types: `<ALPHANUM>`, `<NUM>`, `<SOUTHEAST_ASIAN>`, `<IDEOGRAPHIC>`, and `<HIRAGANA>`.

White space tokenizer

This splits the text stream at white spaces only. However, it will not split the text at any punctuation (like the standard tokenizer). Therefore, all of the punctuation will remain as is inside the generated tokens.

Factory class: `solr.WhitespaceTokenizerFactory`

Arguments:

- `rule` (default: `java`): A rule that considers white space as a delimiter.
- `java`: Uses `Character.isWhitespace(int)` (https://docs.oracle.com/ javase/8/docs/api/java/lang/Character.html#isWhitespace-int-)
- `unicode`: Uses unicode's `WHITESPACE` property

Example:

```
<fieldType name="text_en" class="solr.TextField"
positionIncrementGap="100">
 <analyzer>
 <tokenizer class="solr.WhitespaceTokenizerFactory" rule="java" />
 </analyzer>
</fieldType>
```

Input: `Please send a mail at dharmesh.vasoya@example.com by 12-11.`

Output: `Please, send, a, mail, at, dharmesh.vasoya@example.com, by, 12-11.`

The input string was split at white spaces but the punctuation (@, .,and –) was preserved in the tokens.

Classic tokenizer

This splits the text field into tokens at white spaces and punctuation. The classic tokenizer behaves in the same way as the standard tokenizer of Solr versions 3.1 and older. Like The standard tokenizer, it does not use the Unicode standard annex UAX#29 word boundary rules. Delimiter characters are discarded, with the following exceptions:

- Dots that are not followed by white spaces are kept as part of the token
- Words are split at hyphens unless there is a number in the word, in which case the token is not split and the numbers and hyphens are preserved
- It preserves internet domain names and email addresses as a single token

Factory class: `solr.ClassicTokenizerFactory`

Arguments: `maxTokenLength` (integer, default 255): Max length of the token characters. Tokens that exceed the number of characters specified by `maxTokenLength` will be ignored.

Example:

```
<fieldType name="text_en" class="solr.TextField"
positionIncrementGap="100">
    <analyzer>
      <tokenizer class="solr.ClassicTokenizerFactory"/>
    </analyzer>
  </fieldType>
```

Input: `Please send a mail at dharmesh.vasoya@example.com by 12-Nov.`

Output: `Please`, `send`, `a`, `mail`, `at`, `dharmesh.vasoya@example.com`, `by`, `12-Nov`

The input string is split at white spaces and punctuation, but the email address `dharmesh.vasoya@example.com` and `12-Nov` are preserved as part of the token.

Keyword tokenizer

This treats the entire text field as a single token. The kyword tokenizer is required in scenarios where we want to match the entire string as it is:

Factory class: `solr.KeywordTokenizerFactory`

Arguments: None

Example:

```
<fieldType name="text_en" class="solr.TextField"
positionIncrementGap="100">
 <analyzer>
 <tokenizer class="solr.KeywordTokenizerFactory"/>
 </analyzer>
 </fieldType>
```

Input: `Please send a mail at dharmesh.vasoya@example.com by 12-Nov.`

Output: `Please send a mail at dharmesh.vasoya@example.com by 12-Nov.`

The entire input string is preserved as a single token.

Lower case tokenizer

The lower case tokenizer considers white spaces and non-letters as delimiters, splits the input string at these delimiters, and then discards all delimiters. Finally, it converts all letters to lowercase.

Factory class: `solr.LowerCaseTokenizerFactory`

Arguments: None

Example:

```
<fieldType name="text_en" class="solr.TextField"
positionIncrementGap="100">
 <analyzer>
 <tokenizer class="solr.LowerCaseTokenizerFactory"/>
 </analyzer>
</fieldType>
```

Input: `Please send a mail at dharmesh.vasoya@example.com by 12-Nov.`

Output: `please, send, a, mail, at, dharmesh, vasoya, example, com, by, nov`

The input string was first split at white spaces and punctuation and then converted to lowercase.

Letter tokenizer

The letter tokenizer discards all non-letter characters from the input string and then generates a token at strings of contiguous letters.

Factory class: `solr.LetterTokenizerFactory`

Arguments: None

Example:

```
<fieldType name="text_en" class="solr.TextField"
positionIncrementGap="100">
 <analyzer>
 <tokenizer class="solr.LetterTokenizerFactory"/>
 </analyzer>
</fieldType>
```

Input: `I haven't received mail by Nov12Sunday`

Output: `I, haven, t, received, mail, by, Nov, Sunday`

All non-letter characters (`'` and `12`) are discarded first, and then tokens are generated by considering strings of contiguous letters.

N-gram tokenizer

This generates n-gram tokens of sizes in the provided range from the input string.

Factory class: `solr.NGramTokenizerFactory`

Arguments: `minGramSize (integer, default 1)`: The minimum n-gram size. `maxGramSize (integer, default 2)`: The maximum n-gram size

> The following condition must be fulfilled when providing gram-size arguments:
> `0 < minGramSize <= maxGramSize`

Example:

```
<fieldType name="text_en" class="solr.TextField"
positionIncrementGap="100">
 <analyzer>
 <tokenizer class="solr.NGramTokenizerFactory" minGramSize="2"
maxGramSize="3"/>
 </analyzer>
 </fieldType>
```

Input: `send me`

Output: se, sen, en, end, nd, nd, d, dm, m, me, me

N-gram tokenizer executes tokenization over the entire input string. Also, it does not consider white spaces as delimiters, so white space characters are also included in the tokenization. In the preceding example, white spaces are preserved as parts of the token after tokenization. The n-gram tokenizer is required in cases where we want to match search words from the start, end, or somewhere in between the string along with white spaces.

For example, the input string is `Please send me a mail at dharmesh.vasoya@example.com` and we want to match `mail at dharmesh.vasoya@example.com`.

Edge n-gram tokenizer

This generates n-gram tokens from the start over the entire input string. Like the n-gram tokenizer, the edge n-gram tokenizer also does not consider white space as a delimiter, so white space is also considered during tokenization.

Factory class: `solr.EdgeNGramTokenizerFactory`

Arguments:

- `minGramSize` (integer, default is 1): The minimum n-gram size
- `maxGramSize` (integer, default is 1): The maximum n-gram size (0 < `minGramSize` <= `maxGramSize`)

In earlier versions, Solr supported an argument side (`front` or `back`; the default was `front`), which generated a token from the provided value. This argument has now been removed and Solr generates the token from the front end of the input string.

Example:

```
<fieldType name="text_en" class="solr.TextField"
positionIncrementGap="100">
 <analyzer>
 <tokenizer class="solr.EdgeNGramTokenizerFactory" minGramSize="2"
maxGramSize="10"/>
 </analyzer>
 </fieldType>
```

Input: `send me`

Output: `se, sen, send, send, send m, send me`

The entire input string is split into n-gram pattern tokens considering size parameters (`minGramSize` (2) and `maxGramSize` (10)) along with white spaces. The edge n-gram tokenizer is required for matching n-characters from the start of the string.

For example, the input string is `Please send me a mail at dharmesh.vasoya@example.com` and we want to match `Please send me a mail` but it will not match.

Understanding filters

We have seen that the analyzer uses a series of tokenizer and filter classes together to transform the input string into a token string, which will be used by Solr in indexing. The job of the filter is different from the tokenizer. The tokenizer mostly splits the input string at some delimiters and generates a token stream. The filter transforms this stream into some other form and generates a new token stream. The input for a filter will be a token stream, not an input string, unlike what we were passing at the time of tokenization. The entire token stream generated through tokenization will be passed to the first filter class in the list. Let's cover filters in detail.

What is a filter?

A filter is a tool provided by Solr that runs a filtering process as follows:

- **Adding**: Adds a new token to the stream, such as adding synonyms
- **Removing**: Removes a token from the stream, such as stop words
- **Conversation**: Converts a token from one form to another form, say uppercase to lower case

When a token stream generated during tokenization is passed to the filter, normally the filter looks at each token sequentially and, as per their behavior, performs one of the preceding activities. It then produces a new token stream. Filters are also derived from `org.apache.lucene.analysis.TokenStream`, so the output of a filter is also a token stream.

We can define a filter by its Java implementation factory class in the `managed-schema.xml` file:

```
<filter class="solr.StandardFilterFactory"/>
```

A filter definition should follow a tokenizer or another filter definition because they take a token stream as input. We can configure filters as a child element of `<analyzer>` following the `<tokenizer>` elements. Here is a simple example configured in the `managed-schema.xml` file inside the field `text_en`:

```
<fieldType name="text_en" class="solr.TextField"
positionIncrementGap="100">
 <analyzer>
 <tokenizer class="solr.StandardTokenizerFactory"/>
 <filter class="solr.StandardFilterFactory"/>
 <filter class="solr.LowerCaseFilterFactory"/>
 </analyzer>
 </fieldType>
```

The preceding example is very simple. Solr comes with a large number of filters to meet most of our search requirements. Let's understand them in detail.

Available filters in Solr

Solr provides the following filters. Let's explore their behavior.

Stop filter

This removes all the words listed inside the `stopwords.txt` file. Removing stop words will reduce the size of the index and improve performance. These are the standard English stop words provided by Solr:

a, an, and, are, ask, at, be, but, by, for, if, in, into, is, it, no, not, of, on, or, such, that, the, their, then, there, these, they, this, to, was, will, with.

We can manage (add or remove) words from the file as per our requirement. We can also create a file for other languages and include it by mentioning the file path in the word argument:

Factory class: `solr.StopFilterFactory`

Arguments:

- `words` (optional): The path of the file that contains a list of stop words, one per line. Blank lines and lines that begin with # will be ignored from the file. The path may be an absolute or relative path.

- format (optional): Indicates the format of the stopword list, for example, format="snowball" for a stopwords list that has been formatted for snowball.
- ignoreCase (true/false, default false): This ignores casing when testing for stop words. If it is true, the stop list should contain lowercase words.

Example:

```
<fieldType name="text_en" class="solr.TextField"
positionIncrementGap="100">
 <analyzer>
 <tokenizer class="solr.StandardTokenizerFactory"/>
 <filter class="solr.StopFilterFactory" words="lang/stopwords_en.txt" />
 </analyzer>
 </fieldType>
```

Input: This is an example

Tokenizer to filter: This, is, an, example

Output: This, example

Example:

```
<fieldType name="text_en" class="solr.TextField"
positionIncrementGap="100">
 <analyzer>
 <tokenizer class="solr.StandardTokenizerFactory"/>
 <filter class="solr.StopFilterFactory" ignoreCase="true"
words="lang/stopwords_en.txt" />
 </analyzer>
 </fieldType>
```

Input: This is an example

Tokenizer to filter: This, is, an, example

Output: example

In the first example, we have not specified the argument `ignoreCase`, but in the second example, we have set it to `true`; so the outputs from both the examples are different. The location of the file `stopwords_en.txt` is `%SOLR_HOME%/example/techproducts/solr/techproducts/conf/lang/stopwords_en.txt`, as we currently understand from Solr's built-in example `techproducts`.

LCF: Converts all uppercase letters to lowercase in the token

Factory class: `solr.LowerCaseFilterFactory`

Arguments: None

Example:

```
<fieldType name="text_en" class="solr.TextField"
positionIncrementGap="100">
 <analyzer>
 <tokenizer class="solr.StandardTokenizerFactory"/>
 <filter class="solr.LowerCaseFilterFactory"/>
 </analyzer>
 </fieldType>
```

Input: `This is An example`

Tokenizer to Filter: `This, is, An, example`

Output: `this, is, an, example`

All uppercase letters from the tokens are converted to lowercase. The sequence order of `LowerCaseFilterFactory` in the filter chain should be significant. If we define LCF before stop filter, Solr will unnecessarily apply lower case filtering on those stop words that are going to be removed in the next step.

 If we need to use LCF in text analysis, then must apply LCF to both the phases of an analyzer (index and query). If we define LCF only in the indexing phase and not in the querying phase, a query for `Soccer` will never match with the indexed term `soccer`.

Classic filter

The classic filter is used with the classic tokenizer. It removes dots from acronyms and 's from possessives.

Factory class: `solr.ClassicFilterFactory`

Arguments: None

Example:

```
<fieldType name="text_en" class="solr.TextField"
positionIncrementGap="100">
 <analyzer>
 <tokenizer class="solr.ClassicTokenizerFactory"/>
 <filter class="solr.ClassicFilterFactory"/>
 </analyzer>
 </fieldType>
```

Input: `Computer's C.P.U. isn't`

Tokenizer to filter: `Computer's, C.P.U., isn't`

Output: `Computer, CPU, isn't`

The classic tokenizer and classic filter together converted `Computer's` to `Computer` by removing 's and reduced `C.P.U.` to `CPU` by removing the dots.

Synonym filter

During filtering, the synonym filter looks for synonymous words in the `synonyms.txt` file. The found synonyms will be added at the place of the original token. All the synonym mappings are configured inside the `synonyms.txt` file.

Factory class: `solr.SynonymFilterFactory`

 The synonym filter is now deprecated in Solr as it does not support multi-term synonym mapping. Solr provides a synonym graph filter as an alternative to the synonym filter with multi-term support.

Synonym graph filter

The synonym graph filter supports single- or multi-token synonyms. The filter maps single- or multi-token synonyms and generates a correct token, which was not supported by the synonym filter.

The synonym graph filter is normally configured at query time, not index time. This will reduce the size of the index. If this filter is configured at index time, after adding any new synonyms to the `synonyms.txt` file, re-indexing of entire documents is required. The synonym graph filter configuration at query time does not require re-indexing for adding new synonyms to `synonyms.txt`. To configure this filter at index time, we must mention the flatten graph filter for treating tokens like the synonym filter.

Also, the configuration order for this filter is important. If we are configuring the synonym graph filter before the ASCII folding filter, then we need to maintain all diacritical words (like `caffé`) in `synonyms.txt` as well:

Factory class: `solr.SynonymGraphFilterFactory`

Arguments:

- `synonyms` (required): The path of a file (`synonyms.txt`) that contains a list of synonyms, one per line. Blank lines and lines that begin with # are ignored. This may be a comma-separated list of absolute paths, or paths relative to the Solr config directory.

  Sample format of `synonyms.txt`:

  A comma-separated list of words. If the token matches any of the words, then all the words in the list are substituted, which will include the original token.

  For example:

  ```
  football, soccer
  dumb, stupid, dull
  ```

  Two comma-separated lists of words with the symbol => between them. If the token matches any word on the left, then the list on the right is substituted. The original token will not be included unless it is also in the list on the right.

For example:

```
country => nation
smart,clever,bright => intelligent,genius
```

- `ignoreCase` (optional; default: `false`): This determines the behavior of the filter in case-sensitive or case insensitive matching from the file. If it is `true`, synonyms will be matched case insensitively.
- `expand` (optional; default: `true`): If this is set to `true`, a synonym will be expanded to all equivalent synonyms. If `false`, all equivalent synonyms will be reduced to the first in the list.
- `format` (optional; default: `solr`): Controls how the synonyms will be parsed. Supported formats are:
    - `solr` (`SolrSynonymParser`)
    - `wordnet` (`WordnetSynonymParser`)
    - We can pass the name of our own `SynonymMap.Builder` subclass.
- `tokenizerFactory`: The name of the tokenizer factory to use when parsing the synonyms file. If `tokenizerFactory` is specified, then analyzer may not be, and vice versa.
- `analyzer` (optional; default: `WhitespaceTokenizerFactory`): The name of the analyzer class to use when parsing the synonyms file. If the analyzer is specified, then `tokenizerFactory` may not be, and vice versa.

Example:

```
<fieldType name="text_en" class="solr.TextField"
positionIncrementGap="100">
 <analyzer>
 <tokenizer class="solr.StandardTokenizerFactory"/>
 <filter class="solr.SynonymGraphFilterFactory" synonyms="synonyms.txt"
ignoreCase="true"/>
 </analyzer>
 </fieldType>
```

Input: He is stupid, not clever

Tokenizer to filter: He, is, stupid, not, clever

Output: He, is, dumb, dull, stupid, not, intelligent,genius

All the matching synonyms (from `synonyms.txt`) are added to the token stream.

If we want to apply the synonym graph filter at index time, we must define `FlattenGraphFilterFactory` in an analyzer definition index.

Example:

```
<fieldType name="text_en" class="solr.TextField"
positionIncrementGap="100">
 <analyzer type="index">
 <tokenizer class="solr.StandardTokenizerFactory"/>
 <filter class="solr.SynonymGraphFilterFactory" synonyms="synonyms.txt"
ignoreCase="true"/>
 <!-- required on index analyzers after synonym graph filters -->
 <filter class="solr.FlattenGraphFilterFactory"/>
 </analyzer>
 <analyzer type="query">
 <tokenizer class="solr.StandardTokenizerFactory"/>
 <filter class="solr.SynonymGraphFilterFactory" synonyms="synonyms.txt"
ignoreCase="true"/>
 </analyzer>
 </fieldType>
```

Input: `He is stupid, not clever`

Tokenizer to Filter: `He, is, stupid, not, clever`

Output: `He, is, dumb, dull, stupid, not, intelligent, genius`

All the matching synonyms (from `synonyms.txt`) are added to the token stream.

ASCII folding filter

You can transform alphabetic, numeric, and symbolic Unicode characters that are not in the Basic Latin Unicode block (the first 127 ASCII characters) into their ASCII equivalents, if one exists.

Factory class: `solr.ASCIIFoldingFilterFactory`

Arguments:

- `preserveOriginal`: A Boolean. The default is `false`. If `true`, the original token is preserved (`caffé --> caffé, cafe`).

Example:

```
<fieldType name="text_en" class="solr.TextField"
positionIncrementGap="100">
 <analyzer>
 <tokenizer class="solr.WhitespaceTokenizerFactory"/>
 <filter class="solr.ASCIIFoldingFilterFactory"
preserveOriginal="false" />
 </analyzer>
 </fieldType>
```

Input: thé caffé

Tokenizer to filter: thé, caffé

Output: the, caffe

Keep word filter

We keep only those tokens that are listed in the keepwords.txt files. This is the inverse of the stop words filter.

Factory class: solr.KeepWordFilterFactory

Arguments:

- words: Required. This is the path of a text file containing the list of keep words, one per line. Blank lines and lines that begin with # are ignored. This may be an absolute path or a simple filename.
- ignoreCase: True or false. The default is false. If it is true, then comparisons are done case insensitively and the word file is assumed to contain only lowercase words.

The following is the sample keepwords.txt file:

```
good
great
excellent
```

Example:

```
<fieldType name="text_en" class="solr.TextField"
positionIncrementGap="100">
 <analyzer>
 <tokenizer class="solr.StandardTokenizerFactory"/>
```

```
<filter class="solr.KeepWordFilterFactory" words="keepwords.txt"
ignoreCase="true"/>
</analyzer>
</fieldType>
```

Input: Good and excellent job

Tokenizer to filter: Good, and, excellent, job

Output: Good, excellent

Here, we have set `ignoreCase="true"` to match the words from the `keepwords.txt` file case insensitively. The patch of `keepwords.txt` is `%SOLR_HOME%/example/techproducts/solr/techproducts/conf/keepwords.txt`. We can configure a file patch as relative or absolute as per our needs.

KStem filter

Solr provides a stemming mechanism though which words are converted to their base form by applying language-specific rules. For that, Solr provides a number of stemming filters. The KStem filter is an English-specific and less aggressive stemmer.

Factory class: `solr.KStemFilterFactory`

Arguments: None

Example:

```
<fieldType name="text_en" class="solr.TextField"
positionIncrementGap="100">
 <analyzer>
 <tokenizer class="solr.StandardTokenizerFactory"/>
 <filter class="solr.KStemFilterFactory"/>
 </analyzer>
 </fieldType>
```

Input: remove removing removed

Tokenizer to filter: remove, removing, removed

Output: remove

From the input string, the KStem filter has transformed three forms of a word to their base form `remove`. The first word `remove` was kept as it is because it is already in its base form, the second word `removing` was transformed to `remove` by cropping `ing` and the third word `removed` was transformed to `remove` by cropping `d`. Solr provides a number of stemmer filters. Selecting these filters completely depends on their behavior and which language we are going to use them for. `PorterStemmer` is one of the popular stemmers. What if we do not want to modify some words by stemming? We configure `KeywordMarkerFilterFactory` before `KStemFilterFactory`. We will cover this soon.

KeywordMarkerFilterFactory

This discards the modification/stemming of words listed in the file `protwords.txt`. Any words in the protected word list will not be modified by any stemmer in Solr.

Arguments:

- `protected`: The path of the file that contains the protected word list, one per line

The following is the sample `protwords.txt` file:

```
removing
transforming
```

Example:

```
<fieldType name="text_en" class="solr.TextField"
positionIncrementGap="100">
 <analyzer>
 <tokenizer class="solr.WhitespaceTokenizerFactory"/>
 <filter class="solr.KeywordMarkerFilterFactory" protected="protwords.txt"
/>
 <filter class="solr.KStemFilterFactory"/>
 </analyzer>
 </fieldType>
```

Input: remove removing removed transforming

Tokenizer to filter: remove, removing, removed, transforming

Output: remove, removing, remove, transforming

Here we can see that the words `removing` and `transforming` are not stemmed by `KStemFilterFactory` because they are mentioned in the file `protwords.txt` and protected by `KeywordMarkerFilterFactory`.

Word delimiter graph filter

This filter splits tokens at word delimiters. This is an alternative to the word delimiter filter. Always use a word delimiter graph filter at query time and not at index time because the indexer can't directly consume a graph at index time; if you still need to use this filter at index time, use it with a flatten graph filter.

The rules for determining delimiters are as follows:

- A change in case within a word: `KnowMore` -> `Know`, `More`. This can be disabled by setting `splitOnCaseChange="0"`.
- A transition from alpha to numeric characters or vice versa: `Alpha1000` -> `Alpha`, `1000` `100MS` -> `100`, `MS`. This can be disabled by setting `splitOnNumerics="0"`.
- Non-alphanumeric characters are discarded: `air-crew` -> `air`, `crew`.
- A trailing `'s` is removed: `Solr's` -> `Solr`.
- Any leading or trailing delimiters are discarded: `-air-crew!!` -> `air`, `crew`.

Factory class: `solr.WordDelimiterGraphFilterFactory`

Arguments: It's not possible to list all the arguments here. Please refer to the Solr document for these.

Example:

```
<fieldType name="text_en" class="solr.TextField"
positionIncrementGap="100">
 <analyzer type="index">
 <tokenizer class="solr.WhitespaceTokenizerFactory"/>
 <filter class="solr.WordDelimiterGraphFilterFactory"/>
 <!-- required on index analyzers after graph filters -->
 <filter class="solr.FlattenGraphFilterFactory"/>
 </analyzer>
 <analyzer type="query">
 <tokenizer class="solr.WhitespaceTokenizerFactory"/>
 <filter class="solr.WordDelimiterGraphFilterFactory"/>
 </analyzer>
</fieldType>
```

Input: `KnowMore air-crew Alpha1000`

Tokenizer to filter: `KnowMore, air-crew, Alpha1000`

Output: `Know, More, air, crew, Alpha, 1000`

This is a simple example of a word delimiter graph filter. However, we can play with this filter by applying much more complex filtering terms.

Understanding CharFilter

During an analysis, the analyzer passes the input string to the first tokenizer in the list. If we want to apply any preprocessing to the input string before passing to the tokenizer, we can do it through `CharFilter`. `CharFilters` can be chained like token filters and placed in front of a tokenizer to add, change, or remove characters from an input string. Here is a list of char filters provided by Solr:

- `solr.MappingCharFilterFactory`
- `solr.HTMLStripCharFilterFactory`
- `solr.ICUNormalizer2CharFilterFactory`
- `solr.PatternReplaceCharFilterFactor`

Understanding PatternReplaceCharFilterFactor

This filter uses regular expressions to replace or change character patterns.

Arguments:

- `pattern`: The regular expression pattern to apply to the incoming text
- `replacement`: The text to use to replace matching patterns

Example:

```
<fieldType name="text_en" class="solr.TextField"
positionIncrementGap="100">
 <analyzer>
 <charFilter class="solr.PatternReplaceCharFilterFactory"
pattern="(\w+)(ing)" replacement="$1"/>
 <tokenizer class="solr.WhitespaceTokenizerFactory"/>
 </analyzer>
 </fieldType>
```

Input: `showing see-ing viewing`

Output: `show, see-ing, view`

As per the behavior of the pattern, `ing` is removed from the end of the words except `see-ing`.

Explaining every char filter is not possible here. Please refer to the Solr documents for these.

Understanding multilingual analysis

So far, we have concentrated on Solr text analysis (analyzers, tokenizers, and filters) irrespective of any language. Solr support multiple language search and this feature puts Solr at the top of the list of search engines. Let's understand how Solr works for multiple language search.

So far all the examples we have covered are in English. The tokenization and filtering rules for English are very simple and straightforward, such as splitting at white spaces or any other delimiters, stemming, and so on. But once we start focusing on other languages, these rules may differ. Solr is already prepared to meet multiple analysis search requirements such as stemmers, synonyms filters, stop word filters, character query correction capabilities normalization, language identifiers, and so on. Some languages require their own tokenizers for complexity of parsing the language, some require their own stemming filters, and some require multiple filters as per the language characteristics. For example, here is an analyzer configured for Greek in `managed-schema.xml`:

```
<fieldType name="text_el" class="solr.TextField"
positionIncrementGap="100">
 <analyzer>
 <tokenizer class="solr.StandardTokenizerFactory"/>
 <!-- greek specific lowercase for sigma -->
 <filter class="solr.GreekLowerCaseFilterFactory"/>
 <filter class="solr.StopFilterFactory" ignoreCase="false"
words="lang/stopwords_el.txt" />
 <filter class="solr.GreekStemFilterFactory"/>
 </analyzer>
 </fieldType>
```

Language identification

At the time of indexing, language identification is required to map text to language-specific fields. Solr uses the langid `UpdateRequestProcessor` for language identification. Two types of `UpdateRequestProcessor` are provided by Solr.

- `TikaLanguageIdentifierUpdateProcessor`: Uses the language identification libraries in Apache Tika
- `LangDetectLanguageIdentifierUpdateProcessor`: Uses the open source Language Detection Library for Java

Configuration of `TikaLanguageIdentifierUpdateProcessor` in `solrconfig.xml`:

```
<processor
class="org.apache.solr.update.processor.TikaLanguageIdentifierUpdateProcess
orFactory">
 <lst name="defaults">
 <str name="langid.fl">title,subject,text,keywords</str>
 <str name="langid.langField">language_s</str>
 </lst>
</processor>
```

Configuration
of `LangDetectLanguageIdentifierUpdateProcessor` in `solrconfig.xml`:

```
<processor
class="org.apache.solr.update.processor.LangDetectLanguageIdentifierUpdateP
rocessorFactory">
 <lst name="defaults">
 <str name="langid.fl">title,subject,text,keywords</str>
 <str name="langid.langField">language_s</str>
 </lst>
</processor>
```

`UpdateRequestProcessor` provides many `langid` parameters. We are not going to explain them here. Determining the language at index time is always preferable over query time. During query time, the input provided by the user may be short and sometimes not meaningful enough to extract language information. At index time, full documents are present, so language identification becomes easier.

Configuring Solr for multiple language search

There are mainly three approaches to configure Solr for multiple language search.

Creating separate fields per language

This is a very simple and straightforward approach, done by creating a separate field per language. Create a per language field in managed-schema.xml.

Example:

```xml
<!-- English -->
<fieldType name="text_en" class="solr.TextField"
positionIncrementGap="100">
 <analyzer>
 <tokenizer class="solr.StandardTokenizerFactory"/>
 <filter class="solr.StopFilterFactory" ignoreCase="true"
words="lang/stopwords_en.txt" />
 <filter class="solr.LowerCaseFilterFactory"/>
 </analyzer>
</fieldType>
<!-- Greek -->
<fieldType name="text_el" class="solr.TextField"
positionIncrementGap="100">
 <analyzer>
 <tokenizer class="solr.StandardTokenizerFactory"/>
 <!-- greek specific lowercase for sigma -->
 <filter class="solr.GreekLowerCaseFilterFactory"/>
 <filter class="solr.StopFilterFactory" ignoreCase="false"
words="lang/stopwords_el.txt" />
 <filter class="solr.GreekStemFilterFactory"/>
 </analyzer>
</fieldType>
<!-- Spanish -->
<fieldType name="text_es" class="solr.TextField"
positionIncrementGap="100">
 <analyzer>
 <tokenizer class="solr.StandardTokenizerFactory"/>
 <filter class="solr.LowerCaseFilterFactory"/>
 <filter class="solr.StopFilterFactory" ignoreCase="true"
words="lang/stopwords_es.txt" format="snowball" />
 <filter class="solr.SpanishLightStemFilterFactory"/>
 <!-- more aggressive: <filter class="solr.SnowballPorterFilterFactory"
language="Spanish"/> -->
 </analyzer>
</fieldType>
```

```
...
<field name="content_en" type="text_en" indexed="true" stored="true" />
<field name="content_el" type="text_el" indexed="true" stored="true" />
<field name="content_es" type="text_es" indexed="true" stored="true" />
```

For creating separate fields per language, the DisMax-style query parser is required, which makes it easy to search across multiple fields. Solr provides built-in support for this query parser. Creating separate fields per language is simple and straightforward and fulfills most of the multi-language search requirements. The approach has a disadvantage too. The index size may increase as we define separate fields per language, and so queries may slow down.

Creating separate indexes per language

In this approach, Solr creates a separate Solr index (Solr Core) per language. Solr supports the creation of multiple cores. Every core contains a unique Solr index. Every core uses separate configuration files, including the `managed-schema.xml` file. During searching, every Solr core searches its own data from its own configuration file. After the search, results from all cores are combined together and then returned as an output of the query. Here is the simple configuration of defining a core per language.

File `en_managed-schema.xml`:

```
<field name="content" type="text_en" indexed="true" stored="true" />
```

File `el_managed-schema.xml`:

```
<field name="content" type="text_el" indexed="true" stored="true" />
```

File `es_managed-schema.xml`:

```
<field name="content" type="text_es" indexed="true" stored="true" />
```

File `solr.xml`:

```
<cores>
  <core name="english" instanceDir="shared" dataDir="../cores/core-
perlanguage/data/english/" schema="en_managed-schema.xml" />
  <core name="greek" instanceDir="shared" dataDir="../cores/core-
perlanguage/data/greek/" schema="el_managed-schema.xml" />
  <core name="spanish" instanceDir="shared" dataDir="../cores/core-
perlanguage/data/spanish" schema="es_managed-schema.xml" />
  <core name="aggregator" instanceDir="shared" dataDir="data/aggregator" />
</cores>
```

During the query, a request is sent to each of the language-specific cores using the shards parameter. Now the search will be independent and parallel with other languages. This will improve the performance of Solr. Here the field "content" is defined differently in each language-specific core, the language analysis also executed as per the configuration of that core. The search performance is better by defining a core per language as the search executes in parallel across multiple smaller indexes. As opposed to this, searching across a growing number of fields in a much larger index (the language-per-field approach) will hurt the performance. However, managing each core per language is somehow difficult.

During multiple language search configuration, selecting the implementation approach completely depends on the search requirements. The separate fields per language approach suits cases where the index size is in control. The separate indexes per language approach suits cases where the former does not satisfy the requirements and we have sufficient environment maintenance capabilities.

Understanding phonetic matching

Phonetic matching algorithms are used to match different spellings that are pronounced similarly by encoding them. Some examples are `Sandeep` and `Sandip`; `Taylor`, `Tailer`, and `Tailor`; and so on. Solr provides several filters for phonetic matching.

Understanding Beider-Morse phonetic matching

Beider-Morse Phonetic Matching (**BMPM**) helps you search for personal names or surnames. It is a very intelligent algorithm compared to soundex, metaphone, caverphone, and so on. Its purpose is to match names that are phonetically equivalent to the expected name. BMPM does not split spellings and does not generate false hits. It extracts names that are phonetically equivalent.

It executes these steps to extract names that are phonetically equivalent:

- Determines the language from the spelling of the name
- Applies phonetic rules to identify the language and translates the name into phonetic alphabets
- In the case of a language not identified from the name, it applies generic phonetics
- Finally, it applies language-independent rules regarding things such as voiced and unvoiced consonants and vowels to further ensure the reliability of the matches

BMPM supports the following languages: English, French, German, Greek, Hebrew written in Hebrew script, Hungarian, Italian, Polish, Romanian, Russian written in Cyrillic script, Russian transliterated into Latin script, Spanish, and Turkish.

Factory class: `solr.BeiderMorseFilterFactory`

Arguments:

- `nameType`: Types of names. Valid values are GENERIC, ASHKENAZI, or SEPHARDIC. If you are not processing Ashkenazi or Sephardic names, use GENERIC.
- `ruleType`: The types of rules to apply. Valid values are APPROX or EXACT.
- `concat`: Defines whether multiple possible matches should be combined with a pipe (|).
- `languageSet`: The language set to use. The value auto will allow the filter to identify the language, or a comma-separated list can be provided.

Example:

```
<fieldType name="text_en" class="solr.TextField"
positionIncrementGap="100">
 <analyzer>
 <tokenizer class="solr.StandardTokenizerFactory"/>
 <filter class="solr.BeiderMorseFilterFactory" nameType="GENERIC"
ruleType="APPROX" concat="true" languageSet="auto" />
 </analyzer>
 </fieldType>
```

Input: `sandeep`

Tokenizer to filter: `sandeep`

Output: `sYndip, sandDp, sandi, sandip, sondDp, sondi, sondip, zYndip, zandip, zondip`

From the generated tokens, token `sandip` is similar to our expectations.

Similar to BMPB, Solr provides many more algorithms with unique behavior for implementing phonetic matching. Following is the list of those algorithms:

- Daitch-Mokotoff soundex
- Double metaphone
- Metaphone
- Soundex
- Refined soundex
- Caverphone
- Kölner Phonetik also known as Cologne Phonetic
- NYSIIS

Explaining each algorithm is not possible, but we can understand their behavior through the Solr Admin console by configuring them in the `managed-schema.xml` file.

Summary

In this chapter, we saw an overview of text analysis, analyzers, tokenizers, filters, and how to configure an analyzer along with tokenizers and filters. We also saw the implementation approach for putting tokenizers and filters together. Then we moved on to multiple search. Here we explored how Solr determines a language, two approaches to creating separate fields and separate indexes per language for multiple-language search, and the pros and cons of each approach. Finally, we understood Solr phonetic matching mechanics using the BMPM algorithm.

In the next chapter, we will see how to do indexing using client API, upload data using index handlers, upload data using Apache Tika with Solr Cell, and detect languages while indexing.

5
Data Indexing and Operations

In the last chapter, we jumped into various text analysis methodologies, such as seeing the use of analyzers, filters, and tokenizers, to have an efficient text analysis.

In this chapter, we will see ways to add data to Solr indexes.

Basics of Solr indexing

In order to make content available for searching, we need to index it first—as simple as that! The process of indexing essentially involves any one of the three activities as shown in this diagram:

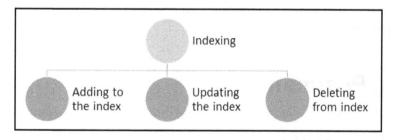

Let's drill down and look at the indexing process, which has the following main actions:

- Adding content to the Solr Index
- Updating the index
- Deleting from the index

Now, there are two basic questions that might arise in your mind:

- From where does Solr accept data to be indexed? Or what are different sources from where data can be indexed?
- How do we index data from the sources that we have identified?

Common sources that the Solr index can get data from are:

- Database tables
- CSV files
- XML files
- Microsoft Word or PDF

The answers to "*How does the Solr index get data from the aforementioned sources?*" are as follows:

- Using client APIs
- Uploading XML files using HTTP requests to the Solr server
- Using the Apache Tika-based Solr Cell framework to ingest proprietary data formats, such as Word or PDF files

Installing Postman

For all HTTP-based service calls, we will be using Postman to invoke such services.

Postman can be downloaded from `https://www.getpostman.com/`. The site provides installation instructions for each of the major operating systems. In this chapter, we will do our exercise based on Windows, so we'll proceed to install the Windows executable.

Once you've downloaded and installed Postman, you should see a screen like this:

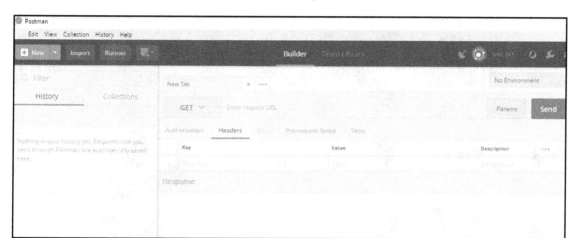

Don't worry! We will get into the details as to how to use Postman later in the chapter. Alternatively, you can use `curl` to do the same, but I prefer Postman due to its easy usability.

Exploring the post tool

In order to index different types of content to the Solr server, Solr provides a command-line tool.

To run this tool in Unix, use the following command:

```
bin/post -c gettingstarted example/exampledocs/books.json
```

For Windows, it gets a bit tricky as `bin/post` is available only as a Unix shell script.

On Windows, we need to use `SimplePostTool`, which is a standalone Java program and can be packaged in `post.jar` located at `example/exampledocs`. Navigate to `example/exampledocs` and issue this command:

```
java -jar post.jar -h
```

We will see the following output:

```
C:\Windows\System32\cmd.exe

::\book\solr\solr-7.2.0\example\exampledocs>java -jar post.jar -h
SimplePostTool version 5.0.0
Usage: java [SystemProperties] -jar post.jar [-h|-] [<file|folder|url|arg> [<file|folder|url|arg>...]]

Supported System Properties and their defaults:
  -Dc=<core/collection>
  -Durl=<base Solr update URL> (overrides -Dc option if specified)
  -Ddata=files|web|args|stdin (default=files)
  -Dtype=<content-type> (default=application/xml)
  -Dhost=<host> (default: localhost)
  -Dport=<port> (default: 8983)
  -Dbasicauth=<user:pass> (sets Basic Authentication credentials)
  -Dauto=yes|no (default=no)
  -Drecursive=yes|no|<depth> (default=0)
  -Ddelay=<seconds> (default=0 for files, 10 for web)
  -Dfiletypes=<type>[,<type>,...] (default=xml,json,jsonl,csv,pdf,doc,docx,ppt,pptx,xls,xlsx,odt,odp,ods,ott,otp,ots,rtf,htm,html,txt,log)
  -Dparams="<key>=<value>[&<key>=<value>...]" (values must be URL-encoded)
  -Dcommit=yes|no (default=yes)
  -Doptimize=yes|no (default=no)
  -Dout=yes|no (default=no)

This is a simple command line tool for POSTing raw data to a Solr port.
NOTE: Specifying the url/core/collection name is mandatory.
Data can be read from files specified as commandline args,
URLs specified as args, as raw commandline arg strings or via STDIN.
Examples:
  java -Dc=gettingstarted -jar post.jar *.xml
  java -Ddata=args -Dc=gettingstarted -jar post.jar '<delete><id>42</id></delete>'
  java -Ddata=stdin -Dc=gettingstarted -jar post.jar < hd.xml
  java -Ddata=web -Dc=gettingstarted -jar post.jar http://example.com/
  java -Dtype=text/csv -Dc=gettingstarted -jar post.jar *.csv
  java -Dtype=application/json -Dc=gettingstarted -jar post.jar *.json
  java -Durl=http://localhost:8983/solr/techproducts/update/extract -Dparams=literal.id=pdf1 -jar post.jar solr-word.pdf
  java -Dauto -Dc=gettingstarted -jar post.jar *
  java -Dauto -Dc=gettingstarted -Drecursive -jar post.jar afolder
  java -Dauto -Dc=gettingstarted -Dfiletypes=ppt,html -jar post.jar afolder
The options controlled by System Properties include the Solr
URL to POST to, the Content-Type of the data, whether a commit
or optimize should be executed, and whether the response should
be written to STDOUT. If auto=yes the tool will try to set type
automatically from file name. When posting rich documents the
file name will be propagated as "resource.name" and also used
as "literal.id". You may override these or any other request parameter
through the -Dparams property. To do a commit only, use "-" as argument.
The web mode is a simple crawler following links within domain, default delay=10s
```

As you can see, we get the full documentation of the post tool.

Issue the following command to run the post tool in Windows:

```
java -Dc=gettingstarted -jar example/exampledocs/post.jar
example/films/films.json
```

This will index content from `films.json` to the server at `localhost:8983`.

In order to index all the documents with the extension XML, issue the following command from the `SOLR_HOME` directory:

```
java -jar example/exampledocs/post.jar -Dc gettingstarted *.xml
```

Let's say you want to delete a document with ID 23 from the `gettingstarted` collection/core; you can issue the following command:

```
java -jar example/exampledocs/post.jar -Dc gettingstarted -Dd
'<delete><id>23</id></delete>'
```

Similarly, we can index `.json` and `.csv` files as shown here:

```
java -jar example/exampledocs/post.jar -Dc gettingstarted *.json
java -jar example/exampledocs/post.jar -Dc gettingstarted *.csv
```

As you can see, there is not much difference in indexing CSV, XML, and JSON documents.

Now let's learn how to index rich documents. Let's say we want to index a Word document; we will issue the following command:

```
java -jar example/exampledocs/post.jar -Dc gettingstarted sample.doc
```

If we want to specify a bunch of documents of type `.pdf` and `.doc` in a folder named `samplefolder`, then we issue the following command:

```
java -jar example/exampledocs/post.jar -Dc gettingstarted -Dfiletypes
doc,pdf samplefolder/
```

Now that we have learned how to use the post tool for indexing, let's see another technique to do the same, known as **index handlers**.

Understanding index handlers

Solr provides a native way to index structured documents such as XML, JSON, and CSV using index handlers.

The default request handler (which is configured by default) is as follows:

```
<requestHandler name="/update" class="solr.UpdateRequestHandler" />
```

Or you can mention them separately in `solrconfig.xml`:

```
<requestHandler name="/update/json" class="solr.UpdateRequestHandler">
    <lst name="invariants">
        <str name="stream.contentType">application/json</str>
    </lst>
</requestHandler>
<requestHandler name="/update/csv" class="solr.UpdateRequestHandler">
    <lst name="invariants">
```

```
        <str name="stream.contentType">application/csv</str>
    </lst>
</requestHandler>
```

Working with an index handler with the XML format

Now let's try to add some content to our index using the XML format. Open the Postman tool and add the URL `http://localhost:8983/solr/gettingstarted/update`, as shown in the following screenshot:

Note that we have selected the method type to **POST**. You also need to add a request header, **Content-Type**, to `text/xml`. Most of this can be done in Postman as we just select values from the dropdown, as shown previously.

Now switch to the **Body** tab and add the following content:

```
<add>
    <doc>
        <field name="title">Harry Potter and Prisoner of
          Azkaban</field>
        <field name="author">J.K. Rowling</field>
    </doc>
</add>
```

For adding any documents to index, the XML schema should have the following elements:

- `<add>`: Specifies that the operation we are going to perform will add one or more documents
- `<doc>`: This has fields that make up the whole document
- `<field>`: Specifies each field to be added for the document

Once you are done with the aforementioned steps, click on the **Send** button in Postman. If everything goes right, you should see the following response:

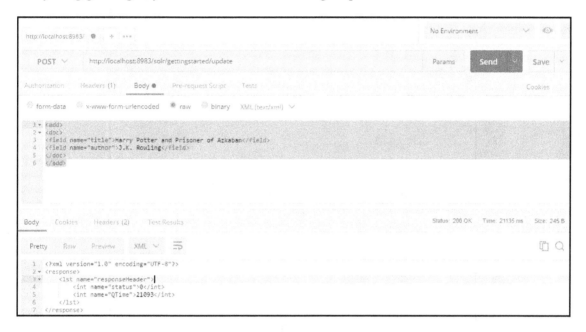

This indicates that the document has been successfully added to the index. In order to verify the documents, you can go to the Solr admin console in the browser, select `gettingstarted`, and then navigate to the **Query** section, as follows:

Once you are on the previous page, click on the **Execute Query** button available at the very bottom of the page. You should see something like this:

```
{
  "responseHeader":{
      "zkConnected":true,
      "status":0,
      "QTime":18,
      "params":{
```

```
     "q":"*:*",
     "_":"1514434725886"}},
"response":{"numFound":3,"start":0,"maxScore":2.0,"docs":[
    {
        "title":["Harry Potter and Chamber of Secrets"],
        "author":["J.K. Rowling"],
        "id":"0bb62d53-20d0-4df2-a385-c08b8658dc28",
        "title_str":["Harry Potter and Chamber of Secrets"],
        "author_str":["J.K. Rowling"],
        "_version_":1587892939487444992},
    {
        "title":["Harry Potter and Prisoner of Azkaban"],
        "author":["J.K. Rowling"],
        "id":"401f8336-88d9-478c-93a2-2de070188a3d",
        "title_str":["Harry Potter and Prisoner of Azkaban"],
        "author_str":["J.K. Rowling"],
        "_version_":1587999318593241088},
    {
        "title":["Harry Potter and Philosophers Stone"],
        "author":["J.K. Rowling"],
        "id":"dcbfd369-2a4b-4e9d-9713-1af373849438",
        "title_str":["Harry Potter and Philosophers Stone"],
        "author_str":["J.K. Rowling"],
        "_version_":1587892903981613056}]
}}
```

As you can see, the document with the title `Harry Potter and Prisoner of Azkaban` is added to the index. I had previously added some other documents, so that's why you are seeing two additional entries.

Now let's try to delete some documents from the index. Open Postman and just replace the content with the following:

```
<delete>
    <id>0bb62d53-20d0-4df2-a385-c08b8658dc28</id>
    <query>title:azkaban</query>
</delete>
```

In Postman, it will look something like this once executed:

What we have done is deleted a couple of records, one with a query where the title is Azkaban and one with the ID 0bb62d53-20d0-4df2-a385-c08b8658dc28. In order to verify this, go to the admin console and click on the **Execute Query** button once again:

As you can see, there is only one entry now as the other two entries have been deleted.

Index handler with JSON

Solr also supports JSON-formatted documents to be indexed. Let's look at a simple example of indexing just one document. To add documents in JSON format on our gettingstarted collection, we need to use the following
URL: http://localhost:8983/solr/gettingstarted/update/json/docs.

Open Postman and create a new request with this URL. See the following screenshot for clarity:

As you can see, we have set **Content-Type** to `application/json`. Now click on the **Body** tab and put the JSON content as follows:

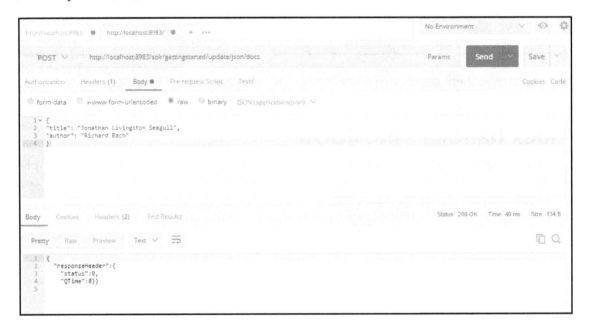

Once you are done, execute the request and it will run to success with the following response:

```
{
  "responseHeader":{
  "status":0,
  "QTime":8}
}
```

The `status` value set to `0` means it is a success. If it is a non-zero value, then it means there is a failure. In order to validate this, go to the Solr admin console and execute the query as we did earlier:

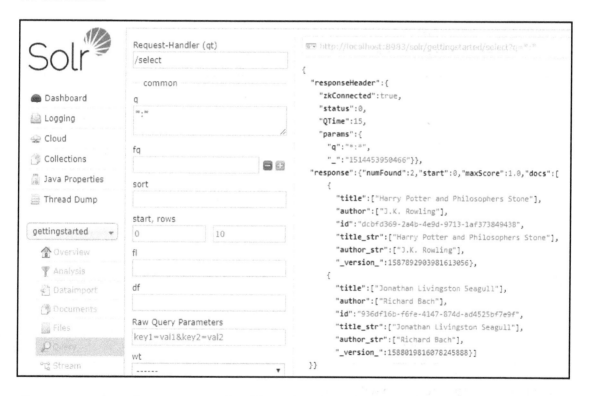

Once you execute the query, you should see that the index also contains the new document that we added using the JSON format.

In order to add multiple documents, you have to pass a JSON array instead of a single document:

```
[
    {
        "title": "Red sails to Capri",
        "author": "Ann Weil"
    },
    {
        "title": "Five Point Someone",
        "author": "Chetan Bhagat"
    }
]
```

The URL has to be `http://localhost:8983/solr/gettingstarted/update/`, as shown in the following screenshot:

You will get a success response with `status` set to 0 once you execute the request. In order to validate, navigate to the Solr admin panel and execute the query:

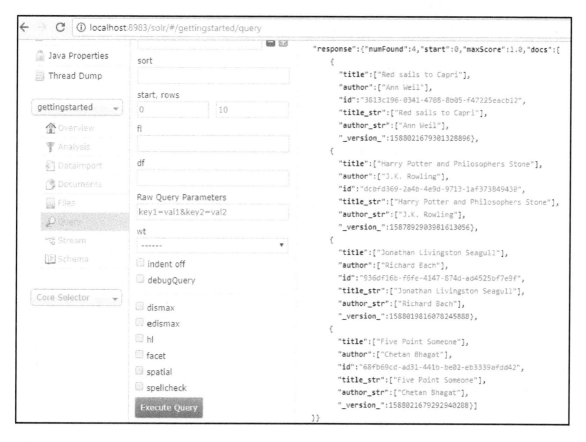

Your response will now have the two documents that you have added and you should see the following documents in the response:

```
{
"responseHeader":{
"zkConnected":true,
"status":0,
"QTime":35,
"params":{
"q":"*:*",
"_":"1514453950466"}},
"response":{"numFound":4,"start":0,"maxScore":1.0,"docs":[
    {
    "title":["Red sails to Capri"],
    "author":["Ann Weil"],
    "id":"3813c196-0341-4708-8b05-f47225eacb12",
    "title_str":["Red sails to Capri"],
    "author_str":["Ann Weil"],
```

```
            "_version_":1588021679301328896},
            {
            "title":["Harry Potter and Philosophers Stone"],
            "author":["J.K. Rowling"],
            "id":"dcbfd369-2a4b-4e9d-9713-1af373849438",
            "title_str":["Harry Potter and Philosophers Stone"],
            "author_str":["J.K. Rowling"],
            "_version_":1587892903981613056},
            {
            "title":["Jonathan Livingston Seagull"],
            "author":["Richard Bach"],
            "id":"936df16b-f6fe-4147-874d-ad4525bf7e9f",
            "title_str":["Jonathan Livingston Seagull"],
            "author_str":["Richard Bach"],
            "_version_":1588019816078245888},
            {
            "title":["Five Point Someone"],
            "author":["Chetan Bhagat"],
            "id":"68fb69cd-ad31-441b-be02-eb3339afdd42",
            "title_str":["Five Point Someone"],
            "author_str":["Chetan Bhagat"],
            "_version_":1588021679292940288}]
        }}
```

You can also add, update, or delete documents in a single operation. To do this, let's try to delete some documents and add a new document:

```
{
    "add": {
    "doc": {
        "title": "Liferay Beginner's Guide",
        "author": "Samir Bhatt"
    }
},
    "delete": { "id":"3813c196-0341-4708-8b05-f47225eacb12" },
    "delete": { "query":"author:rowling" }
}
```

Here, we are executing both `add` and `delete` operations in a single request. We have added a new book, deleted a book with `id`, and deleted a book with `query` where the author is `rowling`.

The request in Postman will look something like this:

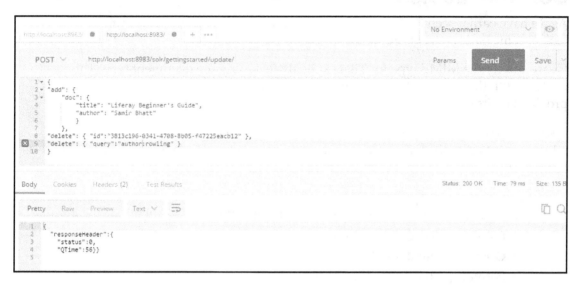

In order to execute this, hit the **Send** button. You will get a success response. In this way, we can add and delete documents in a single operation.

Apache Tika and indexing

We have seen how to index data from a standard file format such as JSON or XML. But what about proprietary file formats such as Word and PDF? Luckily, Solr comes to the rescue with the use of the Apache Tika project. The Tika framework provides a way to incorporate various file formats such as Word and PDF.

Internally, Tika uses the Apache PDFBox parser to parse PDF and Apache POI for the Word format. Solr provides ExtractingRequestHandler, which makes use of Tika to upload binary files and to index as well as extract data.

This framework in Solr is known as Solr Cell, which is an abbreviation of Solr content extraction library, the name when this framework was under development.

Solr Cell basics

As we have earlier seen that, the Solr Cell framework leverages the Tika framework. Let's look at some basic concepts about this.

Please specify the MIME type for Tika explicitly to specify the document type. This has to be done with the `stream.type` parameter or else Tika will decide the document type provided on its own.

Tika creates some additional metadata on its own, such as `Title`, `Author`, and `Subject`, which respects `DublinCore`. Some of the file types where metadata can be extracted are as follows:

- HTML
- XML and derived formats such as XHTML, OOXML and ODF
- Formats of MS Office document types
- **OpenDocument (ODF)**
- Formats with iWorks document
- PDF
- Email formats
- Crypto formats
- **Rich Text Format (RTF)**
- Electronic publication
- Packaging and compression formats such as `.tar`, `.zip`, and `.7zip` files
- Text format
- Help formats
- Feed and syndication formats (RSS and atom feeds)
- Audio formats
- JARs and Java class files
- Video formats
- Cad formats
- Scientific formats
- EXE programs and libraries
- Image formats
- Source code
- Font formats

All extracted text from any of these formats is mapped with content field. Along with these formats, Tika's metadata fields can be mapped to Solr fields.

First, Tika produces an XHTML stream, which is passed to the SAX `ContentHandler`, and then Solr acts on various SAX events; finally it creates the fields to index. Since there is an XML-based parser, we can apply an XPath expression to XHTML to filter the content.

Indexing a binary using Tika

Now let's get our hands dirty and start putting Tika to use. For this example, we will use the `gettingstarted` schema. I will just start one cloud node that created earlier for demo purposes.

To start only one node, issue a command as follows. Note that the path of the node may change as per your setup:

```
solr start -cloud -p 8983 -s
E:\book\solr\solr-7.2.0\example\cloud\node1\solr
```

We will index a sample PDF provided by Solr. The PDF is available at `SOLR_HOME/example/exampledocs` by the name of `solr-word.pdf`.

Open Postman and create a new POST request with the URL `http://localhost:8983/solr/gettingstarted/update/extract?literal.id=doc1&commit=true`. Upload the file in the **binary** section. Finally submit the request as follows:

You will see that the request is successful, with `status` code 0. In order to verify what data has been indexed, we can use Postman to query for PDF documents using the following URL: `http://localhost:8983/solr/gettingstarted/select?q=pdf`.

You will see a response as follows:

```
{
  "responseHeader":
      {
          "zkConnected": true,"status": 0,"QTime": 46,"params": {"q": "pdf"}
      },
    "response": {"numFound": 1,"start": 0,"maxScore": 0.55955875,
      "docs": [{"id": "doc1",
          "date": ["2008-11-13T13:35:51Z"],
          "pdf_docinfo_custom_aapl_keywords": ["solr, word, pdf"],
          "pdf_pdfversion": [1.3],
          "pdf_docinfo_title": ["solr-word"],
          "xmp_creatortool": ["Microsoft Word"],
          "stream_content_type": ["text/plain"],
          "access_permission_can_print_degraded": [true],
          "subject": ["solr word"],
          "dc_format": ["application/pdf; version=1.3"],
          "pdf_docinfo_creator_tool": ["Microsoft Word"],
          "access_permission_fill_in_form": [true],
          "pdf_encrypted": [false],
          "dc_title": ["solr-word"],
          "modified": ["2008-11-13T13:35:51Z"],
          "cp_subject": ["solr word"],
          "pdf_docinfo_subject": ["solr word"],
      .
      .
      .
```

While making the request, we specified `literal.id=doc1`, which tells Solr to use `doc1` as the unique ID for this particular document.

Other parameters that Solr's extracting request handler accepts are covered in this table:

Parameter	Description
capture	This captures XHTML elements having specified names for supplementary addition to the document. This parameter is useful to copy chunks of XHTML into a separate field.
captureAttr	Indexes attributes of Tika XHTML elements to separate fields, which are named after the element.

commitWithin	The time, in milliseconds, to commit the document.
date.formats	Defines date format patterns for identification in the documents.
defaultField	The default field will be used only when the uprefix parameter is unspecified and a field can't be determined.
extractOnly	This is false by default. If the value is true, it returns the extracted content from Tika, with no need to index the document.
extractFormat	The extraction format to be used, the default being XML. We can change it to text if needed.
fmap.source_field	Used to map one field name to another.
ignoreTikaException	This is used to ignore exceptions during processing.
literal.fieldname	Whatever value is specified in literal.fieldname is used for populating the field with this particular name. If the field is multivalued, then the data can also be multivalued.
literalsOverride	Literal field values will override other values having the same field name if set to true; otherwise, literal values that are defined with literal.fieldname will be added at the end.
lowernames	By setting this to true, the entire set of field names will be mapped to lowercase letters with underscores.
multipartUploadLimitInKB	Used to set a limit on the document size to be uploaded.
passwordsFile	The file path to password mappings will be set here.
resource.name	Used to specify the optional name of the file.
resource.password	The password for the PDF (which is password protected) is defined using resource.password.
tika.config	The file path used to specify Tika's configuration file.
uprefix	Used to prefix fields that have not been defined in the schema with the given prefix.
xpath	Used to filter based on the XPath expression during extraction from Tika XHTML content.

Language detection

Solr uses the langid `UpdateRequestProcessor` to identify languages and then map from text to the language-specific field while indexing.

There are two implementations provided by Solr for language detection:

- Tika language detection
- Langdetect language detection

Language detection configuration

The configuration for language detection is done in `solrconfig.xml` and both Tika as well as langdetect language detection use the same parameters, as follows:

```
<processor
class="org.apache.solr.update.processor.TikaLanguageIdentifierUpdateProcess
orFactory">
    <lst name="defaults">
        <str name="langid.fl">title,subject,text,keywords</str>
        <str name="langid.langField">language_s</str>
    </lst>
</processor>
<processor class=
"org.apache.solr.update.processor.LangDetectLanguageIdentifierUpdateProcess
orFactory">
    <lst name="defaults">
        <str name="langid.fl">title,subject,text,keywords</str>
        <str name="langid.langField">language_s</str>
    </lst>
</processor>
```

As you can see, both the configurations use the same parameters, the only difference being the `processor` class. The list of parameters is given here:

Parameter	Description
langid	Used to enable language detection by setting the value to true.
langid.fl	This is a required parameter, which can contain either comma-delimited or space-delimited fields to be processed using `langid`.
langid.langField	This is a required parameter used to specify the field for the returned language code.

langid.langsField	The same as langid.langField, but in this case, it is used to specify the field for a list instead of a single language code.
langid.overwrite	If you enable this parameter, then the content of the langField and langsFields fields will be overwritten provided they already have a value. By default, the value is set to false.
langid.lcmap	Contains a space-separated list that specifies the language code mappings (colon-delimited) to apply to the detected languages.
langid.threshold	Used to set a threshold between 0 and 1, and the language identification score must reach the threshold. Only then is langid accepted. The default value is 0.5.
langid.whitelist	Used to specify the allowed language identification codes list.
langid.map	Used to enable field name mapping. The default value is false.

Client APIs

There are various client APIs available to add data to Solr indexes. This table shows the available client APIs:

Language	Description
Python	There are two output formats: • The first output format is specifically designed for Python • The second format is JSON
Java	A library named SolrJ is available for working with Java
Ruby	A specific output format for Ruby is available and this extends the JSON format
JavaScript	Out-of-the-box support for JSON is available, which makes it very easy to work with JavaScript

More details on the client API will be covered in a later chapter.

Summary

In this chapter, we saw various techniques to index data. We went through index handlers and how they help us in indexing data using XML and JSON formats. We made use of the Solr Cell framework to index binary data formats. We then saw how language detection works. We finally touched on various client APIs available for indexing, though this will be covered in detail in a later chapter.

In the next chapter, we will see in detail how searching works in Solr. We will cover faceting, spell checking, highlighting, ranking, pagination, and many other features related to searches.

6
Advanced Queries – Part I

In the previous chapter, we learned how to build indexes using various methods. In this chapter, we will see how Solr's search works. Solr comes with a large searching kit; by configuring elements from this kit, it provides users with an extensive search experience and returns impressive results with a helpful interface.

Here is a list of search functionalities provided by Solr, that put Solr in the list of desirable search engines:

- Highlighting
- Spell checking
- Reranking
- Transformation of results
- Suggested words
- Pagination on results
- Expand and collapse
- Grouping and clustering
- Spatial search
- More like this word
- Autocomplete

We will look at some of these functions in detail later in this chapter, but first let's understand every component that performs an important role during searches and generates impressive results.

Search relevance

Relevance is a measurement of the user's satisfaction with the response to their search query. It completely depends on the context of the search. Sometimes, the same document can be searched by different classes of people for different context. For example, the search query *higher tax payer in India* can be searched by:

- An income tax department in the context of their duty
- Chartered accountants in the context of their professional interest
- Students in the context of gaining knowledge

The comprehensiveness of any response depends on the context of the search. Sometimes, the context is high, such as searching for legal information; sometimes, it is low, when someone is searching for context such as specific dance steps. So, during Solr configuration, we need to take care of this too.

There are two terms that play an important role in relevance:

- **Precision**: Precision is the percentage of documents in the returned results that are relevant.
- **Recall**: Recall is the percentage of relevant results returned out of all relevant results in the system. Retrieving perfect recall is insignificant, for example, returning every document for every query.

From this example, we can conclude that precision and recall totally depend on the context of the search. Sometimes, we need 100% recall, say when searching for legal information. Here, all the relevant documents should be returned in the response. While in other scenarios, there is no need to return all documents. For example, when searching for dance steps, returning all the documents will overwhelm the application.

Through faceting, query filters, and other search components, the application can be configured with the flexibility to help end users get their searches, in order to return the most relevant results for users. We can configure Solr to balance precision and recall to meet the needs of a particular user community.

Velocity search UI

Solr provides a user interface through which we can easily understand the Solr search mechanism. Using velocity search UI, we can explore search features such as faceting, highlighting, autocomplete, and geospatial searching. Previously we have seen an example of `techproducts`; let's browse its products through velocity UI. You can access the UI through `http://localhost:8983/solr/techproducts/browse`, as shown in the following screenshot:

Solr uses response writer to generate an organized response. Here velocity UI uses velocity response writer. We will explore response writer later in this chapter.

Query parsing and syntax

In this section, we will explore some query parsers, their features, and how to configure them with Solr. Solr supports some query parsers. Here is the list of parsers supported by Solr:

- **Standard query parser**
- **DisMax query parser**
- **Extended DisMax (eDisMax) query parser**

Each parser has its own configuration parameters for clubbing with Solr. However, there are some common parameters required by all parsers. First let's take a look at these common parameters.

Common query parameters

The following are the common query parameters supported by standard query parser, DisMax query parser, and extended DisMax query parser:

Parameter	Behavior	Default value
defType	Selects the query parser: `defType=dismax`	Lucene (standard query parser)
sort	Sorts the search results in either ascending or descending order. The value can be specified as `asc` or `ASC` and `desc` or `DESC`. Sorting is supported by numerical or alphabetical content. Solr supports sorting by field clones. **Example:** • `salary asc`: Sorts based on salary (high to low). • `name desc`: Sorts based on names (z → a). • `salary asc name desc`: First sorts by salary high to low. Within that, it sorts the result set again sorts by name (z → a).	desc
start	Specifies the starting point from where the results should begin displaying.	0
rows	Specifies the maximum number of documents to be returned to the client from the complete result set at a time.	10
fq	Limits the result set to the documents matched by the filter query (`fq`) without affecting the score.	

fl	Specifies the field list to be returned inside the response for each matching document. The fields can be specified by a space or comma. For example: • `fl=id name salary`: Returns only `id`, `name`, and `salary` • `fl=id,name,salary`: Returns only `id`, `name`, and `salary` Indicating `fl=*` will return all the fields. We also can return the `score` of fields for each document by mentioning the `score` string along with the fields. For example: • `fl=id score`: Returns the `id` field and the `score` • `fl=* score`: Returns all the fields in each document along with each field's `score`	`*`
debug	Returns debug information about the specified value. For example: • `debug=query` will return debug information about the query • `debug=timing` will return debug information about the processing time of the query • `debug=results` will return debug information about the score results (explain) • `debug=all` or `debug=true` will return all debugging information for the request	Not including debugging information
explainOther	This specifies a Lucene query that will return debugging information with the explain information of each document matching to that Lucene query, relative to the original query (specified by the q parameter). For example: `q=soccer&debug=true&explainOther=id:cricket` The preceding query calculates the scoring explain info of the top matching documents and compares with the explain info for the documents matching `id:cricket`.	blank
wt	Specifies a response writer format. Supported formats are `json`, `xml`, `xslt`, `javabin`, `geojson`, `python`, `php`, `phps`, `ruby`, `csv`, `velocity`, `smile`, and `xlsx`.	`json`
omitHeader	Tells Solr to include or exclude header information from the returned results; `omitHeader=true` will exclude the header information from the returned results.	`false`
cache	This tells Solr to cache results of all queries and filter queries. If set to `false`, it will disable result caching.	`true`

Apart from the preceding common parameters for parsers, `timeAllowed`, `segmentTerminateEarly`, `logParamsList`, and `echoParams` are also common parameters which are used by all the parsers. We are not detailing these parameters here.

Standard query parser

Standard query parser, also known as **Lucene query parser**, is the default query parser for Solr.

Advantage

The syntax is easy and differently structured queries can easily be created using standard query parser.

Disadvantage

Standard query parser does not throw any syntax error. So, identifying syntax errors is a little tough.

The following parameters are supported by standard query parser. We can configure them in `solrconfig.xml`:

Parameter	Behavior	Default value
q	Specifies a query using standard query syntax. This is a mandatory parameter for any request.	
q.op	Specifies the default operator for query expressions, which overrides the default operator configured inside the schema. Possible values are AND or OR.	
df	Specifies a default field, which overrides the default field definition inside the schema.	
sow	If this is set to `true`, it splits on white spaces.	false

Standard query parser response: The following is the sample response provided by the standard query parser when we search for `field id=SP2514N`

URL: `http://localhost:8983/solr/techproducts/select?q=SP2514N&wt=json`

In Solr admin console, while running a query to search a product with `id=SP2514N` displays the response as follows:

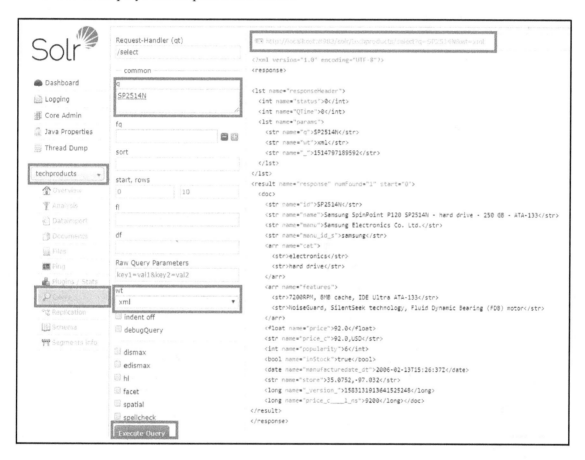

The response code is as follows:

```
{
  "responseHeader":{
  "status":0,
  "QTime":0,
  "params":{
  "q":"SP2514N",
```

```
"wt":"json",
"_":"1515346597997"}},
"response":{"numFound":1,"start":0,"docs":[
{
"id":"SP2514N",
"name":"Samsung SpinPoint P120 SP2514N - hard drive - 250 GB - ATA-133",
"manu":"Samsung Electronics Co. Ltd.",
"manu_id_s":"samsung",
"cat":["electronics",
"hard drive"],
"features":["7200RPM, 8MB cache, IDE Ultra ATA-133",
"NoiseGuard, SilentSeek technology, Fluid Dynamic Bearing (FDB) motor"],
"price":92.0,
"price_c":"92.0,USD",
"popularity":6,
"inStock":true,
"manufacturedate_dt":"2006-02-13T15:26:37Z",
"store":"35.0752,-97.032",
"_version_":1583131913641525248,
"price_c____l_ns":9200}]
}}
```

In the same way, now the query id=SP2514N; and we need only two fields, id and name, in response.

URL: `http://localhost:8983/solr/techproducts/select?fl=id,name&q=SP2514N&wt=json`.

Response:

```
{
"responseHeader":{
"status":0,
"QTime":17,
"params":{
"q":"SP2514N",
"fl":"id,name",
"wt":"json",
"_":"1515346597997"}},
"response":{"numFound":1,"start":0,"docs":[
{
"id":"SP2514N",
"name":"Samsung SpinPoint P120 SP2514N - hard drive - 250 GB - ATA-133"}]
}}
```

We can format the response by setting the `wt` parameter as `json`, `xml`, `xslt`, `javabin`, `geojson`, `python`, `php`, `phps`, `ruby`, `csv`, `velocity`, `smile`, or `xlsx`.

Searching terms for standard query parser

A query string to standard query parser contains terms and operators. There are two types of terms:

- **Single term**: A single word, such as `soccer` or `volleyball`
- **A phrase**: A group of words surrounded by double quotes, such as `apache solr`

We can combine multiple terms with Boolean operators to form complex queries.

Term modifiers

Solr supports many term modifiers that add flexibility or precision during searching. These term modifiers are wildcard characters, characters for making a search fuzzy, and so on.

Wildcard searches

The standard query parser supports two types of wildcard searches within a single term. They are single (?) and multiple (*) characters. They can be applied to single terms only, and not to search phrases. For example:

Wildcard search type	Special character	Search example
Single character (matches a single character)	?	Searching for a string `te?t` will match `test` and `text`.
Multiple characters (matches zero or more sequential characters)	*	Searching for string `tes*` will match `test`, `testing`, and `tester`. The wildcard characters can be used at the beginning, middle, or end of a term. For example, the string `te*t` will match `test` and `text`, and `*est` will match `pest` and `test`.

Fuzzy searches

In fuzzy searching, instead of matching exact terms, Solr searches terms that are likely similar to a specified term. The tilde (~) symbol is used at the end of a single word in fuzzy search. For example, to search for a term similar in spelling to roam, use a fuzzy search; `roam~` will match terms like roam, roams, and foam.

The `distance` parameter (optional) specifies the maximum number of modifications that take place between 0 and 2. The default value is 2. For example, searching for `roam~1` will search the terms such as roams and foam but not foams because it has a modification distance of 2.

Proximity searching

Proximity searching searches for terms within a specific distance of each other. To implement a proximity search, specify a tilde (~) symbol with a numeric value at the end of a search phrase. For example, to search for `soccer` and `volleyball` within 20 words of each other in a document, do this:

```
"soccer volleyball"~20
```

The distance value specifies the term movements needed to match the specified phrase.

Range searches

In range searches, documents are searched based on a provided range (upper and lower bound) for a specific field. All the documents whose values for the specified field fall in a given range will be returned. The range search can be inclusive or exclusive of the range. For example, here the range query matches all documents whose `price` field has a value between 1000 and 50000, both inclusive:

```
price:[1000 TO 50000]
```

Along with date and numerical fields, we can specify the range as words as well. For example:

```
title:{apache TO lucene}
```

The preceding range configuration will search all documents whose titles are between apache and lucene, but not including apache and lucene:

- **Inclusive**: Square brackets [&]. Documents are searched by including the upper and lower bound.
- **Exclusive**: Curly brackets { & }. Documents are searched between the upper and lower bound, but excluding the bounds.

Combining inclusive and exclusive is also possible, where one end is inclusive and the other is exclusive, for example, price:[5 TO 20}.

Boolean operators

Here is a list of Boolean operators supported by standard query parser:

Operator	Symbol	Description
AND	&&	Requires both terms to match. For example, we search documents that contain soccer and volleyball: • "soccer" AND "volleyball" • "soccer" && "volleyball"
NOT	!	Requires that the following term not be present. For example, we search for documents that contain the phrase soccer but do not contain volleyball: • "soccer" NOT "volleyball" • "soccer" ! "volleyball"
OR	||	Requires one of the terms to match. This is a default conjunction operator, for example, searching for documents that contains either soccer or volleyball: • "soccer" OR "volleyball" • "soccer" || "volleyball"
	+	Requires that the following term be present, for example, searching for documents that must contain soccer and that may or may not contain volleyball: +soccer volleyball
	−	Prohibits the following term, for example, searching for documents that contain soccer but not volleyball: +soccer -volleyball

Please note that the Boolean operators AND and NOT must be specified in uppercase.

Escaping special characters

Solr treats these characters with a special meaning when they are used in a query:

```
+   -   &&   ||   !   ( )   { }   [ ]   ^   "   ~   *   ?   :   /
```

Using a backslash character(\) before the special character will notify Solr not to treat it as a special character but as a normal character. For example, for the search string (1+1) :2 the plus and parentheses, and colon can be ignored as special characters and will be treated as normal characters like this:

```
\(1\+1\)\:2
```

Grouping terms

Solr supports groups of clauses using parentheses to form subqueries that control the Boolean logic for a query.

This example will form a query that searches for either soccer or volleyball and world cup:

```
(soccer OR volleyball) AND "world cup"
```

Two or more Boolean operators can also be specified for a single field. Simply specify the Boolean clauses within parentheses. For example, this query will search for the field that contains both soccer and volleyball:

```
game:(+soccer +volleyball)
```

Dates and times in query strings

We need to use an appropriate date format whenever we are running a query against any date field. Search queries for exact date values will require quoting or escaping because : is listed as a special character for the parser:

```
createddate:2001-01-11T23\:45\:40.60Z

createddate:"2001-01-11T23:45:40.60Z"

createddate:[2001-01-11T23:45:40.60Z TO *]

createddate:[1999-12-31T23:45:40.60Z TO 2001-01-11T00:00:00Z]

timestamp:[* TO NOW]

publisheddate:[NOW-1YEAR/DAY TO NOW/DAY+1DAY]

createddate:[2001-01-11T23:45:40.60Z TO 2001-01-11T23:45:40.60Z+1YEAR]

createddate:[2001-01-11T23:45:40.60Z/YEAR TO 2001-01-11T23:45:40.60Z]
```

Adding comments to the query string

Comments can also be added to the query string. Solr supports C-style comments in the query string. Comments may be nested. For example:

```
soccer /* this is a simple comment for query string */ OR volleyball
```

The DisMax Query Parser

The DisMax query parser processes simple phrases (simple syntax). The DisMax query provides an interface that looks similar to Google. The DisMax Query Parser supports the simplified syntax of the Lucene query parser. Quotes can be used for grouping phrases. The DisMax Query Parser escapes all Boolean operators to simplify the query syntax, except the operators AND and OR, which can be used to determine mandatory and optional clauses.

Advantages

It produces syntax error messages. It also provides additional boosting queries, boosting functions, and filtering queries for search results.

DisMax query parser parameters

Apart from common parameters, the following is a list of all parameters supported by the DisMax Query Parser. All the default values for these parameters are configured in `solrconfig.xml`:

Parameter	Behavior
q	Specifies a query string with no special characters and treats Boolean operators + and – as term modifiers. Wildcard characters like * are not supported by this parameter: • q=apache • q="Apache Lucene"
a.alt	Defines an alternate query when the main query parameter q is not specified or blank. This parameter is mainly used to match all documents to get faceting counts.
qf	The qf parameter assigns a boost factor to a specific field to increase or decrease its importance in the query. For example, qf="firstField^3.4 secondField thirdField^0.2" assigns firstField a boost of 3.4, keeps secondField with the default boost, and assigns thirdField a boost of 0.2. These boost factors make matches in firstField much more significant than matches in secondField, which becomes much more significant than matches in thirdField.
mm	The minimum parameter defines the minimum number of optional clauses that must match. Words or phrases specified in the q parameter are considered as optional clauses unless they are preceded by a Boolean AND or OR. Possible values for the mm parameter are integer (positive and negative), percentage (positive and negative), simple, or multiple conditional expressions. The default value for mm is 100%, which means all clauses must match.
pf	The **Phrase Fields (pf)** parameter boosts the score of a document when all the terms in the q parameter appear in close proximity.

ps	The **Phrase Slop (ps)** parameter specifies the number of positions a term is required to move to match a phrase specified in a query with the `pf` parameter.
qs	Similar to the `ps` parameter for the `pf` parameter, the **Query Phrase Slop (qs)** defines the amount of slop on phrase queries explicitly included in the user's query string with the `qf` parameter.
tie	The tie breaker parameter specifies a float value (which should be something much less than 1) to use as a tiebreaker when a query term is matched in more than one field in a document.

bq	The **Boost Query (bq)** parameter specifies an additional and optional query clause that will be added to the user's main query to influence the score. For example, if you want to add a relevancy boost for recent documents:
	`q=apache`
	`bq=date:[NOW/DAY-1YEAR TO NOW/DAY]`
	Multiple `bq` parameters can also be used when a query needs to be parsed as separate clauses with separate boosts.

bf	The **Boost Functions (bf)** parameter specifies functions (with optional boosts) that will be added to the user's main query to influence the score. Any function supported natively by Solr can be used along with a boost value. For example, if you want to show the most recent documents first, this is the syntax: `bf=recip(rord(createddate),1,100,100)`

We have seen all the configuration parameters for DisMax Query Parser and now we are ready to run a search using DisMax query parser.

The query ID is `SP2514N` and all DisMax Parser parameters are default, which means we are not specifying values in those parameters.

The URL
is `http://localhost:8983/solr/techproducts/select?defType=dismax&q=SP2514N&wt=json`

The following shows the Solr admin console showing an example for DisMax query parser:

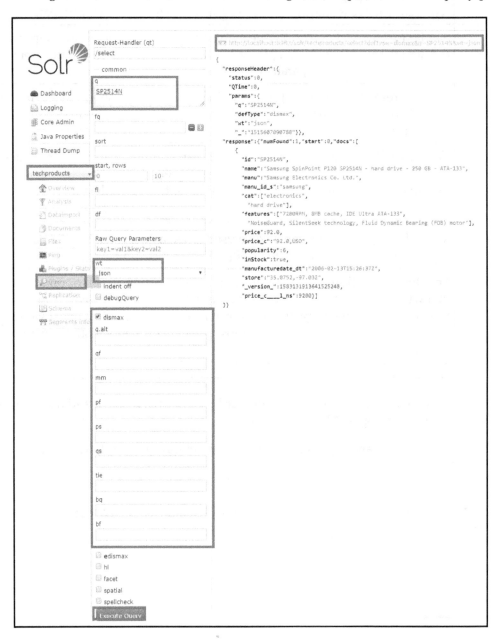

Response:

```
{
  "responseHeader":{
  "status":0,
  "QTime":0,
  "params":{
  "q":"SP2514N",
  "defType":"dismax",
  "wt":"json",
  "_":"1515607090788"}},
  "response":{"numFound":1,"start":0,"docs":[
  {
  "id":"SP2514N",
  "name":"Samsung SpinPoint P120 SP2514N - hard drive - 250 GB - ATA-133",
  "manu":"Samsung Electronics Co. Ltd.",
  "manu_id_s":"samsung",
  "cat":["electronics",
  "hard drive"],
  "features":["7200RPM, 8MB cache, IDE Ultra ATA-133",
  "NoiseGuard, SilentSeek technology, Fluid Dynamic Bearing (FDB) motor"],
  "price":92.0,
  "price_c":"92.0,USD",
  "popularity":6,
  "inStock":true,
  "manufacturedate_dt":"2006-02-13T15:26:37Z",
  "store":"35.0752,-97.032",
  "_version_":1583131913641525248,
  "price_c____l_ns":9200}]
  }}
```

Example: Retrieve only field id and name with score

URL:
http://localhost:8983/solr/techproducts/select?defType=dismax&q=SP2514N
&fl=id,name,score

Response:

```
{
  "responseHeader":{
  "status":0,
  "QTime":1,
  "params":{
  "q":"SP2514N",
  "defType":"dismax",
  "fl":"id,name,score"}},
```

```
"response":{"numFound":1,"start":0,"maxScore":2.6953351,"docs":[
{
"id":"SP2514N",
"name":"Samsung SpinPoint P120 SP2514N - hard drive - 250 GB - ATA-133",
"score":2.6953351}]
}}
```

Use `fl=*` to retrieve all the fields.

Example: Now we search for query iPod, assigning boosting to the `fields` features and cat.

URL:
http://localhost:8983/solr/techproducts/select?defType=dismax&q=iPod&qf
=features^10.0+cat^0.5

Response:

```
{
   "responseHeader":{
     "status":0,
     "QTime":1,
     "params":{
       "q":"iPod",
       "defType":"dismax",
       "qf":"features^10.0 cat^0.5"}},
   "response":{"numFound":1,"start":0,"docs":[
       {
         "id":"IW-02",
         "name":"iPod & iPod Mini USB 2.0 Cable",
         "manu":"Belkin",
         "manu_id_s":"belkin",
         "cat":["electronics",
           "connector"],
         "features":["car power adapter for iPod, white"],
         "weight":2.0,
         "price":11.5,
         "price_c":"11.50,USD",
         "popularity":1,
         "inStock":false,
         "store":"37.7752,-122.4232",
         "manufacturedate_dt":"2006-02-14T23:55:59Z",
         "_version_":1583131913695002624,
         "price_c____l_ns":1150}]
   }}
```

Example: Boost results that have a field that matches a specific value.

URL: `http://localhost:8983/solr/techproducts/select?defType=dismax&q=iP`
`od&bq=cat:electronics^5.0`

In the same way, we can construct a URL for other parameters as well.

eDisMax Query Parser

The eDisMax Query Parser is an improved version of the DisMax Query Parser. Along with supporting all the features provided by DisMax Query Parser, it supports the following:

- Lucene query parser syntax
- Improved smart partial escaping in the case of syntax errors
- Improved proximity boosting by using word shingles
- Advanced stop word handling
- Improved boost function
- Pure negative nested queries
- We can specify which fields the end user is allowed to query, and specify to disallow direct fielded searches

eDisMax Query Parser Parameters: Along with the common parameters, we have these eDisMax Query Parser parameters:

Parameter	Behavior	Default Value
sow	Split on whitespace. Possible values are true and false. Once we set this to true, text analysis will be done for every individual whitespace-separated term.	False
mm.autoRelax	Relax the clauses in case of some of the clauses removed like stop words and search wont get impacted due to any clause removal. We need to take care when using the mm.autoRelax parameter because sometimes we may get unpredictable results. Possible values are true and false.	False
boost	A multivalued list of strings parsed as queries, with scores multiplied by the score from the main query for all matching documents.	

lowercaseOperators	Treats lowercase and and or the same as the operators AND and OR.	False
pf2	A multivalued list of fields with optional weights. It's similar to pf, but based on pairs of word shingles.	
pf3	A multivalued list of fields with optional weights, based on triplets of word shingles. It is similar to pf, except that instead of building a phrase per field out of all the words in the input, it builds a set of phrases for each field out of each triplet of word shingles.	
ps	The ps parameter specifies how many term positions the terms in the query can be off by to be considered a match on the phrase fields.	
ps2	Similar to ps but overrides the slop factor used for pf2. If not specified, ps is used.	
ps3	Similar to ps but overrides the slop factor used for pf3. If not specified, ps is used.	
stopwords	Tells Solr to disable StopFilterFactory configured in query analyzer. Possible values are true and false. False will disable StopFilterFactory.	True
uf	Specifies which schema fields the end user is allowed to explicitly query.	Allow all fields or uf=*

Examples: Searching for music or camera and boosting by popularity.

URL: http://localhost:8983/solr/techproducts/select?defType=edismax&q=music+OR+camera&boost=popularity

Response:

```
{
  "responseHeader":{
  "status":0,
  "QTime":1,
  "params":{
  "q":"music OR camera",
  "defType":"edismax",
  "boost":"popularity"}},
  "response":{"numFound":2,"start":0,"docs":[
```

```
{
"id":"9885A004",
"name":"Canon PowerShot SD500",
"manu":"Canon Inc.",
"manu_id_s":"canon",
"cat":["electronics",
"camera"],
"features":["3x zoop, 7.1 megapixel Digital ELPH",
"movie clips up to 640x480 @30 fps",
"2.0\" TFT LCD, 118,000 pixels",
"built in flash, red-eye reduction"],
"includes":"32MB SD card, USB cable, AV cable, battery",
"weight":6.4,
"price":329.95,
"price_c":"329.95,USD",
"popularity":7,
"inStock":true,
"manufacturedate_dt":"2006-02-13T15:26:37Z",
"store":"45.19614,-93.90341",
"_version_":1583131913780985856,
"price_c____l_ns":32995},
{
"id":"MA147LL/A",
"name":"Apple 60 GB iPod with Video Playback Black",
"manu":"Apple Computer Inc.",
"manu_id_s":"apple",
"cat":["electronics",
"music"],
"features":["iTunes, Podcasts, Audiobooks",
"Stores up to 15,000 songs, 25,000 photos, or 150 hours of video",
"2.5-inch, 320x240 color TFT LCD display with LED backlight",
"Up to 20 hours of battery life",
"Plays AAC, MP3, WAV, AIFF, Audible, Apple Lossless, H.264 video",
"Notes, Calendar, Phone book, Hold button, Date display, Photo wallet,
Built-in games, JPEG photo playback, Upgradeable firmware, USB 2.0
compatibility, Playback speed control, Rechargeable capability, Battery
level indication"],
"includes":"earbud headphones, USB cable",
"weight":5.5,
"price":399.0,
"price_c":"399.00,USD",
"popularity":10,
"inStock":true,
"store":"37.7752,-100.0232",
"manufacturedate_dt":"2005-10-12T08:00:00Z",
"_version_":1583131913706536960,
"price_c____l_ns":39900}]
}}
```

In the same way, we can configure all the eDisMax parser parameters and explore the search functionality.

Response writer

The user who is searching is mainly interested in the search output/response. Rather than providing output in only a single format, if we allow them to select their choice of output/response format and return a response in that format, it will really make the user happy. The good news is that Solr provides various response writers for the end user's convenience.

Once the user runs a search, along with providing matching results, Solr provides a formatted and well-organized output result that becomes easy and attractive for the end user. Solr handles this through a response writer. Solr supports these response writers:

- JSON (default)
- Standard XML
- XSLT
- Binary
- GeoJSON
- Python
- PHP
- PHP serialized
- Ruby
- CSV
- Velocity
- Smile
- XLSX

We can select the response writer by providing an appropriate value to the `wt` parameter. These are the response writer values for `wt`:

Response writer	wt parameter value
JSON	`json`
Standard XML	`xml`
XSLT	`xslt`

Binary	`javabin`
GeoJSON	`geojson`
Python	`python`
PHP	`php`
PHP serialized	`phps`
Ruby	`ruby`
CSV	`csv`
Velocity	`velocity`
Smile	`smile`
XLSX	`xlsx`

Let's explore some of these response writers in detail.

JSON

JSON response writer converts results into JSON format. This is a default response writer for Solr, so if we do not set the `wt` parameter, the default output will be in JSON format. We can configure the `MIME type` for any response writer in the `solrconfig.xml` file. The default `MIME type` for JSON response writer is `application/json`; however, we can override it as per our search needs. For example, we can override the `MIME type` configuration in `techproducts solrconfig.xml`:

```
<queryResponseWriter name="json" class="solr.JSONResponseWriter">
<!-- For the purposes of the tutorial, JSON responses are written as
plain text so that they are easy to read in *any* browser.
If you expect a MIME type of "application/json" just remove this override.
-->
<str name="content-type">text/plain; charset=UTF-8</str>
</queryResponseWriter>
```

JSON response writer parameters

This is a list of JSON response writer parameters that we need to configure to get a response in the expected format:

Parameter	Behavior	Value	Description

json.nl	Controls the output format of `NamedList`, where the order is more important than access by name. `NamedList` is currently used for field faceting data.	flat (default)	`NamedList` is represented as a flat array, with alternating names and values.
			Input:
			`NamedList("a"=1, "bar"="foo", null=3, null=null)`
			Output:
			`["a",1, "bar","foo", null,3, null,null]`

		map	`NamedList` can have optional keys and repeated keys. It preserves the order.
			Input:
			`NamedList("a"=1, "bar"="foo", null=3, null=null)`
			Output:
			`{"a":1, "bar":"foo", "":3, "":null}`

		arrarr	`NamedList` is represented as an array of two element arrays.
			Input:
			`NamedList("a"=1, "bar"="foo", null=3, null=null)`
			Output:
			`[["a",1], ["bar","foo"], [null,3], [null,null]]`

		arrmap	NamedList is represented as an array of JSON objects.
			Input:
			`NamedList("a"=1, "bar"="foo", null=3, null=null)`
			Output:
			`[{"a":1}, {"b":2}, 3, null]`

		arrntv	NamedList is represented as an array of name type value JSON objects.
			Input:
			`NamedList("a"=1, "bar"="foo", null=3, null=null)`
			Output:
			`[{"name":"a","type":"int","value":1},`
			`{"name":"bar","type":"str","value":"foo"},`
			`{"name":null,"type":"int","value":3},`
			`{"name":null,"type":"null","value":null}]`

json.wrf	Adds a wrapper function around the JSON response. Useful in AJAX with dynamic script tags for specifying a JavaScript callback function.	function	

Example: Searching for `id=SP2514N`.

URL: `http://localhost:8983/solr/techproducts/select?q=SP2514N&wt=json`.

Response:

```
{
 "responseHeader":{
 "status":0,
 "QTime":1,
 "params":{
 "q":"SP2514N",
 "wt":"json",
 "_":"1514797189592"}},
 "response":{"numFound":1,"start":0,"docs":[
 {
 "id":"SP2514N",
 "name":"Samsung SpinPoint P120 SP2514N - hard drive - 250 GB - ATA-133",
 "manu":"Samsung Electronics Co. Ltd.",
 "manu_id_s":"samsung",
 "cat":["electronics",
 "hard drive"],
 "features":["7200RPM, 8MB cache, IDE Ultra ATA-133",
 "NoiseGuard, SilentSeek technology, Fluid Dynamic Bearing (FDB) motor"],
 "price":92.0,
 "price_c":"92.0,USD",
 "popularity":6,
 "inStock":true,
 "manufacturedate_dt":"2006-02-13T15:26:37Z",
 "store":"35.0752,-97.032",
 "_version_":1583131913641525248,
 "price_c____l_ns":9200}]
 }
}
```

We can analyze response writer using the Solr console admin as well. Go to the Solr console admin, select **techproducts**, and click on the **Query** tab. Insert your text query in the `q` field, select the `wt` parameter as `json` and click on the **Execute Query** button at the bottom. The query URL and response output will be displayed as follows:

Solr console admin, response writer configuration, and output

Standard XML

The standard XML response writer is the most common and usable response writer in Solr.

Standard XML response writer parameters:

Parameter	Behavior	Default Value
version	The version parameter determines the XML protocol used in the response. The advantage of setting this parameter is that the response format remains the same even if the Solr version gets an upgrade.	The default value is the latest supported one. The only currently supported version value is 2.2.

stylesheet	It includes a <?xml-stylesheet type="text/xsl" href="..."?> declaration in the XML response.	Solr does not return any style sheet declaration by default.
indent	Indenting the XML response for a more human-readable format.	By default, Solr will not indent the XML response.

Example: Searching for query id=SP2514N and retrieving a response in XML format.

Solr admin console, searching for product id=SP2514N, and retrieving the response in XML format:

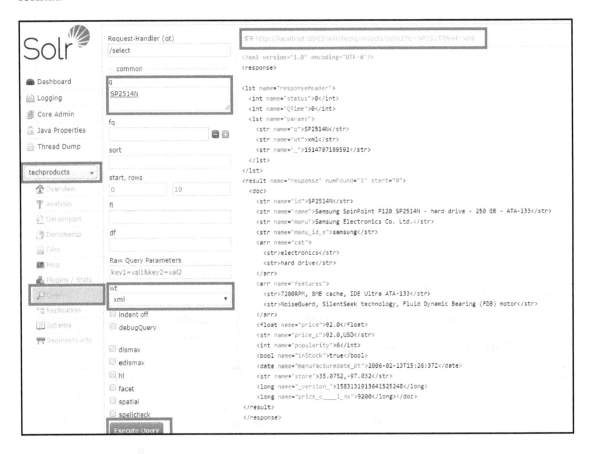

URL: `http://localhost:8983/solr/techproducts/select?q=SP2514N&wt=xml`

Response:

```xml
<?xml version="1.0" encoding="UTF-8"?>
<response>
<lst name="responseHeader">
 <int name="status">0</int>
 <int name="QTime">0</int>
 <lst name="params">
 <str name="q">SP2514N</str>
 <str name="wt">xml</str>
 <str name="_">1514797189592</str>
 </lst>
</lst>
<result name="response" numFound="1" start="0">
 <doc>
 <str name="id">SP2514N</str>
 <str name="name">Samsung SpinPoint P120 SP2514N - hard drive - 250 GB -
ATA-133</str>
 <str name="manu">Samsung Electronics Co. Ltd.</str>
 <str name="manu_id_s">samsung</str>
 <arr name="cat">
 <str>electronics</str>
 <str>hard drive</str>
 </arr>
 <arr name="features">
 <str>7200RPM, 8MB cache, IDE Ultra ATA-133</str>
 <str>NoiseGuard, SilentSeek technology, Fluid Dynamic Bearing (FDB)
motor</str>
 </arr>
 <float name="price">92.0</float>
 <str name="price_c">92.0,USD</str>
 <int name="popularity">6</int>
 <bool name="inStock">true</bool>
 <date name="manufacturedate_dt">2006-02-13T15:26:37Z</date>
 <str name="store">35.0752,-97.032</str>
 <long name="_version_">1583131913641525248</long>
 <long name="price_c____l_ns">9200</long></doc>
</result>
</response>
```

CSV

This returns the results in CSV format. Some information (like facet) will be excluded from the CSV response. The CSV response writer supports multi-valued fields as well as pseudo-fields, and the output of this CSV format is compatible with Solr's CSV update format.

CSV response writer parameters:

Parameter	Behavior	Default value
csv.encapsulator	Specifies a character to be used as an encapsulator in the response	"
csv.escape	Specifies the items to be escaped from the response	None
csv.separator	Specifies the separator for the CSV response	,
csv.header	Indicates whether to print header information in the CSV response or not	true
csv.newline	Used to start a new line from this parameter value	\n
csv.null	Specifies the value to be returned in the response instead of returning null	Zero-length string

Example: Searching for query id=SP2514N and retrieving the response in .csv format.

Solr admin console, searching for product id=SP2514N, and retrieving the response in .csv format:

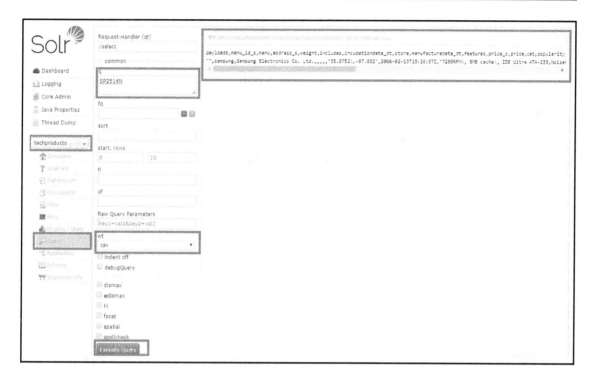

URL: `http://localhost:8983/solr/techproducts/select?q=SP2514N&wt=csv`

Response:

```
payloads,manu_id_s,manu,address_s,weight,includes,incubationdate_dt,store,m
anufacturedate_dt,features,price_c,price,cat,popularity,name,inStock,id,com
pName_s
"",samsung,Samsung Electronics Co.
Ltd.,,,,,"35.0752\,-97.032",2006-02-13T15:26:37Z,"7200RPM\, 8MB cache\, IDE
Ultra ATA-133,NoiseGuard\, SilentSeek technology\, Fluid Dynamic Bearing
(FDB) motor","92.0\,USD",92.0,"electronics,hard drive",6,Samsung SpinPoint
P120 SP2514N - hard drive - 250 GB - ATA-133,true,SP2514N,
```

Velocity

Solr supports a velocity response writer, which is used in Velocity UI to demonstrate some core search features: **faceting**, **highlighting**, **autocomplete**, and **geospatial** searching. velocity response writer is an optional plugin available in the `contrib/velocity` directory.

To use velocity response writer, we must include its `.jar` file and all dependencies in the `lib` folder, and configure in `solrconfig.xml` as follows:

```
<queryResponseWriter name="velocity" class="solr.VelocityResponseWriter">
 <str name="template.base.dir">${velocity.template.base.dir:}</str>
<!--
 <str name="init.properties.file">velocity-init.properties</str>
 <bool name="params.resource.loader.enabled">true</bool>
 <bool name="solr.resource.loader.enabled">false</bool>
 <lst name="tools">
 <str name="mytool">com.example.MyCustomTool</str>
 </lst>
-->
</queryResponseWriter>
```

Here, we have not configured the initialization and request parameters but as per our needs, we can configure them.

We have almost finished looking at search configuration components such as relevance, various query parsers, and response writers. Now let's take a deep dive and and explore various search result operations: faceting, clustering, highlighting, and so on.

Faceting

Faceting is the mechanism provided by Solr to categorize results in a meaningful arrangement on indexed fields. Using faceting, the end user will be provided with categorized results, along with a matching count for that search. Now the user can explore the search results, drill down to any result, and thus find an exactly matching result in which they are interested.

There are many types of faceting provided by Solr. Here is a list of faceting types that Solr currently supports:

- Range faceting
- Pivot (decision tree) faceting
- Interval faceting

We will explore these later in this chapter. But to configure any faceting in Solr, first we have to configure the related parameters. So let's understand faceting parameters first.

Common parameters

These are the common parameters for all types of faceting:

Parameter	Behavior	Default value
facet	Enable or disable faceting.	false
facet.query	Specifies a faceting query, which overrides Solr's default faceting query and returns a faceting count.	

Field-value faceting parameters

Field-value parameters are used to trigger faceting based on the indexed terms in a field. By default, all field-value faceting parameters can be specified on a per field basis with the syntax of f.<fieldname>.facet.<parameter>:

Parameter	Behavior	Default value
facet.field	Identifies a field that should be treated as a facet. At least one field must have this parameter; otherwise, none of the other field-value faceting parameters will have any effect.	
facet.prefix	Limits facet values to terms beginning with the string specified.	
facet.contains	Limits facet values to terms containing the string specified.	

`facet.contains.ignoreCase`	If `facet.contains` is used, the `facet.contains.ignoreCase` parameter causes cases to be ignored when matching the given substring against the candidate facet terms.	
`facet.limit`	Specifies the maximum number of constraint counts that should be returned for the facet fields. The possible values are positive and negative. Providing any negative value indicates that Solr will return an unlimited number of constraint counts.	`100`
`facet.sort`	Determines the ordering of the facet field constraints. Possible values are: • `count`: Sorts constraints based on the count (high to low) • `index`: Sorts constraints based on their index order The default sorting is based on the index, but if the limit parameter (`facet.limit`) is greater than zero, the default sorting will be the count.	
`facet.offset`	Allows paging through facet values. The offset defines how many of the top values to skip instead of returning later facet values.	`0`
`facet.mincount`	Specifies the minimum counts required for a facet field to be included in the response. If a field's counts are less than the minimum, the field's facet is not returned.	`0`
`facet.missing`	Specifies whether or not the count of all matching documents that do not have any values is to be returned in the facet's field.	`false`

facet.method	Specifies the type of algorithm or method Solr should use when faceting a field. The available methods in Solr are: • enum: Iterates over all the terms in the index, calculating a set intersection with those terms and the query. This method is faster for fields that contain fewer values. • fc: Iterates over documents that match the query and finds the terms within those documents. The fc method is faster for fields that contain many unique values. • fcs: Performs per-segment field faceting for single-valued string fields. This method performs better faceting if the index is changing constantly. It also accepts a threads local param, which can speed up faceting.	fc
facet.enum.cache.minDf	Specifies the minimum number of documents required to match a term before filterCache should be used for that term. The default is 0, which means filterCache should always be used.	0
facet.exists	To cap facet counts by 1, specify facet.exists=true. This parameter can be used with facet.method=enum or when it's omitted. It can be used only on on-trie fields (such as strings). It may speed up facet counting on large indices and/or high-cardinality facet values.	false
facet.excludeTerms	Removes the specified terms from facet counts but keeps them in the index.	
facet.threads	Specifies the number of threads to execute for faceting the fields in parallel. Specifying the thread count as 0 will not create any threads, and only the main request thread will be used. Specifying a negative number of threads will create up to Integer.MAX_VALUE threads.	

Range faceting

Range faceting can be done on date fields and numeric fields.

Range faceting parameters:

Parameter	Behavior	Default value

`facet.range`	Specifies the field for which Solr should create range facets. For example:
	`facet.range=salary&facet.range=rank`
	`facet.range=createdDate`	

`facet.range.start`	Specifies from where (lower bound) the range starts. For example:
	`f.salary.facet.range.start=10000.0&f.rank.facet.range.start=1`
	`f.createdDate.facet.range.start=NOW/DAY-30DAYS`	

`facet.range.end`	Specifies where (upper bound) the range ends. For example:
	`f.salary.facet.range.end=100000.0&f.rank.facet.range.end=50`
	`f.createdDate.facet.range.end=NOW/DAY+30DAYS`	

`facet.range.gap`	The size of each range will be added to the `lower` bound successively until the `upper` bound is reached.	
`facet.range.hardend`	A Boolean parameter that specifies how Solr should handle cases where `facet.range.gap` does not divide evenly between `lower` bound and `upper` bound. If it is `true`, the last range constraint will have the `facet.range.end` value as an `upper` bound. If `false`, the last range will have the smallest possible `upper` bound greater than `facet.range.end` such that the range is the exact width of the specified range gap.	`false`
`facet.range.include`	Determines how to compute range faceting between the lower bound and upper bound. Possible values are: • `lower`: All gap-based ranges include their `lower` bound • `upper`: All gap-based ranges include their `upper` bound • `edge`: The first and last gap ranges include their `edge` bounds (`lower` for the first one, `upper` for the last one) even if the corresponding `upper`/`lower` option is not specified • `outer`: The `before` and `after` ranges will be inclusive of their bounds even if the first or last ranges already include those boundaries • `all`: Includes all options—`lower`, `upper`, `edge`, and `outer`.	
`facet.range.other`	Specifies that, in addition to the counts for each range between `lower` bound and `upper` bound, counts should be computed for these options as well: • `before`: All records with field values lower than `lower` bound of the first range • `after`: All records with field values greater than the `upper` bound of the last range • `between`: All records with field values between the start and end bounds of all ranges • `none`: Do not compute any counts • `all`: Compute counts for `before`, `between`, and `after`	

	Specifies a faceting method:	
`facet.range.method`	• `filter`: Generates the ranges based on other `facet.range` parameters. • `div`: Iterates all the documents that match the main query, and for each of them, it finds the correct range for the value. Not supporting for `DateRangeField` field type or when we have used `group.facets`.	`filter`

Example: Search query for `iPod` with faceting enabled and range for the field price from `1000` to `100000`

URL: `http://localhost:8983/solr/techproducts/select?defType=edismax&q=ipod&fl=id,name,price&facet=true&facet.range=price&facet.range.start=10&facet.range.end=20&facet.range.gap=5`

Response:

```
{
  "responseHeader":{
  "status":0,
  "QTime":1,
  "params":{
  "facet.range":"price",
  "q":"ipod",
  "defType":"edismax",
  "facet.range.gap":"5",
  "fl":"id,name,price",
  "facet":"true",
  "facet.range.start":"10",
  "facet.range.end":"20"}},
  "response":{"numFound":3,"start":0,"docs":[
  {
  "id":"IW-02",
  "name":"iPod & iPod Mini USB 2.0 Cable",
  "price":11.5},
  {
  "id":"F8V7067-APL-KIT",
  "name":"Belkin Mobile Power Cord for iPod w/ Dock",
  "price":19.95},
  {
  "id":"MA147LL/A",
  "name":"Apple 60 GB iPod with Video Playback Black",
  "price":399.0}]
  },
  "facet_counts":{
  "facet_queries":{},
  "facet_fields":{},
  "facet_ranges":{
  "price":{
```

```
"counts":[
"10.0",1,
"15.0",1],
"gap":5.0,
"start":10.0,
"end":20.0}},
"facet_intervals":{},
"facet_heatmaps":{}}}
```

Pivot faceting

Pivot faceting is similar to pivot tables in the latest spreadsheets. Pivot faceting provides a facility to generate an aggregate summary from fetched faceting results on multiple fields:

Parameter	Behavior	Default value
facet.pivot	Specify the field on which you want to apply pivoting	
facet.pivot.mincount	Specify the minimum number of documents that need to match in order for the facet to be included in the results	1

Example: In our `techproducts`, we need the stock availability based on the popularity of a category

URL: `http://localhost:8983/solr/techproducts/select?q=*:*&facet.pivot=cat,popularity,inStock&facet.pivot=popularity,cat&facet=true&facet.field=cat&facet.limit=5&rows=0&facet.pivot.mincount=2`

Response:

```
{
"facet_counts":{
"facet_queries":{},
"facet_fields":{
"cat":[
"electronics",14,
"currency",4,
"memory",3,
"connector",2,
"graphics card",2]},
"facet_dates":{},
```

```
"facet_ranges":{},
"facet_pivot":{
"cat,popularity,inStock":[{
"field":"cat",
"value":"electronics",
"count":14,
"pivot":[{
"field":"popularity",
"value":6,
"count":5,
"pivot":[{
"field":"inStock",
"value":true,
"count":5}]}]
}]}}}
```

Interval faceting

Interval faceting is similar to range faceting, but it allows us to set variable intervals and count the number of documents that have values within those intervals in the specified field. Interval faceting is likely to be better with multiple intervals for the same fields, while a facet query is likely to be better in environments where a filter cache is more effective:

Parameter	Behavior	Default value
`facet.interval`	To specify a field where we want to apply the interval. It can be used multiple times for multiple fields in a single request. For example: `facet.interval=price&facet.interval=popularity`	
`facet.interval.set`	To specify a set of intervals for the field. It can be specified multiple times to indicate multiple intervals. For example: `f.price.facet.interval.set=[0,10]&f.price.facet.interval.set=(10,100]` (1,100) -> include values greater than 1 and lower than 100 [1,100) -> include values greater or equal to 1 and lower than 100 [1,100] -> include values greater or equal to 1 and lower or equal to 100	

Example: Faceting query for field `price >=10` and `price < 20`

URL: `http://localhost:8983/solr/techproducts/select?q=*:*&facet=true&facet.interval=price&f.price.facet.interval.set=[10,20)`

Response:

```
"facet_counts":{
"facet_queries":{},
"facet_fields":{},
```

```
"facet_ranges":{},
"facet_intervals":{
"price":{
"[10,20)":2}},
"facet_heatmaps":{}
}
```

Highlighting

Solr supports a feature called **highlighting** that helps end users who are running a query to scan results quickly. Providing a matching term in bold and highlighted the format makes it an extremely satisfying experience for the user. With highlighting, the user can quickly determine the terms they are searching for or make a decision that the provided results do not match their expectations, and lets them move to next query.

Solr comes with a great configuration for highlighting. There are many parameters for **fragment sizing, formatting, ordering, backup.alternate behavior**, and **categorization**. Fragments or snippets are parts of the response that contain matching terms.

Highlighting parameters

Solr provides a large list for highlighting fragments. The following are the basic parameters required to start highlighting:

Parameter	Behavior	Default value
hl	A Boolean parameter to enable/disable highlighting. hl=true will enable highlighting.	false
hl.method	To specify a method to implement highlighting. Available methods are unified, original, and fastVector.	original

Highlighter

Highlighter is nothing but a highlighting implemented method that actually performs the activity. There are three methods available for highlighting. They are unified, original, and fastVector. To implement highlighting, first we need to specify one method to hl.method. If we do not select any method, the default original method performs the activity.

There are many parameters supported by highlighters. Sometimes, the implementation details and semantics will be a bit different, so we can't expect identical results when switching highlighters. Normally, highlighter selection is done via the `hl.method` parameter, but we can also explicitly configure an implementation by class name in `solrconfig.xml`. Let's explore highlighters in detail.

Unified highlighter (hl.method=unified)

Unified highlighter is the new highlighter from Solr 6.4. This is the most flexible highlighter and supports the most common highlighting parameters. It can handle any query accurately, even `SpanQueries`. The greatest benefit of using this highlighter is that we can add more configurations to speed up highlighting on large data documents. We can also add multiple configurations on a per field basis.

Original highlighter (hl.method=original)

Original highlighter is the default highlighter, also known as **standard highlighter** or **default highlighter**. The advantage of this highlighter is its capability of highlighting any query accurately and efficiently, like `unified` highlighter, but it is very slow compared to `unified` highlighter.

The `original` highlighter is much slower at highlighting on large text fields or complex text analysis because it reanalyzes the original text at query time. It supports full-term vectors, but compared to `unified` highlighter and `fastVector` highlighter, it is very slow. Also it does not have a breakiterator-based fragmenter, which can cause problems in some languages.

FastVector highlighter (hl.method=fastVector)

FastVector Highlighter (**FVH**) is faster than `original` highlighter because it skips the analysis step when generating fragments. Sometimes, FVH is not able to highlight some of the fields; in such cases, it will do a conjunction with the `original` highlighter to match the requirement. For such cases, we need to set `hl.method=original` and `f.yourTermVecField.hl.method=fastVector` for all fields that should use the FVH.

Boundary scanners

Sometimes, `fastVector` highlighter will truncate highlighted words, so the output after highlighting may be incomplete or improper. To resolve this issue, we need to configure a boundary scanner in `solrconfig.xml`. There are two types of boundary scanners available in Solr. We have to specify a boundary scanner using the parameter `hl.boundaryScanner`.

The breakIterator boundary scanner

The `breakIterator` boundary scanner scans term boundaries by considering the language (`hl.bs.language`) and boundary type (`hl.bs.type`) and provides expected, accurate, and complete output without any loss of characters. It is used most often. To implement the `breakIterator` boundary scanner, we need to add the following code snippet to the highlighting section in the `solrconfig.xml` file:

```
<boundaryScanner name="breakIterator"
class="solr.highlight.BreakIteratorBoundaryScanner">
 <lst name="defaults">
 <str name="hl.bs.type">WORD</str>
 <str name="hl.bs.language">en</str>
 <str name="hl.bs.country">US</str>
 </lst>
</boundaryScanner>
```

Possible values for the `hl.bs.type` parameter are WORD, LINE, SENTENCE, and CHARACTER.

The simple boundary scanner

The simple boundary scanner scans term boundaries by the specified maximum character value (`hl.bs.maxScan`) and common delimiters such as punctuation marks (`hl.bs.chars`). To implement it, we need to add the following code snippet to the highlighting section in `solrconfig.xml`:

```
<boundaryScanner name="simple" class="solr.highlight.SimpleBoundaryScanner"
default="true">
 <lst name="defaults">
 <str name="hl.bs.maxScan">10</str >
 <str name="hl.bs.chars">.,!?\t\n</str &gt;
 </lst >
</boundaryScanner>
```

Example: Querying for `ipod`, highlighting for the field `name` using `fastVector` highlighter

URL: `http://localhost:8983/solr/techproducts/select?hl=true&hl.method=fastVector&q=ipod&hl.fl=name&fl=id,name,cat`

Response:

```
{
  "responseHeader":{
  "status":0,
  "QTime":4,
  "params":{
  "q":"ipod",
  "hl":"true",
  "fl":"id,name,cat",
  "hl.method":"fastVector",
  "hl.fl":"name"}},
  "response":{"numFound":3,"start":0,"docs":[
  {
  "id":"IW-02",
  "name":"iPod & iPod Mini USB 2.0 Cable",
  "cat":["electronics",
  "connector"]},
  {
  "id":"F8V7067-APL-KIT",
  "name":"Belkin Mobile Power Cord for iPod w/ Dock",
  "cat":["electronics",
  "connector"]},
  {
  "id":"MA147LL/A",
  "name":"Apple 60 GB iPod with Video Playback Black",
  "cat":["electronics",
  "music"]}]
  },
  "highlighting":{
  "IW-02":{
  "name":["<em>iPod</em> & <em>iPod</em> Mini USB 2.0 Cable"]},
  "F8V7067-APL-KIT":{
  "name":["Belkin Mobile Power Cord for <em>iPod</em> w/ Dock"]},
  "MA147LL/A":{
  "name":["Apple 60 GB <em>iPod</em> with Video Playback Black"]}}}
```

The highlighting section includes the ID of each document and the field that contains the highlighted portion. Here we have used the `hl.fl` parameter to say that we want query terms highlighted in the `name` field. When there is a match to the query term in that field, it will be included for each document ID in the list. In the same way, we can explore highlighting more by configuring different parameters.

Summary

In this chapter, we learned the concept of relevance and its terms: Precision and Recall. Then we looked at the velocity search UI. We saw the common parameters for various query parsers and explored each query parser (standard, DisMax, and eDisMax) in detail. After that, we looked at various response writers in detail: JSON, standard XML, CSV, and velocity response writer. We also explored Solr term modifiers, wildcard parameters, fuzzy search, proximity search, and range search.

We looked at all Boolean operators. Then we learned about various faceting parameters and faceting types such as range, pivot, and interval faceting. At the end, we saw Solr highlighting mechanisms, parameters, highlighters, and boundary scanners.

In the next chapter, or rather the second part of this chapter, we will learn more search functionalities such as spell checking, suggester, pagination, result grouping and clustering, and spatial search.

7
Advanced Queries – Part II

We started understanding the concept of relevance and its terms precision and recall in the previous chapter. Then we learned about various query parsers, their parameters, and how we can configure them. In the same way, we explored various response writers, their parameters, and how we can configure them. We also looked at velocity search UI. Then we learned about various faceting parameters and faceting types, such as range faceting, pivot faceting, and interval faceting. At the end, we saw the Solr highlighting mechanism, parameters, various highlighters, and boundary scanners.

In this chapter, we will learn about more search functionalities such as spellchecking, suggester, pagination, result grouping and clustering, and spatial search. Let's start with the spellchecking feature of Solr.

Spellchecking

We have seen that Solr provides magical support for searching. Solr provides a strong index building mechanism, unifiable search configurations, and providing interesting and expected formatted results by executing various transformation steps on the query output. Spellchecking is an advantageous feature provided by Solr for those who make mistakes while typing a query or may enter an incorrect or inappropriate input. Sometimes, we have this experience while searching on Google. If we enter sokcer, then Google provides a hint: **Did you mean: soccer?** Or sometimes, typing socer will directly show results for soccer rather than displaying any hints.

Likewise, there are some scenarios where we need to be careful about the input word:

- If a user enters input search terms with incorrect spelling and there is no matching document available, we use the Solr spellcheck feature, displaying a message that searching for `soccer` instead of `socer` will give the user a hassle-free experience of searching without worrying much about the spelling.
- A user enters less terms for search which is not sufficient to fetch more or sufficient matching documents at that time if any suggestion terms available which contains more matching documents then we can instruct the user by giving a message like `Did you mean xxxxx`. But if the suggestion terms have the same or lesser-matching documents than the query terms, then no message should be shown.
- When no index is available for the entered search terms, no suggestions should be given to the user.

To take advantage of the Solr spellchecking feature, we need to tell the request handle to check spelling during processing. Here is the configuration of the Solr default request handler to enable spellchecking while processing a request:

```
<requestHandler name="/select" class="solr.SearchHandler">
<lst name="defaults">
<str name="echoParams">explicit</str>
<int name="rows">10</int>
<str name="spellcheck.dictionary">default</str>
<str name="spellcheck.dictionary">wordbreak</str>
<str name="spellcheck">on</str>
<str name="spellcheck.extendedResults">true</str>
<str name="spellcheck.count">10</str>
<str name="spellcheck.alternativeTermCount">5</str>
<str name="spellcheck.maxResultsForSuggest">5</str>
<str name="spellcheck.collate">true</str>
<str name="spellcheck.collateExtendedResults">true</str>
<str name="spellcheck.maxCollationTries">10</str>
<str name="spellcheck.maxCollations">5</str>
</lst>
<arr name="last-components">
<str>spellcheck</str>
</arr>
</requestHandler>
```

The preceding configuration is sufficient for enabling spellchecking and performs spellchecking for all queries processed through this request handler, for example, searching for `cemera` instead of `camera`.

URL: `http://localhost:8983/solr/techproducts/select?q=cemera:`

```
{
  "responseHeader":{
  "status":0,
  "QTime":7,
  "params":{
  "q":"cemera"}},
  "response":{"numFound":0,"start":0,"docs":[]
  },
  "spellcheck":{
  "suggestions":[
  "cemera",{
  "numFound":1,
  "startOffset":0,
  "endOffset":6,
  "origFreq":0,
  "suggestion":[{
  "word":"camera",
  "freq":1}]}],
  "correctlySpelled":false,
  "collations":[
  "collation",{
  "collationQuery":"camera",
  "hits":1,
  "misspellingsAndCorrections":[
  "cemera","camera"]}]}
}
```

From the preceding response, we can see that Solr returns the spellcheck container, along with suggested words and the correct spelling in response. Here we have searched for an incorrect word (`cemera`) but in the response, the correct spelling has been returned as a spellcheck-suggested word.

However, you don't need to provide any spellchecking-related parameters to the query string. Still, if you want to disable spellchecking for any specific query, you can use `spellcheck=false` and disable spellchecking for that particular query. For example:

URL:
`http://localhost:8983/solr/techproducts/select?q=cemera&spellcheck=false:`

```
{
  "responseHeader":{
  "status":0,
  "QTime":0,
```

```
"params":{
"q":"cemera",
"spellcheck":"false"}},
"response":{"numFound":0,"start":0,"docs":[]
}}
```

Spellchecking is not executed for this query though we have searched for an incorrect spelling.

It is always advisable to perform spellchecking last because we still want the default search components, such as query, facet, and debug, to execute during query processing. This can be done easily by setting `spellcheck.collate=true`. This is a collation parameter that tells Solr to run spellchecking last because generating the collation query requires an already executed query.

Spellcheck parameters

As we discussed earlier in this chapter, we do not need to pass any parameter to enable or configure a parameter with a query string. Configuring them with any request handler in the `solrconfig.xml` file will enable them. Let's understand all our parameters:

Parameter	Behavior	Default value
`spellcheck`	Enables or disables spellchecking.	`false`
`spellcheck.q` or `spellcheck.q`	Specifies the query for spellchecking. It will be used if `spellcheck.q` is specified, or else the original input query will be used.	
`spellcheck.build`	Boolean parameter that tells Solr to generate a dictionary if it does not exist. Dictionary building will take additional time in query processing, so it is advisable not to pass this parameter with every request.	`false`

`spellcheck.reload`	A Boolean parameter that tells Solr to reload the spellchecker implementation.	
`spellcheck.count`	Specifies the maximum number of suggestions a spellchecker should return in the response for a specific query term. The default value is 1 if the parameter is not set and is 5 if the parameter is set but no value is assigned.	1
`spellcheck.onlyMorePopular`	Specifying this as true will tell Solr to return only those suggestions that have more hits than the original query.	
`spellcheck.maxResultsForSuggest`	Specifies a threshold count based on the number of documents matched from the user's original query. For example, if we have set this to 5 and a user's original query returns >= 5 matching documents, Solr will disable the suggestion automatically.	
`spellcheck.alternativeTermCount`	Specifies the number of suggestions to be returned from the index and/or dictionary for each query term. It will also enable context-sensitive spelling suggestions.	

`spellcheck.extendedResults`	Boolean variable that tells Solr to return additional details about the spellcheck results. For example, setting this to true will return the frequency of the original terms and of suggestions from the index.	
`spellcheck.collate`	If true, this parameter tells Solr to create a new query (collation query) from the suggested spelling correction. The collation query can be executed by clicking on the link **Did you mean ...** ? Returning results is guaranteed, so Solr must execute the collation query in the background before returning results to users.	
`spellcheck.maxCollations`	The maximum number of collation queries Solr will generate. The default is 1. It will work only if `spellcheck.collate` is true.	1
`spellcheck.maxCollationTries`	Specifies the number of times Solr should try for collation before giving up. Specifying a lower value will improve performance as Solr will not provide suggestions in all cases.	

`spellcheck.maxCollationEvaluations`	Specifies the maximum number of word correction combinations for evaluating a correct collation that will run against an index.	`10000`
`spellcheck.collateExtendedResults`	A boolean value that tells Solr whether to return a response in expanded format or not. Setting this to true will return the response in expanded format. It will work only if `spellcheck.collate` is true.	`false`
`spellcheck.collateMaxCollectDocs`	Specifies the maximum number of documents to be collected for testing of collations against the index. The default value for this parameter is `0`, which means that all documents should be collected.	`0`
`spellcheck.collateParam.*Prefix`	Used to specify an additional parameter that you want to be considered by the Spellchecker when internally validating collation queries.	
`spellcheck.dictionary`	Specifies the dictionary name to be used by Solr for spellchecking.	`default`

`spellcheck.accuracy`	Specifies the accuracy level to decide whether the results provided after spellchecking are sufficient or not. Possible values are float values between 0 and 1.	`Float.MIN_VALUE`
`spellcheck.<DICT_NAME>.key`	Specifies a key/value pair for dictionary implementation of spellcheck.	

Implementation approaches

Solr provides many approaches for implementing spellchecking. Let's get a brief overview of these approaches.

IndexBasedSpellChecker

The `IndexBasedSpellChecker` builds a parallel index based on the Solr index and performs spellchecking using this parallel index. For this, a field needs to be defined as a basis for the index terms. The easiest way is to copy terms from some fields (subject, description, and so on) to another field created for spellchecking. Here is a simple example of the `IndexBasedSpellChecker` approach configured in `solrconfig.xml`:

```
<searchComponent name="spellcheck" class="solr.SpellCheckComponent">
 <lst name="spellchecker">
 <str name="classname">solr.IndexBasedSpellChecker</str>
 <str name="spellcheckIndexDir">./spellchecker</str>
 <str name="field">content</str>
 <str name="buildOnCommit">true</str>
 <!-- optional elements with defaults
 <str
name="distanceMeasure">org.apache.lucene.search.spell.LevensteinDistance</s
tr>
 <str name="accuracy">0.5</str>
 -->
 </lst>
</searchComponent>
```

The attribute `classname` defines the approach to be used for spellchecking. If we do not define this attribute, `solr.IndexBasedSpellChecker` is the default one used for spellchecking.

DirectSolrSpellChecker

The `DirectSolrSpellChecker` performs spellchecking directly using the terms from the Solr index without building a parallel index like `IndexBasedSpellChecker`. As `DirectSolrSpellChecker` does not build any indexes, suggestion terms are always up to date as with the Solr main index. Here is an example configured in `solrconfig.xml`:

```
<searchComponent name="spellcheck" class="solr.SpellCheckComponent">
 <lst name="spellchecker">
 <str name="name">default</str>
 <str name="field">name</str>
 <str name="classname">solr.DirectSolrSpellChecker</str>
 <str name="distanceMeasure">internal</str>
 <float name="accuracy">0.5</float>
 <int name="maxEdits">2</int>
 <int name="minPrefix">1</int>
 <int name="maxInspections">5</int>
 <int name="minQueryLength">4</int>
 <float name="maxQueryFrequency">0.01</float>
 <float name="thresholdTokenFrequency">.01</float>
 </lst>
</searchComponent>
```

FileBasedSpellChecker

The `FileBasedSpellChecker` evaluates spellings from an external file dictionary. This is useful when Solr works as a spellchecking server. This is also useful where spelling suggestions are not on the base of actual terms. To implement `FileBasedSpellChecker`, modify `solrconfig.xml` as follows:

```
<searchComponent name="spellcheck" class="solr.SpellCheckComponent">
 <lst name="spellchecker">
 <str name="classname">solr.FileBasedSpellChecker</str>
 <str name="name">file</str>
 <str name="sourceLocation">spellings.txt</str>
 <str name="characterEncoding">UTF-8</str>
 <str name="spellcheckIndexDir">./spellcheckerFile</str>
 <!-- optional elements with defaults
 <str
```

```
name="distanceMeasure">org.apache.lucene.search.spell.LevensteinDistance</s
tr>
 <str name="accuracy">0.5</str>
 -->
 </lst>
</searchComponent>
```

The `sourceLocation` parameter holds the path of the file that contains the spelling dictionary. The `characterEncoding` parameter specifies the character-encoding algorithm.

WordBreakSolrSpellChecker

The `WordBreakSolrSpellChecker` performs spellchecking by breaking and/or combining query terms. This is useful for terms where users put whitespaces at incorrect places. For example, to search for `group dance choreographer`, a user may enter `groupdance choreographor` as a search term. It also provides shard support. Here is the configuration in `solrconfig.xml` for this approach:

```
<searchComponent name="spellcheck" class="solr.SpellCheckComponent">
 <lst name="spellchecker">
 <str name="name">wordbreak</str>
 <str name="classname">solr.WordBreakSolrSpellChecker</str>
 <str name="field">lowerfilt</str>
 <str name="combineWords">true</str>
 <str name="breakWords">true</str>
 <int name="maxChanges">10</int>
 </lst>
</searchComponent>
```

Distributed spellcheck

Solr supports spellchecking on distributed indexes also. The following are the two parameters that are required for the request handler (excluding request handler `/select`) to implement spellchecking on distributed indexes:

Parameter	Behavior
shards	Specifies the shards in distributed indexing configuration.
shards.qt	Specifies a request handler for requesting to shards. This parameter is not required by the `/select` request handler.

For example, to search for the word `cemera` on distributed indexing (`shard1` and `shard2`), the following is the URL:

```
http://localhost:8983/solr/techproducts/spell?spellcheck=true&spellchec
k.build=true&spellcheck.q=cemera&shards.qt=/spell&shards=solr-
shard1:8983/solr/techproducts,solr-shard2:8983/solr/techproducts
```

Suggester

In the preceding section, we have seen how Solr handles incorrectly spelled terms and then returns the correct output for them. Let's move one step ahead and provide a feature wherein the user always enters correct spellings but we want to be a step ahead and provide list of suggestions using whatever the user has already typed. This can be achieved by a Solr tool called suggester. The suggester suggests terms when the user types words. During the implementation of the suggester, we need to consider these two things:

- It must be very fast as we need to display suggestions on the user's characters type
- The suggestions should be ranked and ordered by term frequency

To configure any suggester, `SuggestComponent` needs to be configured in `solrconfig.xml`. Here is a simple configuration of a suggester:

```xml
<searchComponent name="suggest" class="solr.SuggestComponent">
<lst name="suggester">
<str name="name">mySuggester</str>
<str name="lookupImpl">FuzzyLookupFactory</str>
<str name="dictionaryImpl">DocumentDictionaryFactory</str>
<str name="field">cat</str>
<str name="weightField">price</str>
<str name="suggestAnalyzerFieldType">string</str>
<str name="buildOnStartup">false</str>
</lst>
</searchComponent>
```

Now this `suggest` search component must be associated with any request handler in `solrconfig.xml`. Previously we used the `/select` request handler, where we configured many components such as spellchecking. Also, the `/select` request handler contains some built-in components: query, faceting, highlighting, and so on. Merging the suggester with other components is not the best approach at all times; sometimes we expect only suggestions and not spellchecking. So, defining a separate request handler for suggestions is the recommended approach. For that, we are defining a separate request handler here and adding the previously defined `suggest` search component to this request handler in `solrconfig.xml`:

```
<requestHandler name="/suggest" class="solr.SearchHandler" startup="lazy">
<lst name="defaults">
<str name="suggest">true</str>
<str name="suggest.count">10</str>
</lst>
<arr name="components">
<str>suggest</str>
</arr>
</requestHandler>
```

Now, all requests coming at the `/suggest` request handler will be treated for suggestions only. This will work as the other request handler and allow us to configure default parameters for suggestion requests.

Suggester parameters

As we have seen, first we need to define a search component and then we need to inject that component with any request handler. Both the sections contain some parameters that fulfill the suggestion requirements. Here is a list of parameters.

Suggester search component parameters are as follows:

Parameter	Behavior	Default value
searchComponent	The name of the search component.	
name	Suggester name, which will be referred with the request handler.	

lookupImpl	Specifies the lookupImpl implementation algorithms used to look up terms in the suggest index. Available implementations are `AnalyzingLookupFactory`, `FuzzyLookupFactory`, `AnalyzingInfixLookupFactory`, `BlendedInfixLookupFactory`, `FreeTextLookupFactory`, `FSTLookupFactory`, `TSTLookupFactory`, `WFSTLookupFactory`, and `JaspellLookupFactory`.	`JaspellLookupFactory`
dictionaryImpl	Specifies a dictionary implementation for suggestions. Available implementations are `DocumentDictionaryFactory`, `DocumentExpressionDictionaryFactory`, `HighFrequencyDictionaryFactory`, and `FileDictionaryFactory`.	`HighFrequency DictionaryFactory`
sourceLocation	Specifies the dictionary file path when a suggestion is implemented using `FileDictionaryFactory`. The main index will be used as the source of terms and weights if this parameter value is empty.	
field	Specifies a field from which the index is to be used as the basis of suggestion terms. The specified field must be stored in the index.	
storeDir	Specifies a path to store the dictionary file.	
buildOnCommit and buildOnOptimize	If this is true, the suggestion dictionary will be rebuilt after a soft commit. If false, the suggestion dictionary will be built only when we provide the suggest.build=true parameter in the URL. Use `buildOnCommit` to rebuild the suggestion dictionary with every soft commit or `buildOnOptimize` to build it only when the index is optimized. This parameter is not recommended if the volume of the indexes is very high; in such a scenario, `suggest.build=true` is recommended.	`false`

`buildOnStartup`	Specifying this to true will build the suggestion directory at the time of Solr start or core reloading. If this parameter is not specified, the suggester will check whether the suggestion directory is present on disk, and build one if it is not found. Enabling (`true`) is not recommended as sometimes it may take too long in build; instead, use `suggest.build=true` for building manually.	`false`

Suggester request handler parameters are as follows:

Parameter	Behavior	Default value
`suggest`	A boolean parameter to enable/disable suggestions.	`true`
`suggest.dictionary`	A mandatory parameter. It specifies the dictionary component configured inside the search component.	
`suggest.q`	Specifies a query to use for suggestions.	
`suggest.count`	Specifies the number of suggestions to be returned.	`10`
`suggest.cfq`	Specifies the **context filter query (CFQ)** used to filter suggestions based on the context field. CFQ is only supported by `AnalyzingInfixLookupFactory` and `BlendedInfixLookupFactory` and only when backed by a `Document*Dictionary`.	
`suggest.build`	If true, it will build the suggester index.	`false`
`suggest.reload`	If true, it will reload the suggester index.	`false`
`suggest.buildAll`	If true, it will build all suggester indexes	`false`
`suggest.reloadAll`	If true, it will reload all suggester indexes.	`false`

All of these parameters are usually configured in the request handler. However, we can override them at query time by passing parameters in the URL.

Running suggestions

We have configured the suggester and request handler for this suggester in
`solrconfig.xml`. Now let's run the configured suggester and examine the response.

Example: Let's search for `elec` and see how many suggestions are returned in response.

URL: `http://localhost:8983/solr/techproducts/suggest?suggest=true&suggest.build=true&suggest.dictionary=mySuggester&suggest.q=elec`:

```
{
  "responseHeader":{
  "status":0,
  "QTime":14},
  "command":"build",
  "suggest":{"mySuggester":{
  "elec":{
  "numFound":3,
  "suggestions":[{
  "term":"electronics and computer1",
  "weight":2199,
  "payload":""},
  {
  "term":"electronics",
  "weight":649,
  "payload":""},
  {
  "term":"electronics and stuff2",
  "weight":279,
  "payload":""}]}}}
}
```

The query `elec` has returned three suggestions under the `mySuggester` section. Here, we
have provided a single dictionary by the parameter `suggest.dictionary=mySuggester`.
In the same way, we can configure multiple dictionaries in `solrconfig.xml` and use them
in a URL like this:

`http://localhost:8983/solr/techproducts/suggest?suggest=true&suggest.build=true&suggest.dictionary=mySuggester&suggest.dictionary=yourSuggester&suggest.q=elec`

Pagination

A query may fetch a number of results for a search. Returning all results at a time and displaying all of them on a single page is not an ideal approach for any search application. Rather, returning the top *N* number of matching results (sorted based on some fields) first is the ideal way for an application. Solr supports a pagination feature whereby we can return a certain number of results rather than all results and display them on the first page. If we can't find the results we are looking for on the first page, we can call the next page of results by running the subsequent request with pagination parameters. Pagination is very helpful in terms of performance because instead of returning all matching results at a time, it will return only a specific number of results; so the result is very quick. Using pagination, we also can determine how many queries are required to fulfill the expectations behind the search; so we can manage relevance accordingly.

How to implement pagination

To implement pagination, we need to configure two parameters in the query request.

- `start`: Indicates from where the results should be returned from the complete result set
- `rows`: Indicates how many results must be returned from the complete result set

We have to specify some value if we have used the start parameter in a request. Keep in mind that the value of the start parameter should be less than the total number of matching results. If we set `start` higher than the total number of matching results found, the query will not return anything.

Example: Search for a `query q=*:*` and get the first five results sorted by ID in ascending order.

URL: `http://localhost:8983/solr/techproducts/select?q=*:*&fl=id,name&start=0&rows=5&sort=id asc:`

```
{
  "responseHeader":{
  "status":0,
  "QTime":0,
  "params":{
  "q":"*:*",
  "fl":"id,name",
  "start":"0",
  "sort":"id asc",
```

```
"rows":"5"}},
"response":{"numFound":32,"start":0,"docs":[
{
"id":"0579B002",
"name":"Canon PIXMA MP500 All-In-One Photo Printer"},
{
"id":"100-435805",
"name":"ATI Radeon X1900 XTX 512 MB PCIE Video Card"},
{
"id":"3007WFP",
"name":"Dell Widescreen UltraSharp 3007WFP"},
{
"id":"6H500F0",
"name":"Maxtor DiamondMax 11 - hard drive - 500 GB - SATA-300"},
{
"id":"9885A004",
"name":"Canon PowerShot SD500"}]
}
}
```

Only five results are returned in the response. Now, if we want the next five results, we set start=5 and rows=5. Please note that the response index starts with zero.

Cursor pagination

Pagination implementation using the start and rows parameters is very easy and straightforward. But when we have very large data volumes, these parameters are not sufficient to implement pagination. For example, consider this:

- During query processing, Solr first loads all the matching documents in memory; then it creates an offset by the start and rows parameters and returns that offset for that query. If the data volume is very large, Solr first loads all matching results in the memory and then applies pagination. So this will create a performance problem.
- In large volumes of data, a request for start=0&rows=1000000 may create trouble for Solr in maintaining and sorting a collection of 1 million documents in memory.

- A request for `start=999000&rows=1000` also creates the same problem. To match the document at the 999001th place, Solr has to traverse through the first 999,000 documents.
- A similar problem exists with SolrCloud, where indexes are distributed. If we have 10 shards, then Solr retrieves 10 million documents (1 million from each shard) and then sorts to find 1,000 documents matching the query parameters.

As a solution to these problems, Solr introduce a feature of pagination—cursor. Cursor does not manage caching on the server but marks the point from where the last document was returned. Now that mark point, called `cursorMark`, is supplied inside the parameters of subsequent requests to tell Solr where to continue from.

To implement pagination through cursor, we need to specify the parameter `cursorMark` with the value of *. Once we implement cursor pagination in Solr, Solr returns the top *N* number of sorted results (where *N* can be specified in the rows parameter) along with an encoded string named `nextCursorMark` in the response. In subsequent requests, the `nextCursorMark` value will be passed as the `cursorMark` parameter. The process will be repeated until the expected result set is retrieved or the value of `nextCursorMark` matches `cursorMark` (which means that there are no more results).

Examples: Fetching all documents.

Using pseudo-code:

```
$params = [ q => $some_query, sort => 'id asc', rows => $r, cursorMark =>
'*' ]
$done = false
while (not $done) {
  $results = fetch_solr($params)
  // do something with $results
  if ($params[cursorMark] == $results[nextCursorMark]) {
    $done = true
  }
  $params[cursorMark] = $results[nextCursorMark]
}
```

Using SolrJ:

```
SolrQuery q = (new
SolrQuery(some_query)).setRows(r).setSort(SortClause.asc("id"));
String cursorMark = CursorMarkParams.CURSOR_MARK_START;
boolean done = false;
while (! done) {
  q.set(CursorMarkParams.CURSOR_MARK_PARAM, cursorMark);
  QueryResponse rsp = solrServer.query(q);
  String nextCursorMark = rsp.getNextCursorMark();
  doCustomProcessingOfResults(rsp);
  if (cursorMark.equals(nextCursorMark)) {
    done = true;
  }
  cursorMark = nextCursorMark;
}
```

Using curl:

```
$ curl '...&rows=10&sort=id+asc&cursorMark=*'
{
  "response":{"numFound":32,"start":0,"docs":[
    // ... 10 docs here ...
  ]},
  "nextCursorMark":"AoEjR0JQ"}
$ curl '...&rows=10&sort=id+asc&cursorMark=AoEjR0JQ'
{
  "response":{"numFound":32,"start":0,"docs":[
    // ... 10 more docs here ...
  ]},
  "nextCursorMark":"AoEpVkRCREIxQTE2"}
$ curl '...&rows=10&sort=id+asc&cursorMark=AoEpVkRCREIxQTE2'
{
  "response":{"numFound":32,"start":0,"docs":[
    // ... 10 more docs here ...
  ]},
  "nextCursorMark":"AoEmbWF4dG9y"}
$ curl '...&rows=10&sort=id+asc&cursorMark=AoEmbWF4dG9y'
{
  "response":{"numFound":32,"start":0,"docs":[
    // ... 2 docs here because we've reached the end.
  ]},
  "nextCursorMark":"AoEpdmlld3Nvbmlj"}
$ curl '...&rows=10&sort=id+asc&cursorMark=AoEpdmlld3Nvbmlj'
{
  "response":{"numFound":32,"start":0,"docs":[
    // no more docs here, and note that the nextCursorMark
    // matches the cursorMark param we used
```

```
    ]},
    "nextCursorMark":"AoEpdmlld3Nvbmlj"}
```

Examples: Fetching *N* Number of documents.

SolrJ:

```
while (! done) {
 q.set(CursorMarkParams.CURSOR_MARK_PARAM, cursorMark);
 QueryResponse rsp = solrServer.query(q);
 String nextCursorMark = rsp.getNextCursorMark();
 boolean hadEnough = doCustomProcessingOfResults(rsp);
 if (hadEnough || cursorMark.equals(nextCursorMark)) {
 done = true;
 }
 cursorMark = nextCursorMark;
}
```

When implementing pagination, we need to take care of a few things:

- If we have used a start parameter in the request, we have to specify some value.
- The field on which we are applying sorting must be unique (uniqueKey field).
- The cursorMark values are calculated based on the sort values of each document, and it may be possible that multiple documents have the same sort values; that will create identical cursorMarks values. Now, Solr will be confused in subsequent requests as to which cursorMark value should be considered. To overcome this, Solr provides an additional field, uniqueKey, used as a clause with a sorting parameter. This uniqueKey guarantees that the documents are returned in deterministic order, and that way each cursorMark will always point to a unique value.
- When documents are sorted based on a Date function, NOW will create confusion for cursor because NOW will create a new sort value for each document in each subsequent request. This will result in never-ending cursors and return the same document every time. To overcome this situation, select a fixed value for the NOW parameter in all requests.

Result grouping

Result grouping is a useful feature in Solr; it returns an optimal mix of search results for a query. Result grouping can be performed based on field values, functions, or queries.

Sometimes, we have multiple similar documents for a single search term, for example, multiple locations for the same hospital, recipes for specific food, plans for term insurance, and so on. In the normal way, if we are searching for one such term, it will return all similar documents and we will have to display all of them on the same page. Through result grouping, we can display only a single document (or the top few or some limited number) for each unique value, and provide a message link with meaningful text and the number of total results found for that query. Clicking on that link will expand the full search result list. This is similar to the expand and collapse features of a search application. Result grouping is just as capable as expand and collapse; additionally it removes duplicate documents from the list. But from a performance point of view, expand and collapse is a better choice than result grouping.

We looked at faceting in the previous chapter. Result grouping also looks similar to faceting, but through faceting, Solr returns a separate facet section along with the counts for each value. Through result grouping, it actually returns the unique values and their counts (like faceting) plus a number of documents that contain each of the specified values. Also, groups returned in the results section are sorted based on the sorting parameter provided inside the query.

Combining grouping with faceting is also possible. Currently, field and range faceting are included in grouped faceting, but date and pivot faceting are not included. The facet counts are calculated based on the first `group.field` parameter and other `group.field` parameters are ignored.

Result grouping parameters

Parameter	Behavior	Default value
group	If true, query results will be grouped.	false
group.field	Specifies the field by which the result will be grouped.	
group.func	Specifies a function name by which the result will be grouped.	

group.query	Specifies a result grouping query that will return a single group of documents.	
rows	Specifies the number of groups to return.	10
start	Specifies starting point from the list of groups.	
group.limit	Specifies the number of results to be returned for every group.	1
group.offset	Specifies starting point from the list of documents of every group.	
sort	Specifies the field based on groups will be sorted.	score desc
group.sort	Specifies the field based on documents will be sorted within each group. The default behaviour is that if group.sort is not specified, the sort parameter value will be used.	
group.format	Specifies the response format after grouping. Possible values for this parameter are simple and grouped.	Advanced grouping format
group.main	A boolean variable that tells Solr to use first the field grouping command as the main result in the response using group.format=simple. A true value will do the same.	false
group.ngroups	A boolean variable that tells Solr to include the number of groups that have matched to the query in result. A true value will do the same.	false
group.truncate	A boolean variable that tells Solr to calculate facet counts based on the most relevant document of each group matching the query. A true value will do the same.	false
group.facet	To enable/disable grouped faceting.	false
group.cache.percent	Enables caching for result grouping by configuring a value greater than zero. The maximum value is 100.	0

Running result grouping

We have explored the result grouping concept and configurations. Now let's execute some examples.

Example: Grouping by field `manu_exact`", which specifies the manufacturers of items in the `techproducts` dataset.

URL: `http://localhost:8983/solr/techproducts/select?fl=id,name&q=solr+m emory&group=true&group.field=manu_exact`

```
{
 "responseHeader":{
 "status":0,
 "QTime":5,
 "params":{
 "q":"solr memory",
 "fl":"id,name",
 "group.field":"manu_exact",
 "group":"true"}},
 "grouped":{
 "manu_exact":{
 "matches":6,
 "groups":[{
 "groupValue":"Apache Software Foundation",
 "doclist":{"numFound":1,"start":0,"docs":[
 {
 "id":"SOLR1000",
 "name":"Solr, the Enterprise Search Server"}]
 }},
 {
 "groupValue":"Corsair Microsystems Inc.",
 "doclist":{"numFound":2,"start":0,"docs":[
 {
 "id":"VS1GB400C3",
 "name":"CORSAIR ValueSelect 1GB 184-Pin DDR SDRAM Unbuffered DDR 400 (PC
3200) System Memory - Retail"}]
 }},
 {
 "groupValue":"A-DATA Technology Inc.",
 "doclist":{"numFound":1,"start":0,"docs":[
 {
 "id":"VDBDB1A16",
 "name":"A-DATA V-Series 1GB 184-Pin DDR SDRAM Unbuffered DDR 400 (PC 3200)
System Memory - OEM"}]
 }},
 {
```

```
"groupValue":"Canon Inc.",
"doclist":{"numFound":1,"start":0,"docs":[
{
"id":"0579B002",
"name":"Canon PIXMA MP500 All-In-One Photo Printer"}]
}},
{
"groupValue":"ASUS Computer Inc.",
"doclist":{"numFound":1,"start":0,"docs":[
{
"id":"EN7800GTX/2DHTV/256M",
"name":"ASUS Extreme N7800GTX/2DHTV (256 MB)"}]
}}]}},
"spellcheck":{
"suggestions":[],
"correctlySpelled":true,
"collations":[]}
}
```

In the same way, grouping can be achieved by specifying a query or queries.

Example: Retrieve the top three results for the field memory for two price ranges of 0.00 to 99.99 and over 100, using group.query.

URL: http://localhost:8983/solr/techproducts/select?indent=true&fl=name ,price&q=memory&group=true&group.query=price:[0+TO+99.99]&group.query=p rice:[100+TO+*]&group.limit=3

```
{
  "responseHeader":{
    "status":0,
    "QTime":2,
    "params":{
      "q":"memory",
      "indent":"true",
      "fl":"name,price",
      "group.limit":"3",
      "group.query":["price:[0 TO 99.99]",
        "price:[100 TO *]"],
      "group":"true"}},
  "grouped":{
    "price:[0 TO 99.99]":{
      "matches":5,
      "doclist":{"numFound":1,"start":0,"docs":[
          {
            "name":"CORSAIR ValueSelect 1GB 184-Pin DDR SDRAM Unbuffered
DDR 400 (PC 3200) System Memory - Retail",
```

```
            "price":74.99}]
      }},
   "price:[100 TO *]":{
     "matches":5,
     "doclist":{"numFound":3,"start":0,"docs":[
         {
           "name":"CORSAIR XMS 2GB (2 x 1GB) 184-Pin DDR SDRAM Unbuffered
DDR 400 (PC 3200) Dual Channel Kit System Memory - Retail",
           "price":185.0},
         {
           "name":"Canon PIXMA MP500 All-In-One Photo Printer",
           "price":179.99},
         {
           "name":"ASUS Extreme N7800GTX/2DHTV (256 MB)",
           "price":479.95}]
      }}},
  "spellcheck":{
    "suggestions":[],
    "correctlySpelled":false,
    "collations":[]}}
```

Result clustering

So far, we have seen Solr searching by the keyword used in search query. Result clustering is the advanced search component of Solr; it first identifies the similarities between documents, and using these similarities, it finds related documents. It is also not necessary for the identified similarities to be present in the query or document.

The clustering component first discovers the results of a search query and identifies similar terms or phrases found within the search results. A clustering algorithm discovers relationships across all the documents from the search result and forms in a meaningful cluster label. Solr comes with several algorithms for clustering implementation.

Result clustering parameters

Parameter	Behavior	Default value
clustering	Enable/disable clustering.	true

`clustering.engine`	Specifies which clustering engine to use. If not specified, the first declared engine will become the default one.	first in a list
`clustering.results`	When true, the component will run a clustering of the search results (this should be enabled).	`true`
`clustering.collection`	When true, the component will run a clustering of the whole document index.	`false`

From the preceding list, some parameters are of the search component and some of them are of the request handler. There are some additional parameters that are specific to engine-level configuration. We can pass these parameters to the query url to modify configurations at query runtime.

Result clustering implementation

Solr's built-in example `techproducts` contains preconfigured components for result clustering, but by default, the configurations are disabled.

The clustering implementation requires the following configurations.

Install the clustering contrib

The clustering contrib extension requires `solr-clustering-*.jar` under `/dist` and all JARs under `contrib/clustering/lib`. Configure the file path according to your system file path in `solrconfig.xml`:

```
<lib dir="${solr.install.dir:../../../..}/contrib/clustering/lib/"
regex=".*\.jar" />
 <lib dir="${solr.install.dir:../../../..}/dist/" regex="solr-clustering-
\d.*\.jar" />
```

Declare the cluster search component

Define the search component for clustering in `solrconfig.xml`:

```
<searchComponent name="clustering" enable="true"
 class="solr.clustering.ClusteringComponent" >
 <lst name="engine">
 <str name="name">lingo</str>
 <str
name="carrot.algorithm">org.carrot2.clustering.lingo.LingoClusteringAlgorit
hm</str>
 <str name="carrot.resourcesDir">clustering/carrot2</str>
 </lst>
 <lst name="engine">
 <str name="name">stc</str>
 <str
name="carrot.algorithm">org.carrot2.clustering.stc.STCClusteringAlgorithm</
str>
 <str name="carrot.resourcesDir">clustering/carrot2</str>
 </lst>
</searchComponent>
```

We can also declare cluster components as engines or a multiple clustering pipeline, which can be selected by specifying the parameter `clustering.engine=<engine name>` in the query URL.

Declare the request handler and include the cluster search component

Define the request handler for the cluster in `solrconfig.xml`:

```
<requestHandler name="/clustering" startup="lazy" enable="true"
class="solr.SearchHandler">
 <lst name="defaults">
 <bool name="clustering">true</bool>
 <bool name="clustering.results">true</bool>
 <!-- Field name with the logical "title" of a each document (optional) -->
 <str name="carrot.title">name</str>
 <!-- Field name with the logical "URL" of a each document (optional) -->
 <str name="carrot.url">id</str>
 <!-- Field name with the logical "content" of a each document (optional) -
->
 <str name="carrot.snippet">features</str>
 <!-- Apply highlighter to the title/ content and use this for clustering.
-->
```

```
<bool name="carrot.produceSummary">true</bool>
<!-- the maximum number of labels per cluster -->
<!--<int name="carrot.numDescriptions">5</int>-->
<!-- produce sub clusters -->
<bool name="carrot.outputSubClusters">false</bool>
<!-- Configure the remaining request handler parameters. -->
<str name="defType">edismax</str>
<str name="qf">
text^0.5 features^1.0 name^1.2 sku^1.5 id^10.0 manu^1.1 cat^1.4
</str>
<str name="q.alt">*:*</str>
<str name="rows">100</str>
<str name="fl">*,score</str>
</lst>
<arr name="last-components">
<str>clustering</str>
</arr>
</requestHandler>
```

Now we are done with cluster configurations. Let's run a cluster for the built-in example `techproducts` by setting `enable="true"` in the `searchComponent` and `requestHandler` configuration. We can enable the same by specifying a JVM system property using the following command:

```
solr start -e techproducts -Dsolr.clustering.enabled=true
```

Let's run a query for electronics using the configured request handler `/clustering` and see the cluster response.

URL: `http://localhost:8983/solr/techproducts/clustering?q=electronics&rows=100`:

```
{
  "responseHeader":{
    "status":0,
    "QTime":32},
  "response":{"numFound":14,"start":0,"maxScore":2.9029632,"docs":[
      . . . .
    . . . .
      ]
  },
  "clusters":[{
      "labels":["DDR"],
      "score":3.037927435185717,
      "docs":["TWINX2048-3200PRO",
        "VS1GB400C3",
        "VDBDB1A16"]},
```

```
  {
    "labels":["iPod"],
    "score":7.317758461138239,
    "docs":["F8V7067-APL-KIT",
      "IW-02",
      "MA147LL/A"]},
  {
    "labels":["Canon"],
    "score":6.785392802370259,
    "docs":["0579B002",
      "9885A004"]},
  {
    "labels":["Hard Drive"],
    "score":10.460153088070832,
    "docs":["SP2514N",
      "6H500F0"]},
  {
    "labels":["Retail"],
    "score":1.629540936033123,
    "docs":["TWINX2048-3200PRO",
      "VS1GB400C3"]},
  {
    "labels":["Video"],
    "score":10.060361253597023,
    "docs":["MA147LL/A",
      "100-435805"]},
  {
    "labels":["Other Topics"],
    "score":0.0,
    "other-topics":true,
    "docs":["EN7800GTX/2DHTV/256M",
      "3007WFP",
      "VA902B"]}]
  }
```

Here we can see a few clusters discovered for the query (q=electronics). Each cluster has a label and the score shows the kindness of the cluster. The score is specific to an algorithm and meaningful only in relation to the scores of other clusters in the same set. A score with a higher value is better.

Spatial search

Location-based data search is a very important requirement nowadays, such as searching for distances from a place, searching a house within a radius, and so on. Solr supports searching for location-based data called spatial or geospatial searches.

This can be implemented by indexing a field in each document that contains a geographical point (a latitude and longitude); and then at query time, we can find and sort documents by distance from a geolocation (latitude and longitude). The matching listings (results) can be displayed on an interactive map, in which we can zoom in/out and move the map center point to find nearby listings using spatial search. Like latitude and longitude, Solr also allows us to index geographical shapes (polygons), which are used to find a document that intersects geographical regions. Spatial search implemented by indexing a field (latitude and longitude) helps to search from a specific point, while implementing by indexing geographical shapes helps to search all documents within a given range. Solr also supports returning the distances of matching documents in a response. We can also apply sorting on distances to provide more useful results to the user.

Spatial search implementation

There are various sequential steps we need to execute in order to implement spatial search.

Field types

First we need to configure field type in managed-schema.xml or schema.xml:

```
<fieldType name="location" class="solr.LatLonPointSpatialField"
docValues="true"/>
```

There are mainly four field types available in Solr that support spatial search:

- LatLonPointSpatialField: The most commonly used field type and an alternative to LatLonType (deprecated) for latitude—and longitude-based search.
- LatLonType: Its non-geodetic twin PointType field type, and this one is deprecated now.

- `SpatialRecursivePrefixTreeFieldType`: RPT supports more advanced search features, such as polygons and heatmaps. `RptWithGeometrySpatialField` is derived from RPT. It is used for geography-based searches. Sorting and boosting are not supported.
- `BBoxField`: Used to search a bounding box. It supports sorting and boosting.

Query parser

Previously, we explored various query parsers that support normal searching. But when it comes to spatial search, we need to configure a special parser that supports spatial search:

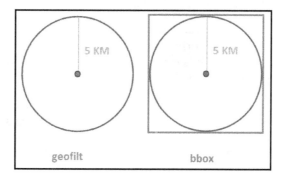

There are two types of spatial search parsers available in Solr.

- `geofilt`: The `geofilt` parser is used to retrieve results based on the geospatial distance from a given point. Please look at the preceding image. Another way of looking at it is that it creates a circular shape filter. For example, to find all documents within 5 kilometers of a given latitude-longitude point, the query will be:

  ```
  &q=:&fq={!geofilt sfield=location}&pt=45.15,-93.85&d=5
  ```

  This filter returns all results within a circle of the given radius around the initial point.

- `bbox`: The `bbox` parser works like `geofilt`, except that it uses the bounding box of the calculated circle. Please look at the preceding diagram. For the same example, the query will be:

  ```
  &q=:&fq={!bbox sfield=location}&pt=45.15,-93.85&d=5
  ```

Spatial search query parser parameters

Both the parsers support the following parameters:

Parameter	Behavior	Default value
d	Specifies a radius distance (usually in kilometers) within the document that should be considered for matching.	
pt	Specifies latitude and longitude for the format as `lat`, `lon`, `x`, `y` for `PointType`, or `x`, `y` for RPT field types.	
sfield	Specifies a spatial field defined in `managed-schema.xml` or `schema.xml`.	
score	If the query is used in a scoring context, this determines what type of scores will be produced. It is not supported by `LatLonType` or `PointType`. Possible values are `none`, `kilometers`, `miles`, `degrees`, `distance`, and `recipDistance`.	none
filter	If set to `false`, parser scoring will be disabled. This is not supported by `LatLonType` or `PointType`.	true

Function queries

In spatial search, along with returning matching documents within a given range, Solr also supports calculation of matching document distances from the search point and merging them in the returning response. Solr even supports sorting and boosting on the calculated distance. To calculate distances, the following are the functions available in Solr:

- `geodist`: This calculates the distance between too points (latitude and longitude)
- `dist`: Calculates the p-norm distance between multidimensional vectors
- `hsin`: This calculates the distance between two points on a sphere
- `sqedist`: Calculates the squared Euclidean distance between two points

From the preceding list, geodist is the most commonly used function for most search cases. It takes three optional parameters: sfield (spatial field defined in managed-schema.xml), latitude, and longitude. For example, we find all cities from the searching point (45.15, -93.85) within a radius of 50 kilometers, calculate their distance from the searched point, and return in the response:

```
&q=:&fq={!geofilt}&sfield=location&pt=45.15,-93.85&d=50&fl=id,city,distance
:geodist()
```

Additionally, we sort by distance ascending. The following is the query:

```
&q=:&fq={!geofilt}&sfield=location&pt=45.15,-93.85&d=50&fl=id,city,distance
:geodist()
&sort=geodist() asc
```

This is the basic overview of spatial search. There are many more spatial searching features available in Solr. Exploring every feature here is not possible. However, we can take this chapter as a reference and explore more spatial search features. Rather than going into more details of spatial search, let's move on to the next chapter.

Summary

In this chapter, we explored and understood various searching functionalities such as spellchecking, suggester, pagination, result grouping, and result clustering. Finally, we looked at spatial search.

So far, we have seen configurations for each one and executed examples by configuring various functionality parameters. Now let's move to the next chapter, where we will see how to configure Solr for production and learn fine-tuning methodologies for better performance. We will explore how to secure Solr and how to take backups. We will configure logging and get an overview of SolrCloud.

Managing and Fine-Tuning Solr

Okay, so you have your brand new car up and running and have been using it judiciously day in and day out, but you don't maintain it properly from time to time! What will happen? Of course, the performance is going to deteriorate over a period of time. Another thing could be that your car supports automatic parking but you never found out how to override the default setting. In such a case, a manual comes in handy for learning and tweaking all the features that your car can provide. Similarly, you need to fine-tune and manage your Solr so as to get the most out of it. This is exactly what we are going to see in this chapter.

JVM configuration

One of the things that you need to take particular care of when you are working on any Java-based application is configuring the JVM optimally, and Solr is no exception.

Managing the memory heap

Anyone who has worked with Java-based applications would have surely come across setting the heap space. We do it using $-Xms$ and $-Xmx$. Suppose I set following the command-line option:

```
-Xms256m -Xmx2048m
```

Here, Xms specifies our initial memory allocation pool, whereas Xmx specifies the maximum memory allocation pool for JVM. In the case we just saw, our JVM will start with 256 MB of memory and will be able to use up to 2 GB of memory.

If we require more heap space, then we can increase -Xms. We can also decide not to give any initial heap space at all and let JVM use the heap space as per the need, but this may increase our startup time. Similarly, failing to set up the maximum heap size properly can result in OutOfMemoryException. Proper garbage collection JVM parameters should be set so that JVM can optimally try to reclaim any available space that already exists in the heap. Also, the size of the heap plays a crucial role in garbage collection. The larger the heap size, the more the time spent by JVM to do garbage collection, leading to *stop the world* conditions.

Managing solrconfig.xml

As we already know now, solrconfig.xml forms the heart of Solr when it comes to configuring Solr.

There are two ways in which this file is modified:

- By making direct changes in solrconfig.xml
- Using the config API to create configoverlay.json, which holds configuration overlays to modify the default values specified in solrconfig.xml

The solrconfig.xml file is used to configure the admin web interface. It can be used to change parameters for replication and duplication. We can change the request dispatcher too using solrconfig.xml. Various listeners and request handlers can be configured using solrconfig.xml.

Go to any of the conf directories for a collection and you will find solrconfig.xml inside. Navigate to SOLR_HOME/server/solr/configsets and you will see various configurations that follow best practices for configuring Solr.

Solr allows you to specify a variable for the property value, which can be replaced at runtime with the following syntax:

```
${propertyname[:default value]}
```

Doing so will allow a default, which can be overridden when Solr is started. If we don't specify a default value, then it we should make sure that the property is specified at runtime or else we will get an error.

For example, take a look at this config:

```
<autoCommit>
    <maxTime>${solr.autoCommit.maxTime:15000}</maxTime>
    <openSearcher>false</openSearcher>
</autoCommit>
```

In the preceding snippet, we have specified to keep the maximum time for doing a hard commit as 15 seconds.

This can be changed at runtime:

```
bin/solr start -Dsolr.autoCommit.maxTime=20000
```

In this way, we can set any Java system property at runtime.

User-defined properties

We can also add `solrcore.properties` in the configuration directory to specify user-defined properties that can be set in `solrconfig.xml`.

For example, `solr.autoCommit.maxTime` can be added to `solrcore.properties`.

 The `solrcore.properties` is deprecated in cloud mode.

On the use of APIs, the Solr core will have its `core.properties` automatically created. In the case of the SolrCloud collection, we can submit our own parameters, which will go into the respective `core.properties`. The only thing to make sure is prefixing the parameter name with `property` as a URL parameter:

```
http://localhost:8983/solr/admin/collections?action=CREATE&name=getting
started&numShards=1&property.user.name=Dharmesh Vasoya
```

This will create `core.properties` with the following entry:

```
user.name=Dharmesh Vasoya
```

Now this property can be used in `solrconfig.xml` as `${user.name}`.

Implicit Solr core properties

The following properties are available as implicit properties for the Solr core:

- `solr.core.config`
- `solr.core.dataDir`
- `solr.core.loadOnStartup`
- `solr.core.name`
- `solr.core.schema`
- `solr.core.transient`

Since implicitly we do not need to specify them in `core.properties`, but they are implicitly available to be used in `solrconfig.xml`.

Managing backups

Going into production, we obviously need a proper backup and restore plan. The last thing we would want is for our hard disk to crash and all our index data to disappear or get corrupted.

Solr provides two ways to back up based on how you are running it:

- Collections API in SolrCloud mode
- Replication handler in standalone mode

Backup in SolrCloud

As mentioned earlier, using the collections API, we can take backups in SolrCloud. Doing so will ensure that the backups are generated across multiple shards; and then, at the time of restore, we use the same number of shards and replicas as the original collection. The commands are listed here:

Command name	Description
`action=BACKUP`	Used to back up Solr indexes and configuration
`action=RESTORE`	Used to restore Solr indexes and configuration

Standalone mode backups

In the case of standalone mode, backups and restoration are done using replication handler. The configuration of replication handler can be customized using our own replication handler in `solrconfig.xml`; however, we will use the out-of-the-box implicit support for replication using the API.

Backup API

In order to back up, we will use the following command to the core that we would like to take a backup of:

```
http://localhost:8983/solr/myschema/replication?command=backup&name=mybacku
p
```

Here, `myschema` is the name of the core that we are working with and `/replication` is the handler to the backup. In the end, you can see we've specified `command=backup` to back up our core.

The `backup` command will bring data from the last committed index. At any point in time, there can be only one backup call being made. Otherwise, we will get an exception if there is a backup process already going on.

A backup request can have the following parameters:

Parameter name	Description
location	The location for the backup. Unless you specify an absolute path, everything will be relative to Solr's instance directory. The snapshot will be created in a directory named `snapshot.<name>`. If you don't specify the name, then the directory name will have a timestamp as the suffix, such as `snapshot.<yyyyMMddHHmmssSSS>`.
numberToKeep	Defines the number of backups. You cannot use this parameter if you have already defined `maxNumberOfBackups` in `solrconfig.xml`.
repository	Defines the name of the repository to be used for the backup. The default will be the filesystem repository.
commitName	Defines the name of the commit that was used while taking a snapshot with the `CREATESNAPSHOT` command.

Backup status

We can monitor the backup operation to check the current status using the following call:

```
http://localhost:8983/solr/myschema/replication?command=details&wt=xml
```

The output will be something like this:

```
<lst name="backup">
    <str name="startTime">Tue Jan 30 14:32:12 DAVT 2018</str>
    <int name="fileCount">15</int>
    <str name="status">success</str>
    <str name="snapshotCompletedAt">Tue Jan 30 14:32:12 DAVT 2018</str>
        <str name="snapshotName">demobackup</str>
</lst>
```

If there is a failure, then we will get `snapShootException` in the response.

API to restore

Similar to taking backups, the restore API requires `command=restore` to be sent to the replication handler on the core, as follows:

```
http://localhost:8983/solr/gettingstarted/myschema?command=restore&name=dem
obackup
```

Executing the preceding command will restore the index snapshot named `demobackup` in the current core. Once the data is fully restored, searches will start reflecting from the restored data.

A restore request can have the following parameters:

Parameter name	Description
`location`	The location of the backup. Unless you specify this, it will look for a backup in Solr's data directory.
`name`	Defines the name of the backed-up index snapshot to be restored.
`repository`	Defines the name of the repository to be used for the backup. The default will be the filesystem repository.

Restore status API

Similar to the backup status API, we have a restore status API to check the restore status:

```
http://localhost:8983/solr/myschema/replication?command=restorestatus&wt=xm
l
```

The output of the API will be as follows:

```
<response>
    <lst name="responseHeader">
        <int name="status">0</int>
        <int name="QTime">0</int>
    </lst>
    <lst name="restorestatus">
        <str name="snapshotName">snapshot.<name></str>
        <str name="status">success</str>
    </lst>
</response>
```

Snapshot API

We can create, restore, and list snapshots of the index using APIs.

The details are shown in tabular format as follows:

API	URL	Parameters
Create snapshot	`http://localhost:8983` `/solr/admin` `/cores?action=CREATESNAPSHOT&` `core=myschema&commitName=commit1`	• `commitName`: The parameter's name to be used for storage • `core`: The name of the core • `async`: The request ID to track this action, which will be processed asynchronously
List snapshot	`http://localhost:8983` `/solr/admin` `/cores?action=LISTSNAPSHOTS&` `core=myschema&commitName=commit1`	• `core`: The name of the core • `async`: The request ID to track this action, which will be processed asynchronously

Delete snapshot	`http://localhost:8983` `/solr/admin` `/cores?action=DELETESNAPSHOT&` `core=techproducts&` `commitName=commit1`	`core`: The name of the core `async`: The request ID to track this action, which will be processed asynchronously `commitName`: To specify the `commitName` to be deleted

JMX with Solr

Java Management Extensions (**JMX**) is a technology that was released in the J2SE 5.0 release; it provides tools for managing and monitoring resources dynamically at runtime. It is used in enterprise applications to make configurable systems and get the state of an enterprise application at any point of time. The resources are represented by **managed beans** (**MBeans**).

Solr can be controlled via the JMX interface; we can make use of VisualVM or JConsole to connect with Solr.

JMX configuration

Solr will automatically identify its location on startup if you have an MBean server running in Solr's JVM or if you start Solr with the `Dcom.sun.management.jmxremote` system property.

Alternatively, you can configure by defining a metrics reporter.

On a remote Solr server, if you need to do JMX-enabled Java profiling, then you have to enable remote JMX access when starting the Solr server.

Open `solr.in.cmd` or `solr.in.sh` in the `SOLR_HOME/bin` directory and set the `ENABLE_REMOTE_JMX_OPTS` property to `true`, along with `RMI_PORT=18983`, to enable remote JMX access.

Logging configuration

Setting up logs is a key part of any enterprise application and Solr is no exception. Luckily, Solr provides many different ways to tweak the default logging configuration.

Log settings using the admin web interface

Using Solr's admin web interface, we can set various log levels. Go to the admin interface by typing the following URL:

```
http://localhost:8983/solr/
```

You should see the following admin screen:

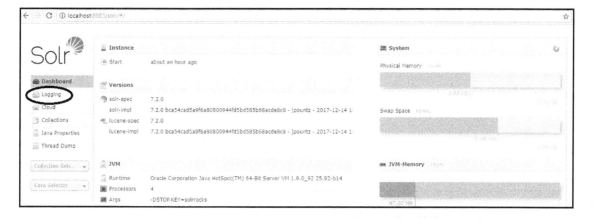

You will see that on the left-hand side, there is a **Logging** option. Click on it and there will be a submenu item called **Level**, which will open up the following screen:

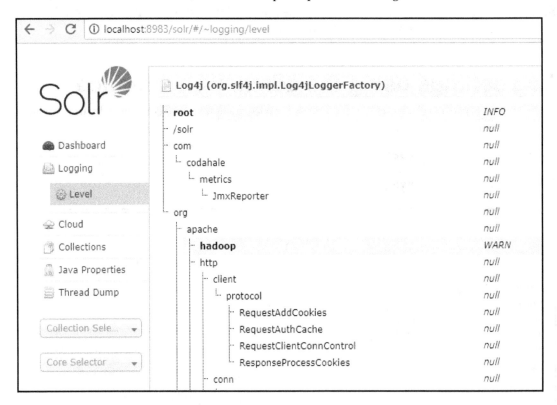

Here, we can set the logging level for many different log categories in a hierarchical order. For example, let's say I want to set `org.apache.http.conn.ssl` to log level and set all the subcategories under it to debug level; I will click on the edit icon next to `ssl`, as shown here:

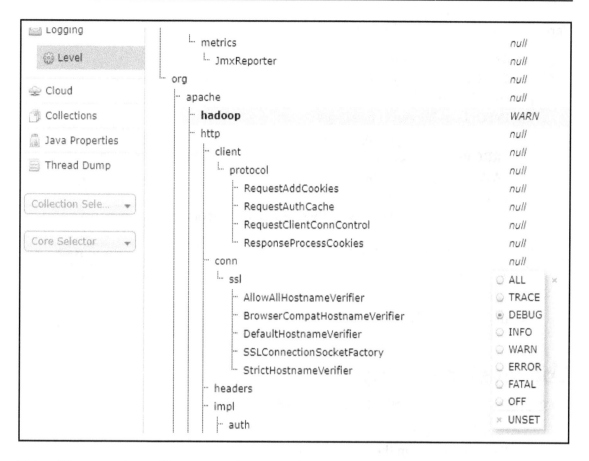

This will open up a small popup with various log levels that we can set.

Any log level set in this manner will be lost during the next restart of the server.

Various log level settings are listed here:

- **ALL**: Logs everything
- **TRACE**: Logs everything but leaves the least important messages
- **DEBUG**: Logs debug-level messages
- **INFO**: Logs info-level messages
- **WARN**: Logs all warning messages
- **ERROR**: Logs all errors
- **FATAL**: Logs every fatal message
- **OFF**: Removes logging
- **UNSET**: Removes the previously selected logging option

You can also set the log level using an API:

```
curl -s http://localhost:8983/solr/admin/info/logging --data-binary
"set=root:WARN"
```

The preceding `curl` command sets the `root` category to the `WARN` level.

Log level at startup

There are two other ways to set up logging temporarily:

- Setting the environment variable
- Pass parameters in the startup script

Setting the environment variable

The first option is to set the environment variable `SOLR_LOG_LEVEL` at startup or put the variable in `SOLR_HOME/bin/solr.in.sh` in the case of Linux and `SOLR_HOME/bin/solr.in.cmd` in the case of Windows.

The values will be one of the log levels that were mentioned earlier.

Passing parameters in the startup script

You can start Solr with parameters telling how much logging would you like:

```
bin/solr start -f -v
```

The preceding script, which has parameter -v, says to start Solr with verbose logging:

```
bin/solr start -f -q
```

The preceding script, which has parameter -q, says to start Solr with quiet logging or print WARN level or more severe logs.

Configuring Log4J for logging

All the logging solutions that we have seen so far are non-permanent settings and are good only until the next restart of the server. To make permanent log changes, we resort to Log4J, which Solr uses for its logging needs.

The Log4J configuration file in our case is the log4j.properties file, which is located in the SOLR_HOME/server/resources directory. All logs are written to the SOLR_HOME/server/logs directory. This path can also be changed using the environment variable SOLR_LOGS_DIR.

Those who have worked with Log4j may know that we can also change log4j.properties to set various logging configurations. There are many settings to decide where you want to print the log, the size of the file generated, what kind of appenders or patterns should be used, and so on.

When we start Solr with the -f option, which stands for foreground, all the logs are written to the console along with the log file. If we are not using the foreground option, then all the logs will be written to solr[port]-console.log.

As mentioned earlier, the log level, the size of the log file, and the logging policy can be changed using log4j.properties.

SolrCloud overview

One of the must have when going to production is clustering for fault tolerance and high availability. Solr's answer to this is SolrCloud, which provides ways to have distributed indexing and search capabilities with central configuration for the entire cluster, and load balancing with failover support.

As mentioned earlier, Solr provides distributed searching. Behind the scenes, Solr makes use of ZooKeeper to manage nodes.

In SolrCloud, data is distributed in multiple shards, which can be hosted on multiple boxes having replicas; this provides redundancy, fault tolerance, and scalability. ZooKeeper holds the strings to manage the shards and replication and to decide which server will handle a specific request.

SolrCloud in interactive mode

Let's set up SolrCloud. Go to the `SOLR_HOME/bin` directory and start the server in interactive mode using the following command:

```
solr -e cloud
```

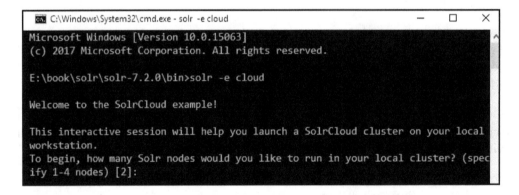

As you can see, an interactive session starts up, asking you how many nodes the cluster should start with, the default being 2. We can start up to 4 nodes, but we will leave it as the default.

```
C:\Windows\System32\cmd.exe

Ok, let's start up 2 Solr nodes for your example SolrCloud cluster.
Please enter the port for node1 [8983]:

Please enter the port for node2 [7574]:

Creating Solr home directory E:\book\solr\solr-7.2.0\example\cloud\node1\solr
Cloning E:\book\solr\solr-7.2.0\example\cloud\node1 into
   E:\book\solr\solr-7.2.0\example\cloud\node2

Starting up Solr on port 8983 using command:
"E:\book\solr\solr-7.2.0\bin\solr.cmd" start -cloud -p 8983 -s "E:\book\solr\solr-7.2.0\example\cloud\node1\solr"

Waiting up to 30 to see Solr running on port 8983
Started Solr server on port 8983. Happy searching!

Starting up Solr on port 7574 using command:
"E:\book\solr\solr-7.2.0\bin\solr.cmd" start -cloud -p 7574 -s "E:\book\solr\solr-7.2.0\example\cloud\node2\solr" -z localhost:9983

Waiting up to 30 to see Solr running on port 7574
Started Solr server on port 7574. Happy searching!
INFO  - 2018-01-28 20:49:55.896; org.apache.solr.client.solrj.impl.ZkClientClusterStateProvider; Cluster at localhost:9983 ready

Now let's create a new collection for indexing documents in your 2-node cluster.
Please provide a name for your new collection: [gettingstarted]

How many shards would you like to split gettingstarted into? [2]

How many replicas per shard would you like to create? [2]

Please choose a configuration for the gettingstarted collection, available options are:
_default or sample_techproducts_configs [_default]

Created collection 'gettingstarted' with 2 shard(s), 2 replica(s) with config-set 'gettingstarted'

Enabling auto soft-commits with maxTime 3 secs using the Config API

POSTing request to Config API: http://localhost:8983/solr/gettingstarted/config
{"set-property":{"updateHandler.autoSoftCommit.maxTime":"3000"}}
Successfully set-property updateHandler.autoSoftCommit.maxTime to 3000

SolrCloud example running, please visit: http://localhost:8983/solr
```

Next, you will be asked to select ports for the two nodes. Leave the default ports of 8983 and 7574 as is and continue. Once both nodes are started, you will be prompted to name the schema, the default being gettingstarted. Leave it as is and continue. As shown in the preceding screen, you are prompted to select the number of shards and replicas. Leave the default value of 2 as is and continue; finally, you will get a message stating that the SolrCloud example is running at http://localhost:8983/solr.

Navigate to the browser and type the specified URL; you will see Solr as follows:

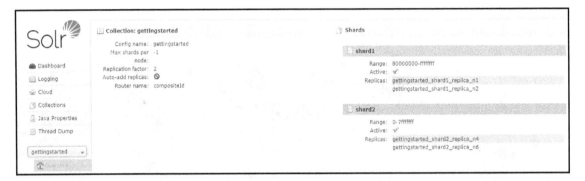

As you can see, the node is started with two shards and a replication factor of two for the gettingstarted schema.

SolrCloud – core concepts

In order to scale, a collection is split or partitioned into various shards having documents distributed, which means shards have subsets of overall documents in the collection. A cluster hosts multiple Solr Documents' collections. The maximum number of documents that a collection can hold and also the parallelization for individual search requests are based on the number of shards a collection has.

When we set up SolrCloud, we created two nodes. A Solr cluster is made up of two or more Solr nodes, and each node can host multiple cores. We also created a couple of shards with a replication factor of two. The greater the number of replicas that each shard has, the more redundancy we are building into the collection. And this determines the overall high availability and the number of concurrent search requests that can be processed.

SolrCloud does not employ the master-slave strategy. Every shard has at least one replica, so at any point in time, one of them acts as a leader based on the first come, first serve principle. If the leader goes down, a new leader is appointed automatically. The document is first indexed in the leader shard replica and then the leader sends the update to all the other replicas.

When a leader is down, by default all the replicas can become leaders; but in order for this to happen, it becomes mandatory that every replica is in sync with the current leader at all times. Any new document that is added to the leader must be sent across all the replicas and all of them have to issue a commit. Imagine what would happen if a replica goes down and there are a large number of updates until the time the replica rejoins the cluster. Obviously, the recovery would be very slow. It all depends on the use case that an organization wants for their syncing strategy. They can keep it as is with real-time syncing, or opt for not syncing in real time or making the replica ineligible for becoming the leader.

We can set the following replica types when creating a new collection or adding a new replica:

Replica type	Description
NRT	**Near real-time** (**NRT**) which is the default and initially the only replica type supported by Solr. The way it works is as follows: it maintains a transaction log and writes new documents locally to its index. Here, any replica of this type is eligible for becoming a leader.
TLOG	The only difference between NRT and TLOG is that while the former indexes document changes locally, TLOG does not do that. The TLOG type of replica only maintains a transaction log, resulting in better speeds compared to NR as there are no commits involved. Just like NRT, this type of replica is eligible to become a shard leader.
PULL	Does not maintain transaction and document changes locally. The only thing it does is pull or replicate the index from the shard leader. Having this replica type ensures that the replica never becomes a shard leader.

We can create different mixes of replica type combos for our replicas. Some commonly used combinations are as follows:

Combination	Description
All NRT replicas	This can be used wherever the update index throughput is less since it involves a commit on every replica during index. Can be ideal for small to medium clusters or wherever the update index throughput is less.
All TLOG replicas	This can be used if we have more replicas per shard, with the replicas being able to handle update requests; NRT is not desired.

TLOG replicas with PULL replicas	This combination is used more often in scenarios where we want to increase the availability of search queries and document updates take the backseat. This will give an outdated result as we are not having NRT updates.

Routing documents

You can specify the router implementation used by a collection using the `router.name` parameter while creating your collection.

By default, the `compositeId` router is used. In this implementation, you can send documents with a prefix in the document ID used to calculate the hash that Solr uses to select the shard for indexing of the document. The prefix can be of your choice but it should be consistent. For example, if you want to find documents of a restaurant chain, you can use the restaurant name as a prefix. If the restaurant chain is `KFC` and document ID is `87364`, the prefix will be something like `KFC!87364`. The exclamation mark is used to differentiate the prefix used to determine the shard where the document will be routed.

Splitting shards

Let's say that you have created a collection in SolrCloud and created two shards initially. Down the line, there are some additional requirements and now you want more shards. You find yourself in the soup, right?

Fear not! the collections API of SolrCloud comes to the rescue. The collections API provides a way to split a shard into two pieces. It does not touch the existing shard at all (which can be deleted later) and the split will create two copies of the data as new shards.

Setting up ignore commits from client applications

Care should be taken in SolrCloud mode: the client application should not send explicit commit requests. Instead, we should set auto commits to make updates visible, ensuring that auto commits happen at regular intervals in the cluster.

However, it is not feasible to go and update all applications to stop them from sending explicit commits. Solr provides `IgnoreCommitOptimizeUpdateProcessorFactory`, which will ignore all explicit commits without touching the client application. The change is done in `solrconfig.xml`, as shown here:

```
<updateRequestProcessorChain name="ignore-commit-from-client"
default="true">
    <processor class="solr.IgnoreCommitOptimizeUpdateProcessorFactory">
        <int name="statusCode">200</int>
    </processor>
    <processor class="solr.LogUpdateProcessorFactory" />
    <processor class="solr.DistributedUpdateProcessorFactory" />
    <processor class="solr.RunUpdateProcessorFactory" />
</updateRequestProcessorChain>
```

In the preceding snippet, we return status 200 to the client but ignore the commit.

Enabling SSL – Solr security

In this example, we will see a basic SSL setup using a self-signed certificate. Enabling SSL ensures that communication between the client and Solr server is encrypted.

Prerequisites

Before generating a self-signed certificate, ensure that you have OpenSSL installed on your machine. To check whether OpenSSL is already installed, type the following command in the Command Prompt:

```
openssl version
```

It should print out the current version of OpenSSL running on your system. If it does not do so, kindly download the latest version of OpenSSL for your operating system and then install it.

We will also make use of JDK's keytool for generating self-signed certificates.

Generating a key and self-signed certificate

JDK provides the `keytool` command to create self-signed certificates. What we will first do is create a keystore using the following command:

```
keytool -genkeypair -alias mysolr -keyalg RSA -keysize 2048 -keypass
solrpass -storepass solrpass -validity 3650 -keystore mysolrkeystore.jks
```

In the preceding command, we are creating a keystore named `mysolrkeystore.jks` using the RSA algorithm, with a key size of `2048` and validity of 10 years. We have also given the alias name of `mysolr` and specified the key password and store password. This will open up an interactive prompt, as shown here:

```
E:\book\solr\solr-7.2.0\keys>keytool -genkeypair -alias mysolr -keyalg RSA -keysize 2048 -keypass solrpass -storepass solrpass -validity 3650 -keystore mysolrkeystore.jks
What is your first and last name?
  [Unknown]:  mastering solr
What is the name of your organizational unit?
  [Unknown]:  knowarth
What is the name of your organization?
  [Unknown]:  knowarth
What is the name of your City or Locality?
  [Unknown]:  ahmedabad
What is the name of your State or Province?
  [Unknown]:  gujarat
What is the two-letter country code for this unit?
  [Unknown]:  in
Is CN=mastering solr, OU=knowarth, O=knowarth, L=ahmedabad, ST=gujarat, C=in correct?
  [no]:  y
```

In the interactive prompt, fill in the rest of the details and voilà! You have your keystore ready.

We will now convert this keystore into PEM format, which is accepted by most clients. This requires a two-step process:

- Converting the keystore from JKS to PKCS12 format
- Final conversion to PEM format

In order to do the first conversion to PKCS12 format, we will still use the JDK keytool. The command is as follows:

```
keytool -importkeystore -srckeystore mysolrkeystore.jks -destkeystore
mysolrkeystore.p12 -srcstoretype jks -deststoretype pkcs12
```

As you can see, we are trying to import the keystore and have specified both source and destination keystore names; finally we've specified the keystore type to be `pkcs12`. You will see an interactive session opening up again:

```
E:\book\solr\solr-7.2.0\keys>keytool -importkeystore -srckeystore mysolrkeystore.jks -destkeystore mysolrkeystore.p12 -srcstoretype jks -deststoretype pkcs12
Enter destination keystore password:
Re-enter new password:
Enter source keystore password:
Entry for alias mysolr successfully imported.
Import command completed:  1 entries successfully imported, 0 entries failed or cancelled
```

As shown here, you will be asked the destination password for the new keystore and also the source keystore password. Keep the password the same as what we entered earlier and you should see that the import will be successfully completed. You will now have `mysolrkeystore.p12` in your directory.

Now, for the final conversion, we will use OpenSSL. Issue the following command:

```
openssl pkcs12 -in mysolrkeystore.p12 -out mysolrkeystore.pem
```

The command is straightforward. You will be presented with options to specify the password once again. Once you have done so, you will see the folder from where you have issued the command with all the three files (jks, pkcs12, and pem keystores), as shown here:

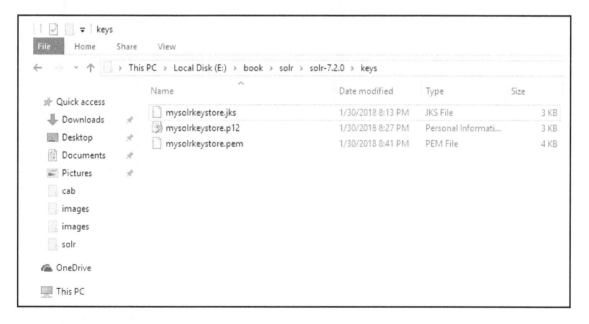

Congratulations!!! You are one step closer to setting up SSL.

Starting Solr with SSL system properties

In order to enable SSL, there are some system properties that you have to turn on. These properties can be found in SOLR_HOME/bin/solr.in.cmd in Windows and SOLR_HOME/bin/solr.in.sh in Unix-based systems.

When you open the file, you will see a set of properties intended for SSL, as highlighted here:

```
97   REM set SOLR_PORT=8983
98
99   REM Enables HTTPS. It is implictly true if you set SOLR_SSL_KEY_STORE. Use this config
100  REM to enable https module with custom jetty configuration.
101  REM set SOLR_SSL_ENABLED=true
102  REM Uncomment to set SSL-related system properties
103  REM Be sure to update the paths to the correct keystore for your environment
104  REM set SOLR_SSL_KEY_STORE=etc/solr-ssl.keystore.jks
105  REM set SOLR_SSL_KEY_STORE_PASSWORD=secret
106  REM set SOLR_SSL_KEY_STORE_TYPE=JKS
107  REM set SOLR_SSL_TRUST_STORE=etc/solr-ssl.keystore.jks
108  REM set SOLR_SSL_TRUST_STORE_PASSWORD=secret
109  REM set SOLR_SSL_TRUST_STORE_TYPE=JKS
110  REM set SOLR_SSL_NEED_CLIENT_AUTH=false
111  REM set SOLR_SSL_WANT_CLIENT_AUTH=false
112
113  REM Uncomment if you want to override previously defined SSL values for HTTP client
114  REM otherwise keep them commented and the above values will automatically be set for HTTP clients
115  REM set SOLR_SSL_CLIENT_KEY_STORE=
116  REM set SOLR_SSL_CLIENT_KEY_STORE_PASSWORD=
117  REM set SOLR_SSL_CLIENT_KEY_STORE_TYPE=
118  REM set SOLR_SSL_CLIENT_TRUST_STORE=
119  REM set SOLR_SSL_CLIENT_TRUST_STORE_PASSWORD=
120  REM set SOLR_SSL_CLIENT_TRUST_STORE_TYPE=
121
```

> As highlighted, there is a section of properties that are related to SSL and they are commented.

Uncomment the lines:

```
set SOLR_SSL_ENABLED=true
set SOLR_SSL_KEY_STORE=E:/book/solr/solr-7.2.0/keys/mysolrkeystore.jks
set SOLR_SSL_KEY_STORE_PASSWORD=solrpass
set SOLR_SSL_KEY_STORE_TYPE=JKS
set SOLR_SSL_TRUST_STORE=E:/book/solr/solr-7.2.0/keys/mysolrkeystore.jks
set SOLR_SSL_TRUST_STORE_PASSWORD=solrpass
set SOLR_SSL_TRUST_STORE_TYPE=JKS
set SOLR_SSL_NEED_CLIENT_AUTH=false
set SOLR_SSL_WANT_CLIENT_AUTH=false
```

Make sure you have changed the keystore path and password as per your configuration.

Once you have done the preceding changes, start Solr using the following command:

```
solr -p 8984 -Dsolr.ssl.checkPeerName=false
```

Once the Solr server is up, navigate to the browser and run the following URL:

```
https://localhost:8984/solr/#/
```

Since it is a self-signed certificate, you may get a message to accept the certificate and continue. Once you continue, you will see the Solr home page:

 Note that you still have a cross mark on `https` since it is a self-signed certificate; it will not have such errors if you are using a proper certificate from GoDaddy or Verisign.

In order to check whether the details of the certificate are the same as you created, click on *F12* to open developer tools if you are using a Chrome browser:

As shown, click on the **Security** tab and then on the **View Certificate** option, which will open a dialog box. Navigate to the **Details** tab and you will see all the details of the certificate that you have created.

Performance statistics

In order to measure performance, Solr provides statistics and metrics; they can read either using Metrics API or by enabling JMX.

Statistics for request handlers

Both search and update request handlers provide various statistics.

The API request path for search is `http://localhost:8983/solr/admin/metrics?group=mycore&prefix=QUERY./select`.

Similarly the API request path for update
is `http://localhost:8983/solr/admin/metrics?group=mycore&prefix=UPDATE./update`.

There are various attributes that can be added at the end of both of these URLs to get various statistics, as listed here:

- `5minRate`: Used to find out the requests per second that have we received in the last 5 minutes.
- `15minRate`: Same as `5minRate`, but here we check for requests per second in the last 15 minutes.
- `p75_ms`/`p95_ms`/`p99_ms`/`p999_ms`: Each of the four attributes represent how much processing time x percentile of the request took. x is to be replaced by the number specified.
- `count`: Number of requests made from the time Solr was time.
- `median_ms`: As the name suggests, this is the median of processing times for all requests.
- `avgRequestsPerSecond`: Average requests per second, just as the name suggests.
- `avgTimePerSecond`: Average time for the requests to be processed.

Just as there are statistics for requests, we have statistics for cache and commits made as well.

Summary

In this chapter, we saw the various tuning parameters needed to take Solr to production. We started off with JVM parameters, and then saw how to manage `solrconfig.xml`. We got an understanding of taking backups, setting up JMX, and configuring logs. Finally, we had an overview of SolrCloud.

In the next chapter, we will see various Client APIs made available by Solr.

9
Client APIs – An Overview

In the previous chapter, we saw the various steps to be configured for production readiness. We also explored the fine-tuning configuration needs to be considered during production setup for better performance. We learned how to secure a Solr, take backups, and configure logs. Then we got an overview of SolrCloud. Now we have a complete configured Solr with all the required configurations to meet any search request. In this chapter, we will learn how Solr can be used with a web application and how to call APIs in different languages. We'll have an overview of various Client APIs supported by Solr.

Client API overview

Solr comes with a bunch of REST APIs, which exposes its features such as query, index, delete, commit, and optimize; it also allows a web application to connect with Solr and perform any operation by calling these APIs. Solr has taken care of these REST APIs such that any web application developed in any programming language can connect to them. A REST API is developed based on the HTTP protocol; so a web application developed in any programming language, such as Java, .NET, Python, and Ruby, can easily connect to and call this API to perform various Solr operations. Using this API, a web application asks Solr to perform some operations, such as querying and indexing. Solr performs those operations and provides a response to the application. Solr also supports various response formats based on programming languages such as Java, JavaScript/JSON, Python, Ruby, PHP, and many more (we have seen this in Chapter 6, *Advanced Queries – Part I*). So it becomes very easy for any programming languages to deal with Solr and to parse a response in expected format. Now Solr is the first choice for web applications developed in any language.

Queries are executed by creating a URL that contains all the query parameters. Solr examines the request URL, performs the query, and returns the response. The default response format is JSON, but we can configure the response format by the wt parameter. The other operations are similar, although in certain cases the HTTP request is a POST operation and contains information beyond whatever is included in the request URL. For example, an index operation may contain a document in the body of the request.

JavaScript Client API

JavaScript client is very easy, simple, and straightforward. We don't need to create any client to connect to Solr. Also, no packages need to be installed for the JavaScript client. JavaScript sends the request to Solr using XMLHttpRequest. Solr processes the request and returns the response in JSON format, which can easily be parsed in JavaScript. We don't need to configure the wt response parameter as Solr, by default, returns the response in JSON format.

Example: Configure hostURL= http://localhost:8983/solr/techproducts/select in JavaScript as follows:

```html
<html>
<head>
<title>Solr Javascript API Example</title>
<script language="Javascript">
//main function called when clicking on search button
function search() {
  //Solr search url
  var hostURL='http://localhost:8983/solr/techproducts/select';
    var xmlHttpReq = false;
    var xmlHttpClient = this;
// Mozilla/Safari
    if (window.XMLHttpRequest) {
        xmlHttpClient.xmlHttpReq = new XMLHttpRequest();
    }
// IE
    else if (window.ActiveXObject) {
        xmlHttpClient.xmlHttpReq = new ActiveXObject("Microsoft.XMLHTTP");
    }
  xmlHttpClient.xmlHttpReq.open('POST', hostURL, true);
    xmlHttpClient.xmlHttpReq.setRequestHeader('Content-Type',
'application/x-www-form-urlencoded');
    xmlHttpClient.xmlHttpReq.onreadystatechange = function() {
        if (xmlHttpClient.xmlHttpReq.readyState == 4) {
            showResponse(xmlHttpClient.xmlHttpReq.responseText);
```

```
        }
    }

    var queryString = appendParams();
    xmlHttpClient.xmlHttpReq.send(queryString);
}

// get entered text in query parameter
function appendParams() {
  var querystring = document.getElementById("querystring").value;
  qstr = 'q=' + escape(querystring)+"&fl=id,name";
  return qstr;
}

//paring and displaying the response
function showResponse(str){
  document.getElementById("responsestring").innerHTML = str;
  var rsp = eval("("+str+")");
  var html = '<strong>Response</strong>';
  html= "</br><strong>Total Found: "+ rsp.response.numFound+"</strong>";
  document.getElementById("result").innerHTML = html;
}
</script>
</head>

<body>
  <div align='center'>
    <p>
      <input id="querystring" name="querystring" type="text"
placeholder='Search Here'>
      <input value="Search" type="button" onClick='search();'>
    </p>
    <div id="result"></div>
    <div id="responsestring"></div>
  </div>
</body>
</html>
```

This is a simple implementation to call the Solr API using JavaScript's XMLHttpRequest. Now if we want to run this code, we create a .html file and paste the preceding code in this file. The created HTML file should reside in the same environment in which Solr is running because modern browsers don't allow cross-site access in JavaScript for security reasons. It may be possible that searching will not work due to an Access-Control-Allow-Origin error. There are various solutions available for this error; it's up to us how we can deal with it.

Now open the HTML file in your browser (supporting `XMLHttpRequest`); a search input box and a button will be displayed. Enter whatever text you want to search and click on the **Search** button. If everything goes well, the Solr API will be called and the response will be displayed as follows. Here we are searching for `ipod`:

ipod   Search

Total Found: 3

{ "responseHeader":{ "status":0, "QTime":1, "params":{ "q":"ipod", "fl":"id,name"}}, "response":{"numFound":3,"start":0,"docs":[{ "id":"IW-02", "name":"iPod & iPod Mini USB 2.0 Cable"}, { "id":"F8V7067-APL-KIT", "name":"Belkin Mobile Power Cord for iPod w/ Dock"}, { "id":"MA147LL/A", "name":"Apple 60 GB iPod with Video Playback Black"}] }, "spellcheck":{ "suggestions":[], "correctlySpelled":false, "collations":[]}}

Response:

```
{
    "responseHeader":{
        "status":0,
        "QTime":1,
        "params":{
            "q":"ipod",
            "fl":"id,name"
        }
    },
    "response":{
        "numFound":3,
        "start":0,
        "docs":[
            {
                "id":"IW-02",
                "name":"iPod & iPod Mini USB 2.0 Cable"
            },
            {
                "id":"F8V7067-APL-KIT",
                "name":"Belkin Mobile Power Cord for iPod w/ Dock"
            },
            {
                "id":"MA147LL/A",
                "name":"Apple 60 GB iPod with Video Playback Black"
            }
        ]
    },
    "spellcheck":{
        "suggestions":[

        ],
        "correctlySpelled":false,
        "collations":[
```

```
        ]
    }
}
```

We've got a JSON response; now we can apply our JavaScript skills to parse and display responses as per the application requirement. Likewise, we can test more capabilities of JavaScript towards the Solr API.

SolrJ Client API

SolrJ is built in Java technologies to connect with Solr from a Java application over HTTP.

Solr and SolrJ both are built-in Java technologies, so communication between them is easy and straightforward. While uploading a document, Solr needs all documents in XML or JSON format. SolrJ uses an internal binary protocol by default, called JavaBin. Normally, the client application sends an update request using HTTP POST with JSON or XML format, but the SolrJ client can send the update request as JSON, XML, or Solr's internal binary JavaBin format. The JavaBin protocol is more efficient than XML or JSON.

Apart from normal communication to Solr, SolrJ also supports load balancing across Solr nodes, automatically discovers locations of Solr servers in a SolrCloud mode, and easily handles bulk indexing for large amounts of data. It is also possible to embed Solr within a Java application and connect to it directly without establishing an HTTP connection to the server.

To create a SolrJ client, we do not need to worry much about the libraries; SolrJ libraries are already available in the Solr structure. Just navigate to `%SOLR_HOME%/dist`. You will find `solr-solrj.jar` (with a specific number); copy that jar and add it to your Java application build path. That's the only library required for your SolrJ implementation! Additionally needed libraries are available inside the `%SOLR_HOME%/dist/solrj-lib` directory; add all those to the Java application class path. Once the configuration is done, we can communicate to Solr using SolrJ.

Here is the simple SolrJ client that connects to the Solr API to run a search query:

```
package com.demo.solr.solrj;

import java.io.IOException;
import org.apache.solr.client.solrj.SolrQuery;
import org.apache.solr.client.solrj.SolrServerException;
import org.apache.solr.client.solrj.impl.HttpSolrClient;
import org.apache.solr.client.solrj.response.QueryResponse;
import org.slf4j.Logger;
```

```
import org.slf4j.LoggerFactory;

public class SolrJSearchClientAPI {
  public static Logger _log =
LoggerFactory.getLogger(SolrJSearchClientAPI.class);

  public static void main(String[] args){
    String hostURL = "http://localhost:8983/solr/techproducts";
    HttpSolrClient solr = new HttpSolrClient.Builder(hostURL).build();
    //set response parser
    //solr.setParser(new XMLResponseParser());
    //query configurations
    SolrQuery query = new SolrQuery();
    query.set("q", "ipod");
    query.set("fl", "id,name");
    /*alternate way to configure fl parameter
     * query.setFields("id","name");*/
    /*select different request handler
     query.setRequestHandler("/spell");*/
    try {
      QueryResponse response = solr.query(query);
      _log.info(response.toString());
    } catch (IOException e) {
      _log.error(e.getMessage());
    } catch (SolrServerException e) {
      _log.error(e.getMessage());
    }
  }
}
```

Response:

```
{responseHeader={status=0,QTime=1,params={q=ipod,fl=id,name,wt=javabin,vers
ion=2}},response={numFound=3,start=0,docs=[SolrDocument{id=IW-02, name=iPod
& iPod Mini USB 2.0 Cable}, SolrDocument{id=F8V7067-APL-KIT, name=Belkin
Mobile Power Cord for iPod w/ Dock}, SolrDocument{id=MA147LL/A, name=Apple
60 GB iPod with Video Playback
Black}]},spellcheck={suggestions={},correctlySpelled=false,collations={}}}
```

To query from the Solr instances running on the cloud using a `zkHostString` key:

```
String zkHostString = "zkServerA:2181,zkServerB:2181,zkServerC:2181/solr";
CloudSolrClient solr = new
CloudSolrClient.Builder().withZkHost(zkHostString).build();
```

Let's run a client that adds a document (builds an index). In our selected core, techproducts, let's add one more product:

```java
package com.demo.solr.solrj;

import java.io.IOException;
import org.apache.solr.client.solrj.SolrServerException;
import org.apache.solr.client.solrj.impl.HttpSolrClient;
import org.apache.solr.client.solrj.response.UpdateResponse;
import org.apache.solr.common.SolrInputDocument;
import org.slf4j.Logger;
import org.slf4j.LoggerFactory;

public class SolrJAddDocumentClientAPI {
  public static Logger _log =
LoggerFactory.getLogger(SolrJAddDocumentClientAPI.class);

  public static void main(String[] args){
    String hostURL = "http://localhost:8983/solr/techproducts";
    HttpSolrClient solr = new HttpSolrClient.Builder(hostURL).build();
    SolrInputDocument document = new SolrInputDocument();
    document.addField("id","HPPRO445");
    document.addField("name","HP Probook 445");
    document.addField("manu","Hewlett Packard");
    document.addField("features", "8GB DDR3LSD RAM");
    document.addField("weight","1.2");
    document.addField("price","800");
    try {
      UpdateResponse response = solr.add(document);
      solr.commit();
      _log.info(response.toString());
    } catch (SolrServerException e) {
      _log.error(e.getMessage());
    } catch (IOException e) {
      _log.error(e.getMessage());
    }
  }
}
```

Through this client, a new product, HP Probook 445, has been added to techproducts. Now if we search for the query q=HP Probook 445, we will get the following response if the product was added successfully:

```
{
  "responseHeader":{
    "status":0,
    "QTime":8,
```

```
      "params":{
        "q":"HP Probook 445"}},
  "response":{"numFound":1,"start":0,"docs":[
      {
        "id":"HPPRO445",
        "name":"HP Probook 445",
        "manu":"Hewlett Packard",
        "features":["8GB DDR3LSD RAM"],
        "weight":1.2,
        "price":800.0,
        "price_c":"800,USD",
        "_version_":1592089897249800192,
        "price_c____l_ns":80000}]
  },
  "spellcheck":{
    "suggestions":[],
    "correctlySpelled":false,
    "collations":[]}
}
```

Here we have added a single product, but if we have a product list (bulk) to add, we can do it like this:

```java
package com.demo.solr.solrj;

import java.io.IOException;
import java.util.ArrayList;
import java.util.List;

import org.apache.solr.client.solrj.SolrServerException;
import org.apache.solr.client.solrj.impl.HttpSolrClient;
import org.apache.solr.client.solrj.response.UpdateResponse;
import org.apache.solr.common.SolrInputDocument;
import org.slf4j.Logger;
import org.slf4j.LoggerFactory;

public class SolrJAddDocumentsClientAPI {
  public static Logger _log =
LoggerFactory.getLogger(SolrJAddDocumentsClientAPI.class);
  public static void main(String[] args) {
    String hostURL = "http://localhost:8983/solr/techproducts";
    HttpSolrClient solr = new HttpSolrClient.Builder(hostURL).build();
    List<SolrInputDocument> documentList = new
ArrayList<SolrInputDocument>();
    SolrInputDocument document1 = new SolrInputDocument();
    document1.addField("id","id1");
    document1.addField("name","product1");
    documentList.add(document1);
```

```
SolrInputDocument document2 = new SolrInputDocument();
document2.addField("id","id2");
document2.addField("name","product2");
documentList.add(document2);
//...
//...
SolrInputDocument documentn = new SolrInputDocument();
documentn.addField("id","idn");
documentn.addField("name","productn");
documentList.add(documentn);
try {
  UpdateResponse response = solr.add(documentList);
    solr.commit();
    _log.info(response.toString());
} catch (SolrServerException e) {
  _log.error(e.getMessage());
} catch (IOException e) {
  _log.error(e.getMessage());
}
  }
}
```

For bulk processes, Solr provides a thread-safe class called
ConcurrentUpdateSolrClient, which first holds all the documents in buffers and then
writes to the HTTP connections.

Using SolrJ, we can delete a document (index) as follows:

```
package com.demo.solr.solrj;

import java.io.IOException;

import org.apache.solr.client.solrj.SolrServerException;
import org.apache.solr.client.solrj.impl.HttpSolrClient;
import org.apache.solr.client.solrj.response.UpdateResponse;
import org.slf4j.Logger;
import org.slf4j.LoggerFactory;

public class SolrJDeleteDocumentClientAPI {
  public static Logger _log =
LoggerFactory.getLogger(SolrJDeleteDocumentClientAPI.class);

  public static void main(String[] args){
    String hostURL = "http://localhost:8983/solr/techproducts";
    HttpSolrClient solr = new HttpSolrClient.Builder(hostURL).build();
    try {
        UpdateResponse response = solr.deleteById("HPPRO445");
```

```
        solr.commit();
        _log.info(response.toString());
    } catch (SolrServerException e) {
      _log.error(e.getMessage());
    } catch (IOException e) {
      _log.error(e.getMessage());
    }
  }
}
```

Now if we search for the query q=HP Probook 445, it should not return any results if it was deleted successfully. In the same way, we delete documents in bulk:

```
solr.deleteById(List<String> ids);
```

After adding/updating/deleting, don't forget to commit the transaction using solr.commit(); otherwise, the indexes will not be affected.

Ruby Client API

Like JavaScript and SolrJ, Ruby can also connect with Solr using the Solr API and performs various operations such as search, indexing, and removal over the HTTP protocol. Solr also provides sufficient API support for the Ruby programming language. So, the application that builds on a Ruby platform can also take advantage of Solr. Solr reverts a query response in Ruby format, which can be interpreted easily in Ruby programming.

For Ruby applications, to communicate with Solr, rsolr is an extensive library. It provides all the functionalities needed to meet your expectations. To install the rsolr dependency, please refer to http://www.rubydoc.info/gems/rsolr. To install rsolr, use this command:

```
gem install rsolr
```

Now let's search using rsolr for the query q=ipod:

```
require 'rsolr'

solr = RSolr.connect :url => 'http://localhost:8983/solr/techproducts'

response = solr.get 'select', :params => {:q =>
'ipod',:fl=>'id,name',:wt=>:ruby}

puts response
```

Response:

```
{"responseHeader"=>{"status"=>0, "QTime"=>2, "params"=>{"q"=>"ipod",
"fl"=>"id,name", "wt"=>"ruby"}}, "response"=>{"numFound"=>3, "start"=>0,
"docs"=>[{"id"=>"IW-02", "name"=>"iPod & iPod Mini USB 2.0 Cable"},
{"id"=>"F8V7067-APL-KIT", "name"=>"Belkin Mobile Power Cord for iPod w/
Dock"}, {"id"=>"MA147LL/A", "name"=>"Apple 60 GB iPod with Video Playback
Black"}]}, "spellcheck"=>{"suggestions"=>[], "correctlySpelled"=>false,
"collations"=>[]}}
```

Solr treats the response format based on the :wt parameter value. For :wt=>:ruby, the
response format will be a hash (a similar object returned by Solr but evaluated as Ruby),
and for :wt=>"ruby", the response will be a string. For other formats, Solr returns the
response as expected.

Now let's try to add a document (index) to Solr:

```
require 'rsolr'

solr = RSolr.connect :url => 'http://localhost:8983/solr/techproducts'

response = solr.add(:id=>'HPPRO445', :name=>'HP Probook 445',
:manu=>'Hewlett Packard', :features=>'8GB DDR3LSD RAM', :weight=>1.2,
:price=>800)

solr.commit

puts response
```

After adding, if we search for the query q=HP Probook 445, it will give the following
response, provided it was added successfully:

```
{"responseHeader"=>{"status"=>0, "QTime"=>4, "params"=>{"q"=>"HP Probook
445", "wt"=>"ruby"}}, "response"=>{"numFound"=>1, "start"=>0,
"docs"=>[{"id"=>"HPPRO445", "name"=>"HP Probook 445", "manu"=>"Hewlett
Packard", "features"=>["8GB DDR3LSD RAM"], "weight"=>1.2, "price"=>800.0,
"price_c"=>"800,USD", "_version_"=>1591126555425243136,
"price_c____l_ns"=>80000}]}, "spellcheck"=>{"suggestions"=>[],
"correctlySpelled"=>false, "collations"=>[]}}
```

After adding/updating/deleting, don't forgot to commit the transaction using
solr.commit(), or else the indexes will not be affected.

We can add multiple documents at a time:

```
require 'rsolr'

solr = RSolr.connect :url => 'http://localhost:8983/solr/techproducts'

response = solr.add([
  { :id => 'id1', :name => "product1"},
  { :id => 'id2', :name => "product2"},
  { :id => 'idn', :name => "productn"}
  ])

solr.commit

puts response
```

Now delete a document using `rsolr`, like this:

```
require 'rsolr'

solr = RSolr.connect :url => 'http://localhost:8983/solr/techproducts'

response = solr.delete_by_id 'HPPRO445'

solr.commit

puts response
```

Now if we search for the query q=HP Probook 445, it should not give any response for the preceding ID if it was deleted successfully. In the same way, we can delete multiple documents in a single transaction:

```
require 'rsolr'

solr = RSolr.connect :url => 'http://localhost:8983/solr/techproducts'

response = solr.delete_by_id ['id1','id2']

solr.commit

puts response
```

Here we have explored various Solr APIs using basic Ruby programming steps. Now, referring to this, we can take a deep dive and add more configurations to Ruby and Solr API connectivity to achieve the expected results.

Python Client API

Solr also comes with APIs that can be connected through applications developed in the Python programming language. Solr supports responses in Python format, which can be easily interpreted in Python programming. As we have seen before for JavaScript, SolrJ, and Ruby, Python also provides all the required packages to perform search, add, delete and so on.

Let's start with search. Here is the simple search configuration for searching a query q=ipod in techproducts:

```
import urllib.request

connection =
urllib.request.urlopen('http://localhost:8983/solr/techproducts/select?q=ip
od&fl=id,name&wt=python')

response = eval(connection.read())

print(response)
```

Response:

```
{'responseHeader': {'status': 0, 'QTime': 51, 'params': {'q': 'ipod', 'fl':
'id,name', 'wt': 'python'}}, 'response': {'numFound': 3, 'start': 0,
'docs': [{'id': 'IW-02', 'name': 'iPod & iPod Mini USB 2.0 Cable'}, {'id':
'F8V7067-APL-KIT', 'name': 'Belkin Mobile Power Cord for iPod w/ Dock'},
{'id': 'MA147LL/A', 'name': 'Apple 60 GB iPod with Video Playback
Black'}]}, 'spellcheck': {'suggestions': [], 'correctlySpelled': False,
'collations': []}}
```

The response format is Python; here, even if we do not set wt=python, Solr will give the response in Python format by default. The eval() function is not recommended in Python because executing arbitrary code inside eval is easy to attack on the server. As a solution, Python provides a package called json or simplejson, which is more secure that eval(). This is the syntax for json:

```
import json
...
...
response = json.load(connection)
```

Now let's add documents to Solr using Python programming. Python provides many libraries for adding documents to Solr through APIs. `pysolr` is one of the rich libraries provided, which gives us a good and simple way to add documents to Solr. We need to add `pysolr` packages like this from the command line:

```
pip install pysolr
```

This is a simple implementation to add a single document to Solr:

```
import pysolr

solr = pysolr.Solr('http://localhost:8983/solr/techproducts', timeout=5)

solr.add([
    {
        'id':'HPPRO445',
        'name':'HP Probook 445',
        'manu':'Hewlett Packard',
        'features':'8GB DDR3LSD RAM',
        'weight':1.2,
        'price':800
    }
])
```

After adding the document through the preceding implementation, searching for q=HP Probook 445 will provide the same response as we have added if the document got added successfully to `techproducts`. Using `pysolr`, we do not need to perform any commit operation as it will be handled internally for any transactions.

In the same way, to add multiple documents at a time, here is a simple implementation:

```
import pysolr

solr = pysolr.Solr('http://localhost:8983/solr/techproducts', timeout=5)

solr.add([
    {
        'id':'id1',
        'name':'product1'
    },
    {
        'id':'id2',
        'name':'product2'
    },
    {
        'id':'idn',
        'name':'productn'
```

```
        }
    ])
```

All the documents will be added successfully inside `techproducts`.

We can delete a document using `pysolr` in Python. This a sample to delete a single document by providing the ID:

```
import pysolr

solr = pysolr.Solr("http://localhost:8983/solr/techproducts", timeout=5)

solr.delete(id='HPPRO445')
```

After deletion, if we search for `q=HP Probook 445`, it should not return the previously added document. Similar is the way to delete multiple documents at a time; here is a sample:

```
import pysolr

solr = pysolr.Solr("http://localhost:8983/solr/techproducts", timeout=5)

solr.delete(id=['id1','id2'])
```

All the documents will be deleted successfully for these IDs.

So we have seen basic Python configurations for operations such as search/add/delete, dealing with the Solr API. The Python programming language supports more detailed configurations to meet the all expectations from any web application. Now, taking this as a reference, we can dive deep and explore Python and Solr bounding in more detail.

Summary

In this chapter, we got a basic overview of various JavaScript, SolrJ, Ruby, and Python supports for Solr API. We explored the basic configurations required to connect with the Solr API for each one of them. Then we designed basic programs for searching, adding, adding in bulk, deleting, and deleting in bulk. We executed them and analyzed the response for each of them.

Index

memory heap, managing 245, 246

L

language detection
  about 164
  configuration 164
logging configuration
  about 253
  admin web interface, using for log settings 253,
    256
  environment variable, setting 256
  log level 256
  Log4J, configuring for logging 257
  parameters, passing in startup script 257
lower case filter (LCF) 105
Lucene 9
Lucene query parser 172

M

managed beans (MBeans) 252
memory heap, JVM
  managing 245
multilingual analysis
  about 136
  language identification 137
  separate fields, creating per language 138
  separate indexes, creating per language 139
  Solr, configuring 138
MySQL
  data, loading 48, 51

N

NASA
  URL 15
Near real-time (NRT) 261

O

Open Test Search
  URL 15
ordering 206

P

pagination
  about 226

cursor pagination 227, 230
  implementing 226
performance
  statistics 268
  statistics, for request handlers 268, 269
phonetic matching
  about 140
  Beider-Morse Phonetic Matching (BMPM) 140,
    142
Phrase Fields (pf) 180
pivot faceting 204
Postman
  installing 144
  URL 144
Public Library of Science (PLOS) 15
Python Client API 283, 284

Q

query parsing
  about 169
  DisMax Query Parser 179
  eDisMax Query Parser 185
  query parameters 170
  standard query parser 172
Query Phrase Slop (qs) 181

R

range faceting 202
relevance 168
response writer
  about 188
  CSV 196
  JSON 189, 192
  standard XML 193
  velocity 198
result clustering
  about 235
  cluster search component, declaring 237
  cluster search component, including 237
  clustering contrib, installing 236
  implementation 236
  parameters 236
  request handler, declaring 237
result grouping

W

well-known text (WKT) 80
White House
  URL 16

X

XML format
  used, for index handlers working 148, 153

www.ingramcontent.com/pod-product-compliance
Lightning Source LLC
Chambersburg PA
CBHW080626060326
40690CB00021B/4832